Mastering ASP.NET Web API

Build powerful HTTP services and make the most of the
ASP.NET Core Web API platform

Mithun Pattankar
Malendra Hurbuns

BIRMINGHAM - MUMBAI

Mastering ASP.NET Web API

First published: August 2017

Production reference: 1110817

Published by Packt Publishing Ltd.
Livery Place
35 Livery Street
Birmingham
B3 2PB, UK.

ISBN 978-1-78646-395-1

www.packtpub.com

Credits

Authors

Mithun Pattankar
Malendra Hurbuns

Reviewer

Vidya Vrat Agarwal

Commissioning Editor

Edward Gordon

Acquisition Editor

Nitin Dasan

Content Development Editor

Siddhi Chavan

Technical Editor

Dhiraj Chandanshive

Copy Editors

Zainab Bootwala
Safis Editing

Project Coordinator

Prajakta Naik

Proofreader

Safis Editing

Indexer

Aishwarya Gangawane

Production Coordinator

Nilesh Mohite

About the Authors

Mithun Pattankar, who hails from Kalaburgi and lives in Bangalore, India, works with the leading MNC as a consultant. He has been developing .NET-based applications for over 12 years now. He has an industry-wide experience in building Desktop Apps (WPF), Web Apps (ASP.NET and client-side frameworks), and Hybrid Mobile apps (Ionic). He is involved in all aspects of application development, and mentors his junior team members. He has been actively working on building ASP.NET Web APIs for different frontends and conducts technical training as well.

Mithun believes in eating sattvic food for healthy living and loves spending time doing socio-spiritual activities. He occasionally blogs on mithunvp.com and can be reached on Twitter at `@mithunpattankar`.

I would like to thank the team at Packt for giving me a wonderful opportunity to write this book. It was truly a great learning experience. Also, thanks to the technical reviewer for providing valuable feedback.

Immense respect and love to my parents for their unconditional love, incredible support, and prayers. Thanks to my sisters with whom I enjoyed growing up.

For her unconditional love, looking after me during late nights while writing this book, and supporting me through thick and thin, I would like to thank my wife from the bottom of my heart.

Lots of love to my cute, adorable son; you're such a blessing for us. Thanks to my best friends for being there every time.

Finally, and most importantly, I would like to dedicate this book to my guru, HDH Pramukh Swami Maharaj, who lived "In the joy of others, lies our own;" only by his blessings and grace, I could accomplish everything in my life.

Malendra Hurbuns is from South Africa, and lives in New Zealand, working for an Australian Company as a senior software developer. He has been developing in .NET for over 15 years. He mentors other developers and is involved in all aspects of development. He loves writing simple code that has a high quality. He is one of the pioneers in web API in his role, and he has implemented many live systems using ASP.NET Web APIs. TDD is also a topic close to his heart. He has worked in the accounting, banking, and simulation industries, which has provided him with a wealth of experience. He is a keen cyclist and swimmer.

Thank you to my mum and dad who have always supported me in my career, and their endurance while I was writing this book, which means a lot to me. Thank you to the team at Packt for guiding me along my first book.

About the Reviewer

Vidya Vrat Agarwal is a .NET passionate, Microsoft MVP, C# Corner MVP, TOGAF Certified Architect, Certified Scrum Master (CSM), author, speaker, Certified MCT, MCPD, MCTS, MCSD.NET, MCAD.NET, and MCSD. He is currently working as a .NET Enterprise architect/consultant in USA. He is passionate about the .NET technology and loves to contribute to the .NET community. He blogs at http://www.MyPassionFor.NETand can be followed on Twitter at @DotNetAuthor. He lives with his wife, Rupali, and two daughters Pearly and Arshika, in Redmond WA.

www.PacktPub.com

For support files and downloads related to your book, please visit `www.PacktPub.com`.

Did you know that Packt offers eBook versions of every book published, with PDF and ePub files available? You can upgrade to the eBook version at `www.PacktPub.com` and as a print book customer, you are entitled to a discount on the eBook copy. Get in touch with us at `service@packtpub.com` for more details.

At `www.PacktPub.com`, you can also read a collection of free technical articles, sign up for a range of free newsletters and receive exclusive discounts and offers on Packt books and eBooks.

`https://www.packtpub.com/mapt`

Get the most in-demand software skills with Mapt. Mapt gives you full access to all Packt books and video courses, as well as industry-leading tools to help you plan your personal development and advance your career.

Why subscribe?

- Fully searchable across every book published by Packt
- Copy and paste, print, and bookmark content
- On demand and accessible via a web browser

Customer Feedback

Thanks for purchasing this Packt book. At Packt, quality is at the heart of our editorial process. To help us improve, please leave us an honest review on this book's Amazon page at `https://www.amazon.com/dp/1786463954`.

If you'd like to join our team of regular reviewers, you can e-mail us at `customerreviews@packtpub.com`. We award our regular reviewers with free eBooks and videos in exchange for their valuable feedback. Help us be relentless in improving our products!

Table of Contents

Preface

Writing web APIs is one of most sought-after programming skills as it provides lightweight HTTP services that reach a broad range of clients. A well-designed web API can be used by various clients such as Desktop, web, and mobile apps; as its HTTP services, it can be used across cross-platform.

ASP.NET Web API 2 is an ideal platform to build REST-based APIs, and it's widely adopted and has been very successful. Microsoft entered the world of open source by introducing cross-platform.NET Core and cross-platform ASP.NET Core technologies.

ASP.NET Core opened a new world of exciting, feature-rich, and lightweight way of developing web applications. With this new technology, we are not confined to the world of Windows OS to build applications. It's truly cross-platform because we don't have to use Visual Studio IDE to develop applications anymore.

ASP.NET Core provides a very innovating approach to build web APIs. In this book, you will learn about the ASP.NET Core anatomy, creating web APIs by exploring the concept of middleware, integrating with databases, applying various security mechanisms, and consuming them in popular web UI frameworks.

This book is written considering both experienced and new developers. A prior knowledge of developing web APIs will be an added advantage, but it's not a prerequisite. It will help you build a truly cross-platform ASP.NET Core Web API and master it. We are using .NET Core 2.0 Preview 2 and ASP.NET Core 2.0 Preview 2, along with Visual Studio 2017 Preview 3 at the time of writing this book, and we do plan to update this book for the final release of ASP.NET Core 2.0.

What this book covers

Chapter 1, *Introduction to Microservices and Service-Oriented Architecture*, discusses the state of service-oriented architecture trends in the industry, as well as what microservices architecture brings to the table.

Chapter 2, *Understanding HTTP and REST*, refreshes the concept of web architecture and describes the core technology and concept behind HTTP and its methods, and you will be introduced to the REST architecture style.

Chapter 3, *Anatomy of ASP.NET Core Web API*, takes you on a journey to understand why web API was incepted, as well as gets you started on creating ASP.NET Core Web API and understanding its anatomy.

Chapter 4, *Controllers, Actions, and Models*, covers the core concept of how a request interacts with a controller, works with the controller dispatch process, customizes the controller dispatch process, and works with the action method results.

Chapter 5, *Implementing Routing*, helps you in understanding how routing maps incoming HTTP requests to its corresponding controller's action methods.

Chapter 6, *Middleware and Filters*, delves deep into one of ASP.NET Core's prominent feature--Middleware and Filters.

Chapter 7, *Perform Unit and Integration Testing*, explains how to write unit tests and perform integration testing for the web API.

Chapter 8, *Web API Security*, explores concepts on identification, authentication, and authorization for the web API.

Chapter 9, *Integration with Database*, integrates with various database using ORM such as EF 6, EF Core, and Dapper.

Chapter 10, *Error Handling, Tracing, and Logging*, explores the ASP.NET Core's in-built logging feature, and shows you how to write efficient error handling code.

Chapter 11, *Optimization and Performance*, explains the asynchronous ways of writing web API, and how to apply the caching technique for a better web API performance.

Chapter 12, *Hosting and Deployment*, deploys the ASP.NET Core Web API on various platforms such as IIS, Stand-alone, Docker, Azure, Linux, and so on. It showcases its true cross-platforms nature.

Chapter 13, *Modern Web Frontends*, consumes the web API developed from previous chapters in UI frameworks such as Angular, Ionic, React, and so on.

What you need for this book

The following software is required to complete the practice exercises given in this book:

- Windows 7 or higher, any Linux-flavor machines, or macOS
- .NET Core 2.0 Preview 2 SDK
- Visual Studio 2017 Preview 3 (any edition)
- Visual Studio Code for non-Windows machines
- OmniSharp for Visual Studio Code
- NodeJS to build modern UI frameworks

- The SQL Server Express edition
- Docker Toolbox
- Postman: Cross-platform REST client
- Your favorite browser

Who this book is for

This book is for .NET developers who want to master ASP.NET Core (Web API) and have played around with previous ASP.NET Web API a little, but don't have an in-depth knowledge of it. You need to know Visual Studio and C#, and have some HTML, CSS, and JavaScript knowledge.

Conventions

In this book, you will find a number of text styles that distinguish between different kinds of information. Here are some examples of these styles and an explanation of their meaning.

Code words in text, database table names, folder names, filenames, file extensions, pathnames, dummy URLs, user input, and Twitter handles are shown as follows: "Running the `dotnet build` command will perform the routine build and generate the `bin` and `obj` folders."

A block of code is set as follows:

```
public class Program
{
  public static void Main(string[] args)
  {
      BuildWebHost(args).Run();
  }
}
```

Any command-line input or output is written as follows:

```
docker run -it -d -p 85:80 packtcontantsAPI
```

New terms and **important words** are shown in bold. Words that you see on the screen, for example, in menus or dialog boxes, appear in the text like this: "Open Visual Studio 2017 IDE, click **New Project** to open project templates dialog."

Warnings or important notes appear like this.

Tips and tricks appear like this.

Reader feedback

Feedback from our readers is always welcome. Let us know what you think about this book-what you liked or disliked. Reader feedback is important for us as it helps us develop titles that you will really get the most out of. To send us general feedback, simply e-mail feedback@packtpub.com, and mention the book's title in the subject of your message. If there is a topic that you have expertise in and you are interested in either writing or contributing to a book, see our author guide at www.packtpub.com/authors.

Customer support

Now that you are the proud owner of a Packt book, we have a number of things to help you to get the most from your purchase.

Downloading the example code

You can download the example code files for this book from your account at http://www.packtpub.com. If you purchased this book elsewhere, you can visit http://www.packtpub.com/support and register to have the files e-mailed directly to you. You can download the code files by following these steps:

1. Log in or register to our website using your e-mail address and password.
2. Hover the mouse pointer on the **SUPPORT** tab at the top.
3. Click on **Code Downloads & Errata**.
4. Enter the name of the book in the **Search** box.
5. Select the book for which you're looking to download the code files.

6. Choose from the drop-down menu where you purchased this book from.
7. Click on **Code Download**.

Once the file is downloaded, please make sure that you unzip or extract the folder using the latest version of:

- WinRAR / 7-Zip for Windows
- Zipeg / iZip / UnRarX for Mac
- 7-Zip / PeaZip for Linux

The code bundle for the book is also hosted on GitHub at `https://github.com/PacktPubl ishing/Mastering-ASP.NET-Web-API`. We also have other code bundles from our rich catalog of books and videos available at `https://github.com/PacktPublishing/`. Check them out!

Errata

Although we have taken every care to ensure the accuracy of our content, mistakes do happen. If you find a mistake in one of our books-maybe a mistake in the text or the code- we would be grateful if you could report this to us. By doing so, you can save other readers from frustration and help us improve subsequent versions of this book. If you find any errata, please report them by visiting `http://www.packtpub.com/submit-errata`, selecting your book, clicking on the **Errata Submission Form** link, and entering the details of your errata. Once your errata are verified, your submission will be accepted and the errata will be uploaded to our website or added to any list of existing errata under the Errata section of that title. To view the previously submitted errata, go to `https://www.packtpub.com/book s/content/support` and enter the name of the book in the search field. The required information will appear under the **Errata** section.

Piracy

Piracy of copyrighted material on the Internet is an ongoing problem across all media. At Packt, we take the protection of our copyright and licenses very seriously. If you come across any illegal copies of our works in any form on the Internet, please provide us with the location address or website name immediately so that we can pursue a remedy. Please contact us at `copyright@packtpub.com` with a link to the suspected pirated material. We appreciate your help in protecting our authors and our ability to bring you valuable content.

Questions

If you have a problem with any aspect of this book, you can contact us at
`questions@packtpub.com`, and we will do our best to address the problem.

1
Introduction to Microservices and Service-Oriented Architecture

With the increase in internet availability, there is an ongoing evolution in data communication techniques. The architectural improvements have been very innovative, scalable, and adoptable across environments. There was a need for software components to be available across the internet with a common interface for communication across different platforms and programming languages.

This led to the concept of creating services easily deployable with scalability, and exposing them over the internet.

Designing functionalities in terms of service was widely adopted; it was a great idea to provide features in the form of services to heterogeneous clients. This concept of using services led to **SOA (Service-Oriented Architecture)**.

In this chapter, we will be looking at the following topics:

- Service in SOA
- Monolithic architecture
- Introduction to Microservices

Services in SOA

A service is a piece of software which provides a functionality to other pieces of software within your system or outside the system.

The other pieces of software (clients) could be anything from a web application (website) to a mobile app (native or hybrid), or a desktop app, or even another service which uses another service in order to carry out a particular type of functionality.

In an e-commerce website context, when a user places an order, the web application communicates with the service to carry out the **create, read, update, and delete (CRUD)** operations on the database.

The communication between the software components (clients) and the service normally happens over a network with some kind of a communication protocol, for example, a mobile app communicating to a service via internet.

A system which uses a service or multiple services in this fashion, is known to have a Service-Oriented Architecture.

The main idea behind this architecture is that, instead of using modules within each client application, it lets us use a service(s) to provide functionality to them. This allows us to have many client applications using the same functionality.

SOA was successful, because of its following characteristics:

- It allows us to scale our software when the demand increases by enabling it to have a copy of the service on multiple servers, so when the traffic comes in, a load balancer redirects that request to a specific instance of the service, and we can have multiple instances of the service. Thus, when the demand increases, increasing the number of instances on the servers helps us scale it.
- SOA boasts of having standardized contracts or interfaces. When a client application calls the service, it calls the service by calling a method. The signature of that method normally doesn't change when the service changes, so we can upgrade our service without having to upgrade our clients as long as the contract and the interface do not change.
- Services are, in fact, stateless, so when a request comes in from a website to our service, that instance of the service does not have to remember the previous request from that specific customer. It, basically, has all the information from the request that it needs in order to retrieve all the data associated with the previous requests within the service, so, the service does not have to remember the previous calls a client has made to that particular instance of the service.

Service implementation

SOA gained popularity due to its implementation of services, which are accessible over standard internet protocols that are independent of OS platforms and programming languages.

Services from a developer POV are nothing but web services hosted on a web server, and which use **SOAP** (**Simple Object Access Protocol**) or JSON for communication. It's interesting to know that a web service can be used as a wrapper for legacy systems for making them network-enabled.

Some of the popular technologies implementing services (SOA) are as follows:

- Web services based on **WSDL** (**Web Service Description Language**) and SOAP
- Messaging, for example, with ActiveMQ, JMS, and RabbitMQ
- WCF (Microsoft's implementation of Web services)
- Apache Thrift
- SORCER
- RESTful HTTP

Service-Oriented Architecture started gaining momentum when the Monolithic architectural approach experience proved to be more painful than thought earlier. Let's briefly understand what Monolithic systems are and their drawbacks that led to adoption of SOA.

Monolithic architecture

Monolithic architecture-based systems existed before the SOA or Microservices movement. These types of systems are exactly the opposite of what SOA tries to achieve.

A typical Monolithic system is an enterprise-based application, and this application might be in the form of a large website with all the working modules packaged in together into one single package, or it might be in the form of a service which talks to a website. It might be packaged as a large executable that is deployed on a machine.

In these systems, we added different components to an application to keep growing; there's no restriction in size, and there's no division. There's always one package which contains everything, and therefore, we end up with a large code base.

The high-level architecture diagram of a Monolithic system would look as follows:

Typical Monolithic architecture

Overheads of Monolithic architecture

In the long run, enterprises faced these shortcomings when they applied Monolithic architecture to their systems:

- Due to the code base being so large, it took the teams longer to develop a new functionality within the application.
- Deployment of a large system can also be challenging, because even for a small bug fix, we have to deploy a new version of the entire system, and therefore, that creates greater risk.
- It's one large code base, so, we're also stuck with one technology stack.
- It makes the overall system less competitive, because we can't easily adopt new technologies which might give us a competitive edge.
- Since the code is in one large package, we might also have high levels of coupling, which means that if a change is made in one part of the system, it might affect another part of the system, because the code is intertwined. This kind of coupling might be present between modules, and also between different services.

- Scaling up this service to meet the demand is quite inefficient. For example, if the Orders module of the system is in demand, we would have to create a copy of the whole package, of the whole service, in order to scale up just the Orders section.
- More powerful servers need to be bought to work efficiently for a large footprint of monolithic apps.
- Unit testing for such a large code base takes time, and regression testing by QA is also a time-consuming process.

 The only one advantage that a Monolithic system has is the fact that we can run the entire code base on one machine, so, when developing and testing, we could probably replicate the entire environment on a machine.

An example of a Monolithic system could be an ASP.NET MVC site where the website itself is the UI layer, and then in the Business layer, you have business logic along with the data access layer. Over the years, if we continue with the same approach, then it will become a Monolithic system.

Introducing Microservices

The Microservices architecture is, basically, service-oriented architecture done well. After years of working with Service-Oriented Architecture, software developers have realized what Service-Oriented Architecture should be like, and this is basically what Microservices architecture is--it's an evolution of the Service-Oriented Architecture.

Microservices are small, autonomous services that perform one function well while working with other services as well.

Microservices introduces a new set of additional design principles, which teach us how to size a service correctly. Previously, there was no guidance on how to size a service, and what to include in a service. The traditional Service-Oriented Architecture resulted in monolithic large services, and because of the size of the service, these services became inefficient to scale up.

Let's look into the advantages of using Microservices.

Lightweight yet scalable

Microservices provide services which are more efficiently scalable, flexible, and which can provide high performance in the areas where performance is required.

An application which is based on the Microservices architecture is, normally, an application which is powered by multiple Microservices, and each one of these provide a set of functions, or a set of related functions, to a specific part of the application. A Microservices architecture normally provides a set of related functions to applications, to client applications, and client services.

Microservices architecture also uses a lightweight communication mechanism between clients and services or between two or more services. The communication mechanism has to be lightweight and quick, because when a Microservices-architected system carries out a transaction, it is a distributed transaction which is completed by multiple services. Therefore, the services need to communicate to each other in a quick and efficient way over the network.

Technology agnostic

The application interface for a Microservice, or the way we communicate to a Microservice, also needs to be technology agnostic. It means the service needs to use an open communication protocol so that it does not dictate the technology that the client application needs to use. And by using open communication protocols, for example, like HTTP REST (JSON based), we could easily have a .NET client application which talks to a Java-based Microservice.

Independently changeable

Another key characteristic of a Microservice is that it is independently changeable. We can upgrade, enhance, or fix a specific Microservice without changing any of the clients or any of the other services within the system.

In the Microservices architecture, each microservice has its own data storage. By modifying one Microservice, we should then be able to deploy that change within the system independently without deploying anything else.

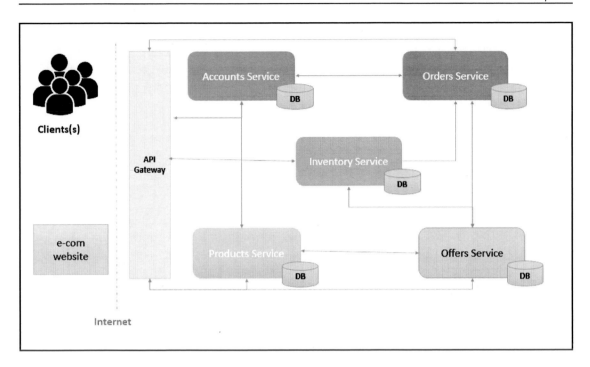

Sample Microservices architecture app

The preceding image depicts a high-level architecture diagram for a Microservices system. This is an example of a typical e-commerce system, and as you can see on the left-hand side, there's a shopping website running in the customer's browser, or it could be a mobile app using the API gateway.

The browser connects to the demo shopping website via the internet--the demo shopping website might be an ASP.NET MVC website running on IIS. All the processing required for all the interactions with the website is actually carried out by a number of Microservices which are running in the background.

Each Microservice has a single focus, or a single set of related functions, has its own data storage, and it's also independently changeable and deployable. So, for example, we could upgrade the Orders service without upgrading any other part of this system.

There might also be multiple instances for each type of Microservice. For example, if the Orders service is in demand, we might have several instances of the Orders service in order to satisfy the demand. And in order to direct a request from the shopping website to the correct instance of an order service, we have an API Gateway which manages and routes a request to the correct Microservice within the system.

So, in this example, when a customer places an order, the shopping website might use multiple services and multiple functions within those services in order to satisfy that transaction. And this is why, in the Microservices architecture, a transaction is normally a distributed transaction, because the transaction is actually satisfied by multiple pieces of software, that is, Microservices.

Benefits of Microservices

The following are the benefits of Microservices:

- Microservices architecture satisfies the need to respond to change quickly. The software market is really competitive nowadays. If your product can't provide a feature that's in demand, it will lose its market share very quickly.
- It fulfills the need for a business-domain-driven design. The architecture of an application needs to match the organization structure, or the structure of the business functions within the organization.
- The Microservices architecture makes use of automated test tools. We've already seen that in a Microservices architecture, transactions are distributed, and therefore, a transaction will be processed by several services before it's complete. The integration between those services needs to be tested, and testing these Microservices together manually might be quite a complex task. Automated test tools help us to perform this integration testing, reducing the manual burden.
- Cloud-compliant Microservices can reduce the burden of deployment and release management.
- The Microservices architecture provides a platform to adopt new technology. Because the systems are made of several moving parts, we can easily change one part, that is, a Microservice from one technology stack to another technology stack in order to get a competitive edge.
- By using asynchronous communication, the distributed transaction does not have to wait for individual services to complete their tasks before it's complete.
- Microservices have shorter development times. Because the system is split up into smaller moving parts, we can work on a moving part individually, can have teams working on different parts concurrently, and because Microservices are small in size and they have a single focus, the teams have less to worry about in terms of scope.
- The Microservices architecture also offers us increased uptime, because when it comes to upgrading the system, we will probably deploy one Microservice at a time without affecting the rest of the system.

Netflix adopted the Microservices architecture; the lessons learnt on architectural designs are summarized in this link along with a video: `https://www.nginx.com/blog/microservices-at-netflix-architectural-best-practices/`.

Summary

The evolution of building services has seen many changes in the past decade with improvements in the internet bandwidth, machine processing power, better frameworks, and so on.

From a developer's point of view, Microservices are REST-based Web APIs either using ASP.NET, Java, PHP, or others. In the upcoming chapters, we will learn the various aspects of developing an ASP.NET Core-based Web API application.

2
Understanding HTTP and REST

REST means Representational State Transfer. The REST architecture style was a PhD dissertation by Roy T. Fielding titled *Architectural Styles and the Design of Network-based Software*. This paper was first published in 2000 after a 6 year study. We can be thankful to Mr. Fielding for the research work and findings.

The modern-day API is modeled around REST, and you will hear people mentioning, *it's not RESTful or questioned, is your API RESTful?*

To create and model a well-defined API, you need to have sound knowledge of REST. For this reason, we will delve a bit deeper into Roy T. Fielding's study.

Roy T. Fielding set out to fix a few problems that showed their head in 1993. Many authors were publishing their work on the web, and they wanted to collaborate. The web became a great place to share and discuss research work. However, no sooner had it got popular did it become troublesome.

There seem to be missing standards in terms of how documents were published and how they could be edited. There were also problems related to infrastructure and speed, and editing and accessing documents was slow.

In this chapter, we will look into the following topics:

- Software architecture
- REST principles
- REST architectural elements
- HTTP
- HTTP/2
- The Richardson maturity model

Software architecture

Software architecture is an abstraction of the runtime elements of a software system during a phase of its operation. A system may be composed of many levels of abstraction and many phases of operation, each with its own software architecture.

Software architecture is defined by a configuration of architectural elements-components, connectors, and data-constrained in their relationships in order to achieve a desired set of architectural properties:

- **Component**: This is is an abstract unit of software instructions and the internal state that provides a transformation of data via its interface
- **Connector** : This is an abstract mechanism that mediates communication, coordination, or cooperation among components
- **Data**: This is an element of information that is transferred from a component, or received by a component, via its connector

The REST architectural style is a combination of several network architectures:

- Data-flow styles:
    - Pipe and filter
    - Uniform pipe and filter
- Replication styles:
    - Replicated repository
    - Cache

- Hierarchical styles:
  - Client-server
  - Layered systems and layered-client-server
  - Client-stateless-server
  - Client-cache-stateless-server
  - Layered-client-cache-stateless-server
  - Remote session
  - Remote data access
- Mobile code styles:
  - Virtual machine
  - Remote evaluation
  - Code-on-demand
  - Layered-code-on-demand-client-cache-stateless-server
  - Mobile agent
- Peer-to-peer styles:
  - Event-based integration
  - C2
  - Distributed objects
  - Brokered distributed objects

REST principles

REST is modeled around starting with nothing and then adding constraints. We will apply constraints to a software architecture, and your architecture will become RESTful.

Client - server

Note that throughout Roy T. Fielding's work, he does not mention that REST has to be applied to the HTTP protocol. In our case, a client server will be the browser as the client and IIS as the server.

Note that the separation of the client and server allows abstraction. These two components can be built independently as well as deployed independently.

Stateless

The next constraint to add is stateless. The server should not contain any state of workflow. In this way, the client is the driver of the information that it wants. When the client asks the server for data, the client needs to pass all the relevant information to the server. This method of designing software creates an abstraction, where the server is unaware of the client; it creates a loose couple design, which is conducive to changes. Later on in the chapter, we will look further into stateless by expanding the idempotent concept.

The client has to keep track of its state. The downside is that the client will have to send more data to the server on each request.

Having the stateless server allows you to scale out, since the server does not store any client-specific data.

Cache

Caching is the next constraint. Whenever the server transmits data that will not change, we refer to the data as static data. The server can cache the data.

When the very first request is made, the server will make a trip to the database in order to fetch the data. This data should then be cached as an application layer. Every subsequent request for that data will be fetched from the cache, saving the server a request to the database, resulting in the response being returned to the client faster.

The uniform interface

This is the constraint that makes REST different from other network architecture patterns. The interfaces exposed by the components are generalized. The server does not have intimate knowledge of its consumers. It serves all requests from clients in the same way. What you get is coarse grained data, as not all consumers would want this amount of data.

To get a uniform interface, four constraints will have to be applied:

- Identifying resources
- Manipulating resources
- Self-descriptive messages
- Hypermedia as the engine of the application state

We will look into these later on.

Layered system

By layering the components, we ensure that each component does not know about the layers that its neighbors connect to. This promotes good security in order to have good boundary walls. It also allows legacy systems to be protected if they are consumed in your architecture, and it allows you to protect new systems:

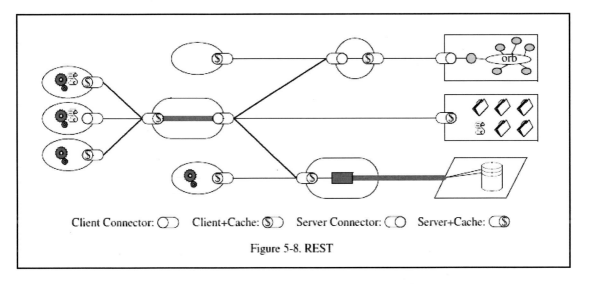

Client Connector: ⬭   Client+Cache: ⑤   Server Connector: ⬭   Server+Cache: ⑤

Figure 5-8. REST

With the layered approach, it leads to many hops between systems, but you have the security boundaries, and components can be updated individually.

Code-on-demand

This is probably the least popular characteristic of REST. It allows the server to provide code to the client by an applet or script that can be executed by the client. This allows the server to provide more functionality to the client post the deployment. The constraint is optional, and we will not explore it in detail.

REST architectural elements

As discussed earlier, REST is not a protocol, and it can be discussed without implementation. The key element of REST is the ability to add constraints to components, connectors, and data.

Data elements

When you select a hyperlink where data needs to be transferred from the server to the client, the client needs to interpret the data and render it into a format to the user. How does the REST principle do this? The REST components transfer the data as well as the metadata to the client, with instructions to help the client compose the resource that it has requested:

Data element	Modern web examples
Resource	The intended conceptual target of a hypertext reference
Resource identifier	URL, URN
Representation	HTML document, JPEG image
Representation metadata	Media type, last modified time
Resource metadata	Source link, alternates, vary
Control data	If-modified-since, cache control

Resources and resource identifiers

A resource is a reference to any information that you wish to share. It could be a picture or a document that you wish to share with your friends. Roy T. Fielding sums up a resource quite precisely. A resource is a conceptual mapping to a set of entities, not the entity that corresponds to the mapping at any particular point in time. More precisely, a resource R is a temporally varied membership function $Mr(r)$, which for time t maps to a set of entities, or values, which are equivalent. The values in the set may be resource representations and/or resource identifiers.

When a resource is used between components, a resource identifier is used by REST to know which resource it is.

Your resource should have a resource identifier when it is used between components, which is used by REST to identify your resource.

Representations

A representation is a combination of the data you want to share and the metadata associated with it. The format of a representation is known as a media type. Media will be discussed in more detail later on in this chapter with some concrete examples. Media types are important when the server sends some data for the client to render; ideally, the server will send the media type first, which will describe to the client how the data should be rendered. As the client receives the data, it can start rendering the representation, which results in a better user experience. This is compared to the client receiving all the data and then receiving instructions on how to render the representation.

Connectors

The types of connectors are client, server, cache, resolver, and tunnel. You can think of connectors as interfaces. They abstract how components communicate. A connector's job in the REST architecture is to enable the retrieving of resource representations as well as exposing resources. REST is stateless; every request will have to carry all the information that is required for the server to process the request from the client.

Let's look at the model that REST uses to process a request. The request can be compared to a stored procedure:

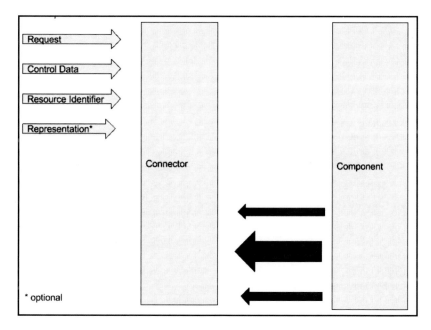

> *Control Data defines the purpose of a message between components, such as the action being requested or the meaning of a response.*

-Architectural Styles and the Design of Network-based Software Architectures by Roy T. Fielding, section 5.2.1.2, page 109

Components

A component in REST architecture would be a web browser on the client and IIS on the server.

HTTP

HTTP stands for Hypertext Transfer Protocol. The very first version was 0.9; then came version 1.0.

The key difference between 1.0 and 1.1 is that the client makes a connection with the server and that connection is reused, whereas in HTTP 1.0, the connection is thrown away and for each request, a new connection is created. HTTP 1.1 is also derived by applying the REST constraints to 1.0.

A basic HTTP message is composed of a header and body.

When the client communicates with the server, it communicates via HTTP. The server responds to the client with messages and code.

HTTP/1.1 status codes

There is a broad range of status codes, which indicate to the client what has occurred with the request that has been processed by the server:

- 2xx: Success
- 200: OK
- 201: Created
- 3xx: Redirection
- 4xx: Client error

- `400`: Bad Request
- `401`: Unauthorized
- `403`: Forbidden
- `404`: Not found
- `409`: Conflict
- `5xx`: Server error
- `500`: Internal server error

We will concentrate on the most common codes and the codes that we will use later on in the book when we implement an API.

An API example

I have used the GitHub API to show the basic HTTP methods. You can sign up to GitHub and get an authentication token if you wish to explore the API. In the next chapter, we will create our own API. In these examples, we act as a consumer of an API. In these examples, I am using Fiddler to make the request. You can use any tool you like; other commonly used tools are Postman, which is built into the Chrome browser or Advanced Rest Client. Idempotent is a term used for REST APIs; simply put, when you call a method, it will return the same data no matter how many times you call it. In the following examples, I will list which methods are idempotent.

HTTP POST example

Our HTTP method is POST, and `https://api.github.com/gists` is our resource. We have a header value in the request as well. `User-Agent` is the header key, with a value of `Awesome-Octocat-App`. This is what the documentation has specified.

You can take note of the request body in the following screenshot:

This is our request for a POST method.

Our response from this request is depicted here. The server has responded with 201, which means that our request was valid, and the server has carried out the operation successfully:

```
HTTP/1.1 201 Created
Server: GitHub.com
```

The server also sends back a resource to us. A new resource has been born and we can fetch data from this.

POST is not idempotent. Idempotent in the REST world implies that as a client when I call an endpoint more than once, I expect to receive the same behavior or I expect to get back the same data. Consider the example where you have to create a contact with a unique email address. The first time you call POST with this email address and other contact details, the server will respond with 201, which means that contact has been created and a unique resource has been published, where you can fetch that data.

If you call a POST method with the same email address, what will happen? The server should return a conflict, 409. The email exists in the data store. So POST is not idempotent:

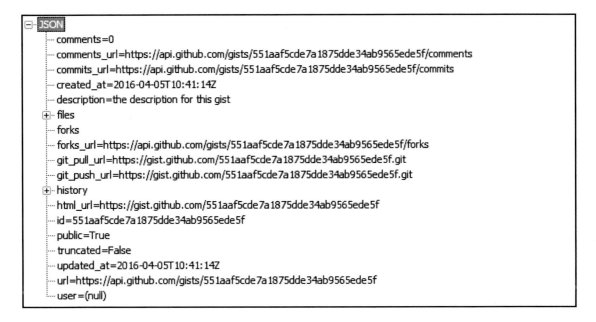

HTTP GET example

Using the resource from the server, we perform GET on the resource:

The server responds with a 200 status, which is OK:

#	Result	Protocol	Host	URL
2	200	HTTPS	api.github.com	/gists/551aaf5cde7a1875...

The server returns the data that we have requested:

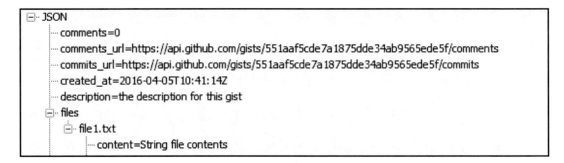

GET is idempotent, when we make the very first time request, we get a response. Making the same request will return the same response. This also ties into the REST principle of stateless. In order for this GET request to return the same data, the server should be stateless.

HTTP PUT example

We can perform an update to our representation with the following URL. Take note of the HTTP verb PUT.

The documentation has said that we can call a PUT method at the following resource and also note the /star as part of the URI. PUT is used to modify our representation. Generally, PUT will have a body. In the gist API for GitHub, they have made it simpler. Generally, the notion is for PUT to look similar to POST, except that the URI contains the identifier that was received when the POST method was called:

PUT behaves similar to POST when a resource does not exist. In our example from POST, if you had to call PUT the very first time with the POST request to create a contact instead, then you would receive 201, informing you that the resource was created. Then, if you had to call the request on PUT again, you will get back 200 with the same data. In this way, PUT is idempotent.

HTTP DELETE example

DELETE is very similar to GET. Our HTTP method is DELETE, and we want to undo the star put we created with PUT. DELETE usually has no body:

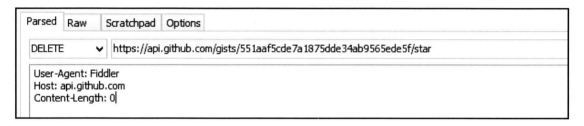

DELETE is idempotent; when you call DELETE, you will get 200 back, indicating that the resource has been deleted. Making this request again will result in 404, resource not found, as the data has been deleted. Making this call again will result in 404. Although the response has changed from 200 to 404, you are still getting back the same behavior and the server is not doing anything different.

Version 2 of HTTP

HTTP/2 is an optimization of HTTP 1.1. Many browsers already support HTTP/2; your Chrome browser does that already.

HTTP/2 is a combination of two specifications: Hypertext Transfer Protocol version 2 (RFC7540) and HPACK- Header Compression for HTTP2 (RFC7541).

When using HTTP/2 over **Transport Layer Security (TLS)**, "h2" is used to indicate the protocol.

The "h2c" string is used when HTTP/2 is used over clear text TCP or when HTTP.1.1 upgrades.

An example of a GET request is as follows:

GET / HTTP/1.1
Host: server.example.com
Connection: Upgrade, HTTP2-Settings
Upgrade: h2c
HTTP2-Settings: <base64url encoding of HTTP/2 SETTINGS payload>

-RCF 7540 Section 3.2

This request is from a client that does not know whether HTTP/2 is supported. It makes a HTTP 1.1 request, but includes an upgrade field in the header, "h2c", and at least one HTTP2-Settings header field:

A server that does not support HTTP/2 will respond as follows:

HTTP/1.1 200 OK
Content-Length: 243
Content-Type: text/html

-RCF 7540 Section 3.2

This looks like a regular HTTP/1.1 response:

A server that does support HTTP/2 will respond as follows:

HTTP/1.1 101 Switching Protocols
Connection: Upgrade
Upgrade: h2c
[HTTP/2 connection ...

-RCF 7540 Section 3.2

A frame is introduced as basis unit in HTTP2. You can think of a frame as a packet that is transferred over the wire. For requests and responses, the HEADER and DATA frames are used as the building blocks, and for HTTP/2 features, the frames are SETTINGS, WINDOWS_UPDATE, and PUSH_PROMISE.

Single connection

A single connection between the server and client can be used by both the server and the client to transport multiple requests. Suppose you have a page that has several components in it, which all fire independent requests to the server-say, one that will get the weather for today, one that will get the latest stock prices, and one that will get the latest headlines. They can all be made with one connection, not three separate connections. This exists for the server as well. What you end with is less connections getting created.

Server push

The server can push data to the client. When the client requests data from the server, the server can figure out that the client will need some other data as well. The server can push this data to the client. The client can always reject the data by signaling to the server that push data should be disabled. This data sent by the server to the client is called a PUSH_PROMISE frame. The data is stored in the client's cache if it implements an HTTP cache.

Multiplexing and streams

A stream is like a tunnel that has many cars passing through it in both directions, with the cars being substituted with frames, and a stream is standalone between a client and a server. In HTTP/2, a connection can have many streams, with frames from one request spread over many streams, though the order of the frames is important.

This is a significant improvement from HTTP 1.1, which uses multiple connections to render a single page.

Stream prioritization

Having multiple streams is great, but sometimes, you want a stream to be addressed ahead of another stream. In HTPP/2, a client can specify the priority of a stream in the HEADERS frame. This priority of the stream can be changed by the client using the Priority frame. In this way, the client can indicate to its peer how it prefers its request to be processed.

Binary messages

Messages are processed faster as they are in a binary format compared to text. Since they are in the native binary format over the wire, they don't need to translate from text to binary by the TCP protocol.

Header compression

As the web has evolved, more data is sent from the server to the client and from the client to the server. HTTP 1.1 does not compress header fields. HTTP works over TCP and a request is sent over this connection, where the headers are large and contain redundant data. TCP works on Slow Start implemented by a network congestion-avoidance algorithm, which places packets over the network. If the headers are compressed, more packets can be sent over the wire. HTTP/2 fixed this problem with header compression, which takes advantage of TCP, resulting in a faster transfer speed of data.

Media types

Commonly referred to as **MIME (Multipurpose Internet Mail Extensions)** types, media types are used to identify the format of an HTTP message body. A media type is of the `{type/subtype}` format; examples are as follows:

- text/html
- image/png
- audio/mpeg
- video/avi

A request can be as follows:

```
GET:
Host:
Accept:application/json, text/javascript
```

The client is specifying which format it can receive data in.

Richardson maturity model

The **Richardson maturity model** (**RMM**) was developed by Leonard Richardson. Commonly referred to as RMM, it is used to upgrade the standard of your API.

Level 0

This is your traditional soap-based web service or the XML-RPC service. It uses HTTP, but it has one method and one URI. This method is usually `POST` and will return a heavy dataset. I am sure all of us have worked with this type of web service or might encounter it at some point. The entire database as a dataset is wrapped in this output.

Level 1

Resources are exposed, but you still have an HTTP method. If you are at Level 0, then changing your web service to return a resource will take you from level 0 to level 1. You still have one HTTP method, but when your method is invoked, your service will pass back a resource:

```
Request:
POST
diet/ate
Response
diet/ate/12789
Request:
POST
diet/ate
Response:
diet/ate/99000
```

There is one endpoint `diet/ate` still, it returns many resources.

Level 2

Level 2 is for the use of HTTP verbs. So in level 1, we introduced resources, and level 2 introduces verbs.

Using the preceding example, when you post what you ate at 10 a.m., the server will give you back a resource. Using this resource, you can perform GET on that resource and see the details of what you ate at 10 a.m.:

```
GET: diet/ate/12789
Response
{
  'time':'10:00',
  'apple':'1',
  'water':'2'
}
```

You can then update these details using PUT; note that we are acting on the same resource.

The request is as follows:

```
PUT: diet/ate/12789
{
  'time':'10:00',
  'tea':'1',
  'muffin':'3'
}
```

You can also delete this resource if you realize later on that you didn't eat at 10 a.m.:

```
DEL : diet/ate/12789
```

We used the same resource with a different verb.

When we created the resource in level 1, we changed POST to return 201 when the resource is created and a 409 conflict if the resource exists.

Part of level 2 uses response codes and does not return 200 for every operation.

Level 3

In level 3, hypermedia is introduced into our responses, commonly referred to as **HATEOAS (Hypertext As The Engine of Application State)**.

Let's go back to the POST example:

```
POST : diet/ate
Response:
{
  "id":"12789",
  "links":[{
```

```
      "rel":"self",
      "href":"http://yoursitename/diet/12789
    },
    {
      "Rel":"self",
      "href":"http://yoursitename/diet/12789"
    },
    "rel":"rating",
    "href":"http://yoursitename/diet/12789/rating/"
    ]
}
```

The point of the link is that it lets the consumer know what actions it can carry out.

Although both endpoints look the same, the consumer will figure out that one is DELETE and the other is PUT.

The last link is the resource to rate the meal you added.

Summary

We looked at the definition of REST and how REST is derived. When you look at the REST architecture, you should be able to depict it in three categories, as explained by Roy T. Fielding. One, the process view, describes how data flows from the client to the several components. Two, the connector view is specific to the exchanging of messages between components specific to resources and resource identification. Three, the data view of how the data that we referred to as representations is transmitted from the server to the client. It is very important to have a good understanding of the REST principles and that REST was applied to HTTP 1.0 in order to derive HTTP 1.1.

HTTP is a living example of the REST principles. Actions such as GET and POST are stateless, which is a principle of REST. The examples show how to construct an HTTP request and what the server sends back as a response. With HTTP/2, we have new features coming through, which makes our transfer speed much faster and our applications more responsive.

The Richardson maturity model explains how APIs are classified; as a developer, you should aim for a level 3 model. If you are a consumer of an API, perhaps you need to choose between several options. RMM will help you make this informed decision.

In this chapter, we did not focus on specific technologies; in the next chapter, we will delve deeper into the ASP.NET Core and what it offers as a framework in order to build web APIs.

3

Anatomy of ASP.NET Core Web API

This chapter starts with a quick recap of MVC. You might be surprised why we need MVC when we are working with web APIs. It's because the ASP.NET Web API is designed based on the MVC principles of Controllers, Models, and Views (the response returned can be treated as a faceless view in the case of a Web API).

Our focus in this chapter is to know why we need a lightweight HTTP-based service technology in the form of a Web API, its evolution to meet the constantly changing industry demands, the entry of Microsoft into the world of Open Source in the form of .NET Core and ASP.NET Core apps, and not limiting ourselves to the world of Windows OS for developing ASP.NET web applications.

In this chapter, we will be looking at the following topics:

- A quick recap of the MVC framework
- Inception of web APIs and their evolution
- Introduction to .NET Core
- An overview of the ASP.NET Core Architecture
- Creating an ASP.NET Core Project using Visual Studio IDE
- Creating an ASP.NET Core Project in Linux/macOS
- Examining the ASP.NET Core project files and structures
- Understanding Request processing
- MVC and web API unification
- Running the ASP.NET Core Web API

A quick recap of the MVC framework

A **Model-View-Controller** (**MVC**) is a powerful and elegant way of separating concerns within an application, and applies itself extremely well to web applications.

With ASP.NET MVC, MVC stands for the following:

- **Models (M)**: These are classes that represent the domain model. Most of them represent the data stored in a database, for example, Employee, Customer, and so on.
- **View (V)**: This is a dynamically generated HTML page as template.
- **Controller (C)**: This is a class that manages the interaction between the View and the Model. Any operation on a View should have a corresponding handling in the Controller like user inputs, render appropriate UI, Authentication, Logging, and so on.

Inception of Web APIs and their evolution

Looking back to the days when the ASP.NET ASMX-based XML web service was widely used for building service-oriented applications, it was the easiest way to create a **SOAP** (**Simple Object Access Protocol**)-based service that could be used by both .NET applications and non-.NET applications. It was available only over HTTP.

In the late 2007, Microsoft released **Windows Communication Foundation** (**WCF**). WCF was and is, even now, a powerful technology for building SOA-based applications. It was a giant leap in the world of the Microsoft .NET world.

WCF was flexible enough to be configured as an HTTP service, remoting service, TCP service, and so on. Using the contracts of WCF, we would keep the entire business logic code base the same, and expose the service as HTTP-based or non-HTTP-based via SOAP/non SOAP.

Until 2010, the ASMX-based XML web service, or WCF service, was widely used in client-server-based applications; in fact, everything was running smoothly.

But the developers of the .NET and non-.NET community started to feel the need for a completely new SOA technology for client-server applications. Some of the reasons behind this were as follows:

- With applications in production, the amount of data used while communicating started to explode, and transferring them over the network was bandwidth consuming.
- SOAP, being lightweight to some extent, started to show signs of payload increase. A few KB SOAP packets would become a few MB of data transfer.
- Consuming the SOAP service in applications led to huge application sizes because of WSDL and proxy generation. This was even worse when it was used in web applications.
- Any changes to the SOAP services led to updating the service proxy to reflect changes. This wasn't an easy task for any developer.
- JavaScript-based web frameworks were released, and gained ground for a much simpler way of web development. Consuming SOAP-based services was not that optimal.
- Hand-held devices, like tablets and smartphones, became popular. They had more focused applications, and needed a very lightweight service-oriented approach.
- Browser-based **Single Page Applications** (SPA) gained ground very rapidly. Using SOAP-based services was quite heavy for these SPA.
- Microsoft released REST-based WCF components, which can be configured to respond in JSON or XML, but still it was built on top of heavy technology of WCF.
- Applications where no longer just large enterprise services, and there was a need for a more focused, lightweight, and easy-to-use service, which could be up and running in a few days.

Any developer who has seen the evolving nature of SOA-based technologies such as ASMX, WCF, or any SOAP-based technology, felt the need to have much lighter, HTTP-based services.

HTTP-only, JSON-compatible **POCO (Plain Old CLR Object)**-based lightweight services was the need of the hour, and the concept of Web APIs started gaining momentum.

Introducing web API

Any method(s) that is accessible over the web using HTTP verbs is called a web API. It is a lightweight way of transmitting data over HTTP, easily consumed by various clients like browsers, desktop apps, handheld devices, or even other SOA applications.

For a web API to be a successful HTTP-based service, it needed a strong web infrastructure like hosting, caching, concurrency, logging, security, and so on. One of the best web infrastructures was none other than ASP.NET.

ASP.NET, either in the form of a Web Form or an MVC, was widely adopted, so the solid base for web infrastructure was mature enough to be extended as a Web API.

Microsoft responded to the community needs by creating ASP.NET Web API--a super-simple yet very powerful framework for building HTTP-only, JSON-by-default web services without all the fuss of WCF.

The ASP.NET Web API can be used to build REST-based services in a matter of minutes, and can be easily consumed with any of the frontend technologies.

It was launched in 2012 with the most basic needs for HTTP-based services like convention-based Routing, HTTP Request, and Response messages.

Later, Microsoft released the much bigger and better ASP.NET Web API 2 along with ASP.NET MVC 5 in Visual Studio 2013.

ASP.NET Web API 2 evolved at a much faster pace with these features:

- Installing of the web API 2 was made simpler by using NuGet; you can create either an empty ASP.NET or MVC project, and then run the following command on the NuGet Package Manager Console:

```
Install-Package Microsoft.AspNet.WebApi
```

- The initial release of the web API was based on convention-based routing, which means that we define one or more route templates, and work around it. It's simple without much fuss, as the routing logic is in a single place, and it's applied across all controllers.
- The real-world applications are more complicated with resources (controllers/actions) having child resources, for example, customers having orders, books having authors, and so on. In such cases, convention-based routing is not scalable.

- Web API 2 introduced a new concept of Attribute Routing, which uses attributes in programming languages to define routes. One straightforward advantage is that the developer has full control over how URIs for the web API are formed.
- Here a is quick snippet of Attribute Routing:

```
Route("customers/{customerId}/orders")]
public IEnumerable<Order>GetOrdersByCustomer(int customerId) { ...
}
```

> For more details on this, read Attribute Routing in ASP.NET Web API 2 at
> https://www.asp.net/web-api/overview/web-api-routing-and-acti
> ons/attribute-routing-in-web-api-2.

- An ASP.NET Web API lives on the ASP.NET framework, which may lead you to think that it can be hosted on IIS only. However, using OWIN self-host, it can be hosted without IIS also.
- If any web API is developed using either the .NET or non-.NET technologies, and is meant to be used across different web frameworks, then enabling CORS is a must.

> A must read on CORS and ASP.NET Web API 2 can be found at this link:
> https://www.asp.net/web-api/overview/security/enabling-cross-
> origin-requests-in-web-api.

- IHTTPActionResult and web API OData improvements are other few notable features which helped web API 2 evolve as a strong technology for developing HTTP-based services.
- ASP.NET Web API 2 has become more powerful over the years with C# language improvements like asynchronous programming using Async/Await, LINQ, Entity Framework Integration, Dependency Injection with DI frameworks, and so on.

ASP.NET into Open Source world

Every technology has to evolve with growing needs and advancements in the hardware, network, and software industry, and the ASP.NET Web API is no exception to that.

Some of the changes that ASP.NET Web API should undergo from the perspectives of the developer community, enterprises, and end users are as follows:

- Although ASP.NET MVC and web API are part of the ASP.NET stack, but their implementation and code base is different. A unified code base reduces the burden of maintaining them.
- It's known that web APIs are consumed by various clients such as web applications, native apps, hybrid apps, and desktop applications using different technologies (.NET or non .NET). But how about developing a web API in a cross-platform way, where the developer need not always rely on Windows OS/Visual Studio IDE.
- The ASP.NET stack should be made open source so that it's adopted on a much bigger scale.
- End users are benefitted with open source innovations.

We saw why web APIs were incepted, how they evolved into a powerful HTTP-based service, and some evolutions that are required. With these thoughts, Microsoft made an entry into the world of Open Source by launching .NET Core and ASP.NET Core.

Introduction to .NET Core

.NET Core is a cross-platform open-source managed software framework. It is built on top of CoreCLR, a complete cross-platform runtime implementation of CLR.

.NET Core applications can be developed, tested, and deployed on cross platforms such as Windows, Linux flavors, and macOS systems.

.NET Core has the following important components:

- **CoreCLR**: This is the .NET Core execution engine which performs the essential tasks of GC, compilation to machine code.
- **CoreFX**: This contains class libraries for collections, filesystem, XML, async, and so on for .NET Core.
- **SDK Tools**: This is a set of SDK tools for day-to-day development experience. Creating projects, build, run, and tests are common developer needs that are part of these SDK tools.

.NET Core shares a subset of the original .NET Framework, plus it comes with its own set of APIs that is not part of the .NET Framework. This results in some shared APIs that can be used by both .NET Core and the .NET Framework.

A .Net Core application can easily work on the existing .NET Framework, but not vice versa.

.NET Core provides a **CLI (Command Line Interface)** for an execution entry point for operating systems, and provides developer services such as compilation and package management.

The following are some interesting points to know about .NET Core:

- .NET Core can be installed on cross platforms like Windows, Linux, and macOS. It can be used in device, cloud, and embedded/IoT scenarios.
- Visual Studio IDE is not mandatory to work with .NET Core, but when working on the Windows OS, we can leverage the existing IDE knowledge.
- .NET Core is modular, which means that, instead of assemblies, developers deal with NuGet packages.
- .NET Core relies on its package manager to receive updates, because cross-platform technology can't rely on Windows updates.
- To learn .NET Core, we just need a shell, text editor, and it's runtime installed.
- .NET Core comes with flexible deployment. It can be included in your app or installed side-by-side user- or machine-wide.
- .NET Core apps can also be self-hosted/run as standalone apps.

.NET Core supports four cross-platform scenarios: ASP.NET Core web apps, command-line apps, libraries, and Universal Windows Platform apps.

It does not support Windows Forms or WPF which render the standard GUI for desktop software on Windows.

At present,only the C# programming language can be used to write .NET Core apps. F# and VB support are on the way.

We will, primarily, focus on the ASP.NET Core web apps, which include MVC and web API. CLI apps and libraries will be covered briefly. As its cross platform, having to install Visual Studio IDE to create applications is not mandatory. In this section, we will install .NET Core, build very a basic .NET Core application, and learn about the different commands for .NET Core.

Install .NET Core SDK

Open the .NET Core (`https://www.microsoft.com/net/core/preview`) website to download the SDK as per your platform of choice. At the time of writing, .NET Core 2 Preview 2 was available.

For the Windows environment, .NET Core 2.0 SDK can be installed in two ways:

- **.NET Core 2.0 and Visual Studio Tooling**: During Visual Studio 2017 installation, an option is provided to install required tooling or .NET Core SDK can also install them. CLI gets installed along with this.
- **.NET Core 2.0 SDK for Windows**: This is the CLI mode of working with .NET Core applications.

If you're using Windows OS, and prefer Visual Studio 2017 IDE, then it's better to leverage your IDE experience..

To work with code, you can also install a text editor like Visual Studio Code. It's a lightweight code editor developed by Microsoft for Windows, Linux, and macOS. It can be downloaded from `https://code.visualstudio.com/`. Other text editors like Vim, Atom, and Sublime can also be used.

For a non-Windows machine, an appropriate .NET Core SDK (refer to this link for your OS of choice: `https://www.microsoft.com/net/core/preview`) and Visual Studio Code (recommended) for working with code should be installed.

Visual Studio for Mac is an exclusive IDE for macOS users, and can be used for .NET Core and ASP.NET Core apps. Download it from `https://www.visualstudio.com/vs/visual-studio-mac/`.

Creating and running a basic .NET Core application

We will focus on learning a few basic concepts of .NET Core, and how to work through the command line. The following steps are cross platform to learn .NET Core. Refer the documentation link for further details at `https://docs.microsoft.com/en-us/dotnet/core/tools/`.

First, let's ensure that everything was installed properly. Open the Console/ Shell (as per your OS of choice), enter the following command to view the CLI commands and tool version, product information, and the runtime environment:

```
> dotnet -info
```

The .NET Core CLI provides the following commands to work with:

new	Initializes a basic .NET project
restore	Restores dependencies specified in the .NET project (Runs automatically in most cases)
build	Builds a .NET project
publish	Publishes a .NET project for deployment (including the runtime)
run	Compiles and immediately executes a .NET project
test	Runs unit tests using the test runner specified in the project
pack	Creates a NuGet package

There are a few more commands as well, go look for them too.

In the command line, type the following command:

```
> dotnet new console --name DemoCoreApp
```

```
d:\code>dotnet new console --name DemoCoreApp
The template "Console Application" was created successfully.

Processing post-creation actions...
Running 'dotnet restore' on DemoCoreApp\DemoCoreApp.csproj...
  Restoring packages for d:\code\DemoCoreApp\DemoCoreApp.csproj.
  Generating MSBuild file d:\code\DemoCoreApp\obj\DemoCoreApp.cs
ps.
  Generating MSBuild file d:\
gets.
  Restore completed in 297.18

Restore succeeded.

d:\code>cd DemoCoreApp

d:\code\DemoCoreApp>code .

d:\code\DemoCoreApp>dir
 Volume in drive D has no lak
```

.NET Core Command in action

Let's understand what's happening here in the preceding screenshot:

- `dotnet new` creates a .NET Core C# console project in the context of directory. It has two files: `program.cs` containing the C# code, and its project file, `csproj`.
- `DemoCoreApp.csproj` is a usual .NET project file containing all the details about the project in an XML format. However, in .NET Core, the projects are highly trimmed due to the use of netcoreapp2.0 as the target framework.
- From .NET Core 2.0, whenever we create, build, or publish a project, `dotnet restore` runs automatically.

As seen in the preceding screenshot, the demo project is open in VS Code; view `program.cs` to see the C# code for outputting the text on the console.

Just as in traditional .NET projects, we build a C# project, the same way, running the `dotnet build` command, will perform the routine build and generate the `bin` and `obj` folders.

Now `dotnet run` will run the C# console application, and display the result `Hello World` on the console.

This C# project can be published and used for deployment by running `dotnet publish`. This will create the `publish` folder under the `bin` directory. This `publish` folder can then be ported to any machine which has .NET Core SDK installed.

We saw a console application built; we can use the same `dotnet new` command to create libraries, web, and xunittest projects, as follows:

```
dotnet new [--type]
```

The `--type` option specifies the template type of the project to be created, that is, console, web, lib, and xunittest.

Using the .NET CLI command `dotnet new web`, you can create a web application that uses .NET Core, and that is called ASP.NET Core.

Introducing ASP.NET Core

ASP.NET Core is a new open-source and cross-platform framework for building modern cloud-based web applications using .NET.

ASP.NET Core is completely open source, you can download it from GitHub (`https://github.com/aspnet/Mvc`). It's cross platform, which means that you can develop ASP.NET Core apps on Linux/macOS, and, of course, on Windows OS.

ASP.NET was first released almost 15 years back with the .NET framework. Since then, it's been adopted by millions of developers for large and small applications.

With .NET Core being cross platform, ASP.NET took a huge leap beyond the boundaries of the Windows OS environment for development and deployment of web applications. Let's look into more details of the cross-platform ASP.NET.

An overview of ASP.NET Core

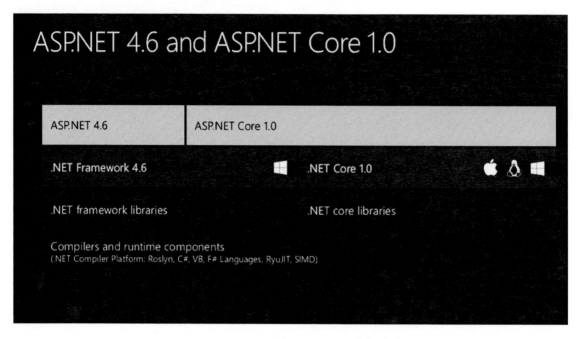

ASP.NET Core Architecture overview

A high-level overview of ASP.NET Core provides following insights:

- ASP.NET Core runs both on Full .NET framework and .NET Core.
- ASP.NET Core applications with full .NET framework can only be developed and deployed on Windows machines.
- When using .NET core, it can be developed and deployed on a platform of choice. The logos of Windows, Linux, and macOS indicate that you can work with ASP.NET Core on those.
- ASP.NET Core, when on a non-Windows machine, uses the .NET Core libraries to run the applications. It's obvious you won't have all the .NET libraries, but most of them are available.
- Developers working on ASP.NET Core can easily switch working on any machine not confined to Visual Studio IDE.
- ASP.NET Core can run with different versions of .NET Core.

ASP.NET Core has many other foundational improvements apart from being cross-platform. The following are the advantages of using ASP.NET Core:

- ASP.NET Core takes a totally modular approach for application development--every component needed to build an application is well factored into NuGet packages. We only need to add the required packages through NuGet to keep the overall application lightweight.
- ASP.NET Core is no longer based on `System.Web.dll`.
- Visual Studio IDE was used to develop ASP.NET applications on Windows OS box. Now, since we have moved beyond the Windows world, we will require IDE/editors/ Tools required for developing ASP.NET applications on Linux/macOS. Microsoft developed powerful lightweight code editors for almost any type of web applications called as Visual Studio Code.
- ASP.NET Core is such a framework that we don't need Visual Studio IDE/ code to develop applications. We can use code editors like Sublime and Vim also. To work with the C# code in editors, install the OmniSharp plugin.
- ASP.NET Core has powerful, seamless integration with modern web frameworks like Angular, Ember, NodeJS, and Bootstrap.
- Using bower and NPM, we can work with modern web frameworks.
- ASP.NET Core apps are cloud ready with the configuration system--it just seamlessly gets transitioned from on-premises to cloud.
- Built-in dependency injection.
- Can be hosted on IIS, or self-hosted in your own process or on Nginx (It is a free, open-source, high-performance HTTP server and reverse proxy for LINUX environment.).
- New lightweight and modular HTTP request pipeline.
- Unified code base for web UI and web APIs. We will see more on this when we explore the anatomy of an ASP.NET Core application.

Creating ASP.NET Core Project using Visual Studio IDE

We will now create an ASP.NET Core Web API application using Visual Studio 2017 IDE. Ensure this prerequisite before starting:

- Install Visual Studio 2017 (do select the .NET Core SDK options while installation). We will be using the community edition all the way. ASP.NET Core 2.0 Preview 2 is used throughout this book

Let's get started with building the ASP.NET Core Web API step by step:

1. Open Visual Studio 2017 IDE, click on **New Project** to open the project templates dialog.
2. Under Visual C# Templates, click on **.NET Core**, and select **ASP.NET Core Web Application** as shown in the following screenshot:

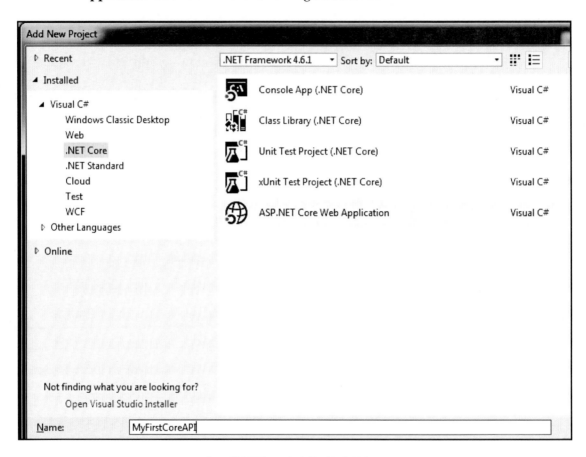

Create ASP.NET Core project in Visual Studio 2017 IDE

 We can also create an ASP.NET Core web application targeting the full .NET framework by web template under the Visual C# section

3. Provide an appropriate project name like `MyFirstCoreApi`, click on **OK**.

Choosing the application type

ASP.NET Core provides us different application templates to start developing applications. These templates give us an optimal project structure to keep everything organized. We have the following types:

- **Empty**: This is simplest form of a project template containing only `Program.cs` and the `Startup.cs` class. Due to the complete modular nature of ASP.NET Core, we can upgrade this empty project to any type of web application.
- **Web API**: This creates the Web API project with controllers, `web.config`, and so on. Our focus will be on this application template.
- **Web Application**: This creates an ASP.NET Core MVC type of project with Controllers, Views, client configurations, `Startup.cs`, and `web.config`.
- **Web Application (Razor pages)**: This creates an ASP.NET Core web app using the Razor pages.
- **Angular, React.js, and React.js with Redux**: This creates JavaScript-framework-based ASP.NET Core web applications.

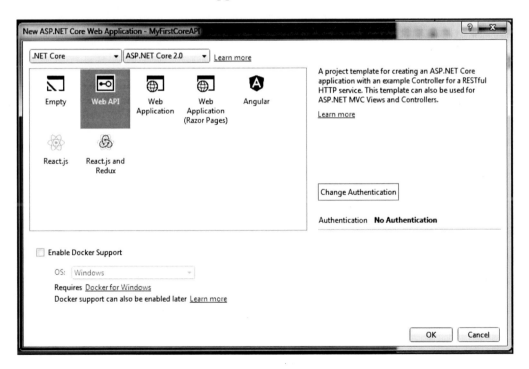

ASP.NET Core Project Templates

It's not mandatory to follow the template project structure provided by ASP.NET Core. When working on large projects, it's best practice to split them into separate projects for maintainability. The default project structure is good enough to understand the interaction between various components.

Selecting authentication type

Every application needs some type of authentication to prevent unauthorized access to the application. In the preceding screenshot, **Change Authentication** will provide the following authentication options:

- **No Authentication**: Choosing this option will not add any authentication packages to the application. However, we can add such packages to completely safeguard our application data when required.
- **Individual User Accounts**: Connecting to an Azure AD B2C application will provide us with all the authentication and authorization data.
- **Work or School Accounts**: Enterprises, organizations, and schools that authenticate users with Office 365, Active Directory, or Azure Directory services can use this option.
- **Windows Authentication**: Applications used in the Intranet environment can use this option.

In the **Change Authentication** option, select **No Authentication**, as shown in this screenshot:

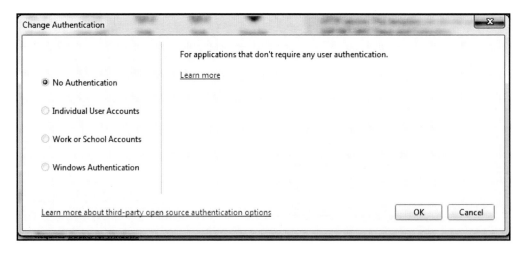

Select Authentication Type for Web API

Click on **OK** to create an ASP.NET Core Web API project; Visual Studio tooling will immediately start restoring the packages needed.

The `dotnet restore` command is executed to restore all the NuGet packages.

We saw how the Visual Studio IDE tooling helps us to create ASP.NET Core applications on Windows OS. This is similar to that when creating ASP.NET (MVC 4/5 and ASPX) applications.

Creating ASP.NET Core web applications on Linux/macOS

ASP.NET Core, being a cross-platform technology, we would need a similar user experience for creating web applications on Linux/macOS. It's well understood that Visual Studio IDE cannot be installed on Linux/macOS, so, there is a different approach for working with ASP.NET Core applications on non-Windows OS.

The following are the software requirements for Linux/macOS machines:

- Install the latest NodeJS version (`https://nodejs.org/en/`).
- Install Visual Studio Code-- a cross-platform lightweight code editor. Sublime, Vim, Atom can also be used (`https://code.visualstudio.com/#alt-downloads`).
- Install .NET Core SDK for Linux/macOS (`https://www.microsoft.com/net/download`).

> On Windows machines too, we can use NodeJS, Visual Studio Code, and .NET Core SDK for working with ASP.NET Core and avoid Visual Studio IDE.

Creating ASP.NET Core web apps with Yeoman

Yeoman is web-scaffolding tool for modern web apps. It is an open source tool that works like Visual Studio templates using the command-line option. The Yeoman command-line tool, yo, works alongside a Yeoman generator.

Yeoman generates a complete project with all the necessary files to run the application, just like VS IDE. Read through the link http://yeoman.io/ to know more.

For installing Yeoman, ensure that NodeJS and NPM are installed from the link in the software prerequisites given earlier.

Open the command line to run the command to install **Yeoman (yo)**. The option -g installs the npm packages globally so that it can be used from any path.

```
npm install -g yo
```

Once Yeoman is installed successfully, we need to install the ASP.NET Core generator for yo. It will help in project creation and the scaffolding of the different components of web applications. In the command line, run the following command:

```
npm install -g generator-aspnet
```

Yeoman scaffolding can only be used with ASP.NET Core web applications for .NET Core.

Creating ASP.NET Core Web API using Yeoman

Ensuring that everything is installed properly, open the command line, type yo aspnet to view the different project templates similar to Visual Studio IDE. We will create a web API application, provide an appropriate name like yowebapidemo, and hit *Enter* to create the project.

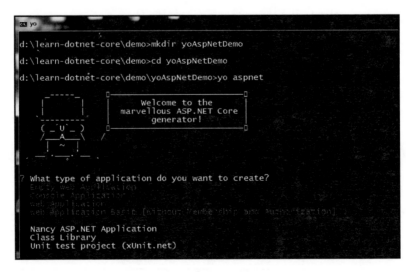

Create ASP.NET Core apps using Yeoman

Once the Yeoman generates the web API project, it displays the list of project files created and the instructions to perform.

 We can even use the .NET Core CLI commands to create an ASP.NET Core Web API project by referring to the link `https://docs.microsoft.c om/en-us/dotnet/core/tools/`.

ASP.NET Core Web API Application structure

We have created a web API project using either Visual Studio IDE on Windows, Yeoman generator, or the .NET Core CLI on Linux/macOS--the application structure will be the same including files, folder, and configuration settings. Let's understand the application structure in detail:

Files and folder	Purpose
The `/Controllers` folder	This is where we put the `Controller` classes that handle the requests
The `Program.cs` file	This is the entry point for application execution using the `Main` method.
The `Startup.cs` file	This is needed to set up the configuration and for wiring up the services that the application will use
The `.csproj` file	This is a C# project file (`.csproj`), which is more lightweight, robust, and easy to use.
The `Appsettings.json` file	This is the Key/ value-based configurations settings file
The `Web.config` file	This is used strictly for IIS configuration, and invokes the app when running on IIS

What about Model classes?

Domain models or POCO classes can be added in the Models folder, or we can create a separate class library for models. The preceding project structure is a good starting point; on larger projects, we can split the controllers, repositories, and domain models into separate class libraries for maintainability.

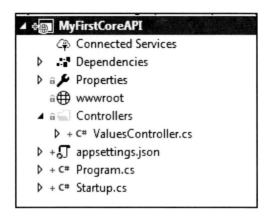

Asp.Net Core Web API project structure

Let's understand in detail the contents of each of these files.

Program.cs

ASP.NET Core web apps are, fundamentally, console applications--isn't it surprising to know that? Just like every console app needs `Main()` to get executed, the .NET Core apps have the `Program.cs` file that contains the `Main()` method.

ASP.NET Core is built on top of .NET Core, which is the reason why we have `program.cs` in the application structure which we just created. Check out this file:

```
using Microsoft.AspNetCore;
using Microsoft.AspNetCore.Hosting;

namespace MyFirstCoreAPI
{
  public class Program
  {
    public static void Main(string[] args)
    {
        BuildWebHost(args).Run();
```

```
    }

    public static IWebHost BuildWebHost(string[] args) =>
        WebHost.CreateDefaultBuilder(args)
        .UseStartup<Startup>()
        .Build();
    }
}
```

You can break down the preceding code as follows:

- Just like any .NET console application needs the `Main()` method to start executing, in the same way, .NET Core runtime will start the application by calling the `Main()` method.
- The `IWebHost` interface is needed to run these console applications as web apps (either as MVC or Web API).
- The `WebHost` class has `CreateDefaultBuilder`, which has preconfigured defaults to run the application. This means that the web app would need a web server (Kestrel), an IIS integration setup, configuration files to read various values, and the `Content Root` folder. All these requirements are preconfigured in this method.
- Although we can implement a custom method, but the default implementation provided is good enough to start. Read through this link to know the `CreateDefaultBuilder` code from the ASP.NET Core GitHub repo at `https://github.com/aspnet/MetaPackages/blob/rel/2.0.0-preview1/src/Microsoft.AspNetCore/WebHost.cs`. Let's look into these methods from the GitHub repo:
    - `UseKestrel ()` is an extension method and acts like a web server to run ASP.NET core apps. It's based on libuv. Kestrel is often called an internal web server responsible for running applications. It's lightweight, fast, and cross-platform. There's more on this at `https://github.com/aspnet/KestrelHttpServer`.
    - `UseContentRoot()` is an extension method for specifying the content root directory to be used by the web host. This is, usually, the current working directory; it can be configured to point to the other folder which contains all the files needed to run applications.
    - When using ASP.NET Core apps, IIS is considered as an external web server exposed to the internet for receiving requests. `UseIISIntegration()` configures the port and the base path the server should listen on when running behind `AspNetCoreModule`.

- `ConfigureAppConfiguration` reads the configuration files, and adds `UserSecrets` and environment variables.
- `ConfigureLogging` sets up the logging to the console as well as the debug window.
- `UseStartup(StartUp)` sets up the class to configure various services such as hitting the request-response pipeline, and so on. Startup is a simple class without any base class, and having two methods, `Configuration` and `Configure`.
- `Build()` builds and prepares `WebHostBuilder` for running the web application.
- `Run()` runs the ASP.NET Core web apps under the Kestrel web server.

Startup.cs

In ASP.NET Core, the Startup class gets called when `webHostBuilder` runs from `Main()`, and is required for all applications.

It's the first line of execution when any request comes, or a response is returned. It performs a bunch of operations, like providing the dependency injection, adding and using various middleware components, and so on.

The `Startup.cs` class must define the `Configure` and `ConfigureServices` methods; they will be called when the host starts running.

The Configure method

ASP.NET Core is totally modular, that is, you can add components if you really need them. With this approach, web apps become lightweight in terms of deployment and performance.

The main objective of the `Configure` method of the `Startup.cs` class is to configure the HTTP request pipeline. In the following code example of `Startup.cs`, you can see that `IApplicationBuilder` uses an extension method to configure the pipeline.

The `UseMvc` extension method adds the routing middleware to the request pipeline, and configures MVC as the default handler, as follows:

```
app.UseMvc();
```

We have created a simple web API, and for that, we are using MVC. You might wonder why MVC when we are working with web APIs? The reason for this is that ASP.NET Core has a unified MVC and web API.

IApplicationBuilder defines a class that provides the mechanisms to configure an application's request pipeline. You can build custom pipeline configurations as middleware, and add them using an extension method to IApplicationBuilder. Chapter 6, *Middleware and Filters,* is dedicated to this.

By default, IApplicationBuilder, IHostingEnvironment and ILoggerFactory are injected by server in a web API or MVC project:

```csharp
using Microsoft.AspNetCore.Builder;
using Microsoft.AspNetCore.Hosting;
using Microsoft.Extensions.DependencyInjection;

namespace MyFirstCoreAPI
{
  public class Startup
  {
    // This method gets called by the runtime. Use this method to add services to
        the container.
    public void ConfigureServices(IServiceCollection services)
    {
      services.AddMvc();
    }

    // This method gets called by the runtime. Use this method to configure the
        HTTP request pipeline.
    public void Configure(IApplicationBuilder app, IHostingEnvironment env)
    {
      app.UseMvc();
    }
  }
}
```

In the next section, we will discuss in detail about ASP.NET Core request pipeline processing, and the roles of middleware.

The ConfigureServices method

The `ConfigureServices` method sets all the services to be available for the application to run using the **dependency injection (DI)**. It adds the services list to the `IServiceCollection` instance, and is called before `Configure`.

The reason why this method gets called first by runtime is because some features such as MVC, Identity, Entity Framework, and so on, need to be added before they are ready for the request pipeline processing. For this reason, in the preceding code, we saw `services.AddMvc()`.

The `ConfigureServices` method helps achieve the dependency injection pattern in ASP.NET Core apps. Let's see a simple example, assuming that we wrote the `NewsOfDay` class by implementing the `INewsOfDay` interface. I want to use the DI pattern so that any other class can easily inject this interface to get the quote of the day.

```
public void ConfigureServices(IServiceCollection services)
{
  // using DI to inject the interface
  services.AddSingleton<INewsOfDay, NewsOfDay>();
}
```

ASP.NET Core supports dependency injection by default; we don't need to use any third-party DI containers such as Unity, StructureMap, Autofac, and so on. However, if the developer feels the need to use other DI containers, they can override the default implementation.

*.csproj

Any .Net developer would be familiar with the `*.csproj` file in the .NET project; in ASP.NET Core applications, we do find this file. It's a very trimmed-down version when compared with the traditional .NET applications.

In the initial version of ASP.NET Core, JSON-based `project.json` file was used for package management, but it was removed to keep in sync with other .NET applications, and to work well with the MSBUILD system.

The `.csproj` file can be now edited in Visual Studio 2017 IDE without reloading the entire project. Right-click on the project file, click on **Edit** to make changes.

Let's see the contents of the ASP.NET Core project's `*.csproj` file:

```
<Project Sdk="Microsoft.NET.Sdk.Web">
 <PropertyGroup>
   <TargetFramework>netcoreapp2.0</TargetFramework>
   <UserSecretsId>aspnet-MyFirstCoreAPI-D0B356AB-BC35-4D73-9576-
     997BC358BEE9</UserSecretsId>
 </PropertyGroup>

 <ItemGroup>
   <Folder Include="wwwroot\" />
 </ItemGroup>

 <ItemGroup>
   <PackageReference Include="Microsoft.AspNetCore.All"
     Version="2.0.0-preview2-final" />
 </ItemGroup>

 <ItemGroup>
   <DotNetCliToolReference
     Include="Microsoft.VisualStudio.Web.CodeGeneration.Tools"
     Version="2.0.0-preview2-final" />
 </ItemGroup>
</Project>
```

You can break down the `*.csproj` file as follows:

- The `TargetFramework` tag points to `netcoreapp2.0`. This is the ASP.NET Core name for .NET Standard 2.0. I recommend you to go to this link to know more about .NET Standard 2.0: `https://blogs.msdn.microsoft.com/dotnet` `/2016/09/26/introducing-net-standard/`.
- `Folder` is instructed to include the `wwwroot` directory in the build process.
- `PackageReference` are the NuGet packages or any custom libraries that will be included in the project. The `Microsoft.AspNetCore.All` meta-package references all of the ASP.NET Core packages with a single version number. Any new version can be updated only by changing this version. Even though you can add them as individual packages, but it's recommended to use `Microsoft.AspNetCore.All`.

Why Microsoft.AspNetCore.All meta-package?

.NET Core 2.0 brings a new feature called the Runtime Store. This, essentially, lets us pre-install packages on a machine in a central location so that we don't have to include them in the published output of individual apps.

ASP.NET Core request processing

ASP.NET (MVC and ASPX) were dependent on `system.web.dll` for all of its request processing. It used to do all the heavy work of browser-server communication, and was tightly coupled with IIS.

ASP.NET Core is designed by completely removing `system.web.dll` to make it cross-platform; this led to a different request processing technique in a completely pluggable way. This removal has also helped in the unification of MVC and the web API stack in ASP.NET.

ASP.NET Core doesn't differentiate between MVC and web API, so the request processing will be common now. In the next section, we will learn more on unification.

The following image shows an overview of the ASP.NET Core request processing:

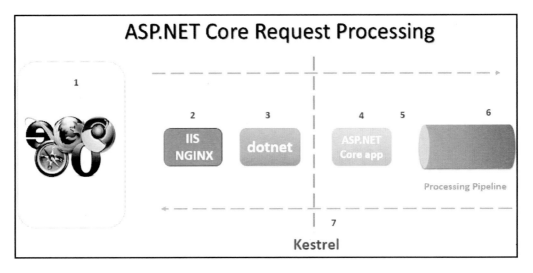

ASP.NET Core request processing

Let's understand the ASP.NET Core request processing step by step.

Various clients like web applications (browsers), native apps, and desktop apps hit the web APIs hosted on external web servers such as IIS/ Nginx. It is interesting to that know that IIS is now part of the external web server, because it does not run the ASP.NET Core application. It only acts as the hosting web server exposed over internet. Nginx is the counterpart of IIS on Linux machines.

IIS/ Nginx calls the dotnet runtime installed on the machine to start the processing request. It's now that the processing comes under .NET core. The `web.config` file is still present in the ASP.NET Core apps for this purpose.

The Dotnet runtime invokes the Kestrel web server (internal web server) to run the application. Kestrel is an open source lightweight cross-platform web server based on libuv; this is one of important steps for making ASP.NET Core apps truly cross-platform.

Kestrel then starts the application through the `Main ()` method present in the application. Remember, the ASP.NET core apps are console applications. The `Main ()` method present in `Program.cs` is the starting point in .NET Core apps.

The `Main ()` method then builds and runs `webHostBuilder`. The request, then, is pushed to the `Configure` method of the `Startup.cs` class; the HTTP request pipeline is configured here. The default web API template project we created earlier has only `app.UseMvc ()` added in the pipeline. We can customize the HTTP request pipeline processing logic in the form of middleware (refer `Chapter 6`, *Middleware and Filters*, for more details):

1. The MVC middleware is built on top of generic Routing middleware for handling requests. At this point, the request is processed, and sent to the appropriate controller for processing.
2. When request processing is completed, the response is sent through the same pipeline in the reverse order. Custom middleware can help us return a response if the request is invalid.

ASP.NET Core request pipeline processing is completely pluggable; the `Configure` method should include only the required middleware instead of the heavy `system.web.dll` that is present in the ASP.NET web stack.

Unified MVC and Web API in ASP.NET Core

One of the major architectural evolutions was the unification of MVC and web API in ASP.NET Core. There is no difference between the MVC and web API controllers in ASP.NET Core.

In the prior ASP.NET stack, the controllers from MVC and web API derived from their respective base controllers as follows:

```
// ASP.NET MVC 5 Controller
public class HomeController : Controller
{
```

```
    // Action Methods
}
// ASP.NET MVC 5 Controller
public class ValuesController : ApiController
{
    // API Action Methods
}
```

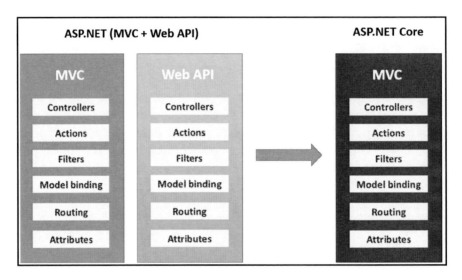

MVC and Web API unification

Both, ASP.NET MVC 4/5 and web API 2, have Controllers, Actions, Filters, Model binding, Routings, and Attributes, but they had different codebases because of following reasons:

- ASP.NET MVC (4/5) depends on `system.web.dll`, which is tied to IIS for hosting. Without IIS, you host an MVC application.
- The ASP.NET Web API was designed to be self-hosted; it wasn't dependent on IIS for hosting.

One of ASP.NET Core's design thoughts was to make it self-hosted and independent of IIS for hosting. In this way, `system.web.dll` was removed so that it can be hosted without IIS. This led to the merging of MVC and web API together to form a single codebase.

In ASP.NET Core, MVC and web API share the same base controller, and so, there is no implementation difference between MVC and web API.

Running the ASP.NET Core Web API project

Our ASP.NET Core Web API was created by Visual Studio 2017 IDE for the Windows environment and Yeoman generator for Linux/ macOS. We will run the application using either IIS Express or the Kestrel server.

Before running the application, let's understand more about the `Values` controller (created by default). Under the `Controllers` folder it has a C# class file named `ValuesController.cs`:

```
using System.Collections.Generic;
using Microsoft.AspNetCore.Mvc;

namespace MyFirstCoreAPI.Controllers
{
  [Route("api/[controller]")]
  public class ValuesController : Controller
  {
    // GET api/values
    [HttpGet]
    public IEnumerable<string> Get()
    {
        return new string[] { "value1", "value2" };
    }

    // GET api/values/5
    [HttpGet("{id}")]
    public string Get(int id)
    {
        return "value";
    }

    // POST api/values
    [HttpPost]
    public void Post([FromBody]string value)
    {
    }

    // PUT api/values/5
    [HttpPut("{id}")]
    public void Put(int id, [FromBody]string value)
    {
    }

    // DELETE api/values/5
    [HttpDelete("{id}")]
    public void Delete(int id)
```

```
        {
        }
    }
}
```

You can break down the preceding code as follows:

- Web APIs are based on the Model, Values, and Controller concept. `ValuesController.cs` is a C# class accessed by clients over HTTP.
- It's derived from the Controller base class, which makes any class an MVC or web API controller
- `[Route("api/[controller]")]` defines the routing strategy. Controllers are accessible based on this configuration
- `ValuesController` provides the following methods that are accessible over HTTP:

Method name	HTTP verb	Remarks
Get()	HttpGet	Returns IEnumerable of strings
Get(int id)	HttpGet	Returns a string based on value
Post([FromBody]string value)	HttpPost	Inserts a string using POST
public void Put(int id, [FromBody]string value)	HttpPut	Updates a string based on Id using PUT
public void Delete(int id)	HttpDelete	Deletes a string record using DELETE

Running the application in Visual Studio IDE

While working with Visual Studio 2017 IDE, we have two ways for running ASP.NET Core apps:

- **Using IIS Express**: If you want to use IIS Express. Press *F5* to start running the application; it opens the selected web browser.
- **Using Kestrel server**: If you want to run through the Kestrel server, select `MyFirstCoreAPI` from run options. Press *F5* to start running the application; it opens the selected web browser, and also the console window.

In these environments, we will use the command-line options to run the application. They use the Kestrel server to run the application.

Running ASP.NET Core Web API on Linux/macOS

Open the console/shell from the project root in your Linux/macOS machine, as follows:

```
dotnet run
```

This preceding command compiles, builds, and runs the application; it also starts listening for requests on `http://localhost:5000`. Open any browser, and paste the URL `http://localhost:5000/api/values` to see the web API returning a response from the values controller.

You would see the application running, and displaying the response in the browser, as seen in the following screenshot:

Response after Web API on browser

We can use Postman to send requests and receive responses from the web API shown. The ports are auto generated and will differ according to machine.

Postman is a tool for using various activities of the API--we will be using this for API testing. You can download it from `https://www.getpostman.com/`.

The response formatters are set as JSON, by default, in ASP.NET Core Web API projects. However, we can customize as per our needs.

How about debugging using Visual Studio Code?

 If you need a similar experience for debugging .NET Core (C#) in Visual Studio Code,
Omnisharp--C# extension for .NET core--should be installed. Refer to this link to set up debugging:
`https://github.com/OmniSharp/omnisharp-vscode/blob/master/debugg`
`er.md`

Further reading

Refer to the following link for detailed information on. NET Core:

- `https://docs.microsoft.com/en-us/dotnet/`

For more on ASP.NET Core, refer to the following:

- `https://docs.asp.net/en/latest/`
- `https://github.com/aspnet/Mvc`
- ASP.NET Monsters series on Channel 9 MSDN
- ASP.NET Community Stand-ups on `https://live.asp.net/`

Summary

We've covered a lot of ground in this chapter. We began with an introduction to MVC, and looked at how ASP.NET Web API has matured through in the last decade. With the background established, we learnt how to use .NET Core and the power of a cross-platform framework.

We understood ASP.NET Core and its architecture, and we set up our systems with .NET Core SDK. We also created a web API using Visual Studio tooling and Yeoman generators. We learned, in detail, about ASP.NET Core request processing and the unification of web API and MVC into a single code base.

In the next chapter, you'll learn more about Model, Views, and Controllers.

4

Controllers, Actions, and Models

The entry point and the flesh of a service are controllers. While handlers are one of the initial classes in the ASP.NET Core pipeline, once the request has passed through ASP.NET and has found an appropriate route, it will be directed to your controller.

Now you are in control of what data you want to send as your response. A controller can contain many methods. Although these may be public methods, not all of them will be available. Enabling HTTP actions on these methods will turn these methods into actions.

In the course of this chapter, you will get a better understanding of controllers and how they tie in with the ASP.NET pipeline. We will create some controllers as well as the actions for these controllers.

In this chapter, we will cover the following topics:

- Introduction to Controllers
- Actions
- Creating Controllers with models

Introduction to controllers

When you add a new controller to your project, ASP.NET automatically loads that controller for you and makes it ready for use. Here are some pointers that you may want to know so that you don't get stuck, or if you want to create a new project and have all your controllers in there:

- Your controller needs to end with the word `Controller`.
- Make sure your class is `public`; needless to say, interfaces and abstract classes will not work. Inherit them from the Microsoft controller class.
- You cannot have the same controller name in different namespaces. ASP.NET allows multiple namespaces for the same controller but both controllers will not be resolved. Best practice is to have unique names for your controllers.

Actions

The web API has many actions, some of which were covered in `Chapter 2`, *Understanding HTTP and REST*, with examples. As a refresher, we will go over them again as we will want to use these actions when we create our controller. The `Action` attributes will be used to decorate a method.

Every action should be thought about from a consumer's point of view; for example, for `Post`, the client is posting something.

If we had created `ShoesController`, the route for this would be as follows:

```
[Route("api/[controller]")]
```

Post

This action is used when we want to create something. The body of the message will contain the data that needs to be saved to a data store:

```
[Route("")]
[HttpPost]
public IActionResult CreateShoes([FromBody] ShoeModel model)
```

The first line is the route, routes should always be declared. They give someone who is reading the code or debugging the code a better understanding of what is happening and how the flow is.

In the second line, we state the `Action` attribute; in this case, it is `Post`, and you don't need to set it all the time. It is a good practice to declare the action.

Get

`Get` is used to retrieve data. In most cases, `Get` is not explicitly stated:

```
[Route("")]
[HttpGet]
public IHttpActionResult GetShoes()
```

This can be declared as follows:

```
[Route("")]
public IHttpActionResult Get()
```

Note the omission of the action.

Put

`Put` is used to update data or create some data if it does not exist:

```
[Route("{id}")]
[HttpPut]
public IHttpActionResult Update(ShowModel model)
```

You will notice the ID as part of the route, it implies that the caller knows which entity they want to update. All we have done is create the method named `Update`; the name can be what you want it to be.

Patch

`Patch` is similar to `Put`, with the difference that you send just the data that has changed the delta and not the whole model:

```
[Route("{id}")]
[HttpPatch]
public IHttpActionResult PatchUpdate(ShowModel model)
```

Delete

`Delete` is used to delete data. All you need is the ID:

```
[Route("{id}")]
[HttpDelete]
public IHttpActionResult Delete(string id)
```

These are the actions that we will use in our controllers. I have looked at the `Actions` attribute separately from the controllers, so we can give it some attention without worrying about the implementation.

Controllers

I fired up VS 2017 community edition and created a new web project. Note that you get to choose which template you want to target. I have selected ASP.NET Core Web Application. Create a new project called `Puhoi`, which is a small town in New Zealand, which makes some diary products. I aim to create a controller for some of their products. It's good to create an example that is tangible and is a real work example. I tend to stay away from something like a book's controller or product's controller.

After creating the project, you will be prompted with a template to choose; select the template highlighted in the following screenshot by selecting ASP.NET Core 2.0:

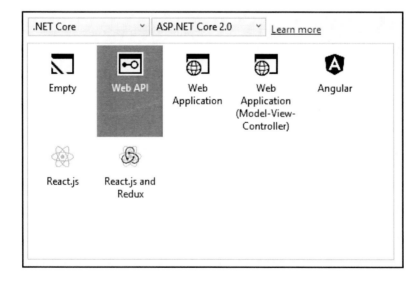

I have created a new Controller, which gets saved in the `Controllers` folder:

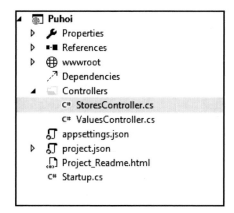

Also, note the route for the controller; it does not contain the name of the controller:

```
namespace Puhoi.Controllers
{
    [Route("api/[controller]")]
    0 references
    public class StoresController : Controller
    {
```

Let's talk about what we want to create and a little bit about Puhoi Cheese. They have a few products, such as milk, cheese, and yoghurt.

Like any company, you would want to list all your products, add new products, and remove products. So if there were a frontend for this, a website, or an app, then they would hook themselves into this API to get the relevant information. Let's go about and build some of this logic. We will not create the backend for this, as it is out of the scope of this chapter.

Let's build the stores controller, which will list some of the top products, such as a department store. Then let's drill down and create a subproduct controller, such as something to list all kinds of cheese. If you don't like cheese, you not going to like this chapter; I apologize beforehand.

Models

We create the models in a separate project, as we want don't want to pollute the API project with everything, it's not a dumping ground. When we create classes, one class has one responsibility and, as soon as they have more than one responsibility, we create this into a new class. Projects should contain classes that have, and share, the same responsibility. We also create a `BaseModel` class that has some common attributes that we want all our models to have and which they should have, because they are related.

```
public  class BaseModel
{
   public Guid Id { get; set; }
}
```

After creating the models project, we have a folder with the model class and our `BaseModel` class:

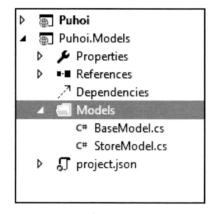

The `StoreModel` class inherits from the `BaseModel` class and the properties represent the model attributes:

```
namespace Puhoi.Models
{
    public class StoreModel : BaseModel
    {
        public string Name { get; set; }
        public int NumberOfProducts { get; set; }
        public string DisplayName { get; set; }
        public string Description { get; set; }
    }
}
```

Now that we have our model, let's add it to our controller and get going. Don't forget to add a reference from your web API to the `Models` project.

Later on, you will also see how we add the models separately. I have refactored our controller to use store model, and this is what it looks like now:

```
[HttpGet]
public IEnumerable<StoreModel> Get()...

[HttpGet("{id}")]
public StoreModel Get(int id)...

[HttpPost]
public void Post([FromBody]StoreModel model)...

[HttpPut("{id}")]
public void Put(Guid id, [FromBody]StoreModel model)...

[HttpDelete("{id}")]
public void Delete(int id)...
```

To summarize, we are returning one or many `StoreModel` on `Get`, and the `Post` and `Put` methods have our model as an input parameter.

Now that we have this in place, what remains is how we should return data for `Get` and transmit data to be stored for `Put` and `Post`.

We can create an in-memory data store and use it as our persistent store. But that's a bit hacky, and you don't really do that in a production system. Maybe we should create a database and pass the data all the way from the API to the database. That's a lot of effort, and the chapter is about controllers. So maybe we create an interface to our data store and pass the data from our API to our interface, and that should be a nice pattern to follow when you are ready to implement you API.

To create a nicely layered architecture and hide some of this code that will hook the API to the data layer, we will create a new Class Library project and add some classes to that library. And these classes will direct data to and from the datastore interface.

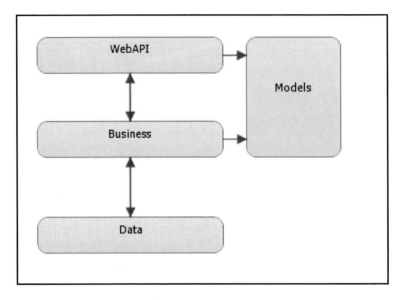

Minimum-layered web API architecture

I have made the diagram generic with a minimal number of components. If you want to, you can create more components. It's important to think about boundary points in your application. Your API project should never reference the data project, and the data project should never reference the API project.

Business

Create a new Class Library project with the name of your application, and then create .Business, as follows:

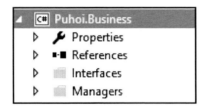

Have the folder structure for it as well.

This is the interface for `IDataStoreManager`:

```
namespace Puhoi.Business.Interfaces
{
  public interface IStoreManager
  {
    HttpModelResult Add(BaseModel model);
    HttpModelResult Update(BaseModel model, Guid id);
    HttpModelResult Get(Guid id);
    HttpModelResult Delete(Guid id);
    HttpModelResult GetAll();
  }
}
```

You need a reference to the models projects and add a reference to `System.Web`.

Note that we are returning `HttpStatusCode`. One might argue why business references `System.Web`, and in the older days, these might be a valid argument. As with our design diagram, `Business` is the layer between web API and the data layer. It will have to know about both, it is a business layer, but it is a web API Business layer.

The `HttpModelResult` class looks like the following:

```
public class HttpModelResult
{
    public HttpStatusCode HttpStatus { get; set; }
    public BaseModel Model { get; set; }
    public IEnumerable<BaseModel> Models {get;set;}
}
```

We now create a concrete class that implements `IStoreManager`. However, we need this to be registered. Many of you would use dependency injection for object creation and use a library like Autofac.

With ASP.NET Core, this is now built in.

Dependency Injection

This is how I have registered our `StoreManager` class:

I have navigated back to our PuhoiAPI project and added the following code in the `Startup.cs` class:

```
// This method gets called by the runtime. Use this method to a
public void ConfigureServices(IServiceCollection services)
{
    // Add framework services.
    services.AddMvc();
    services.AddTransient<IStoreManager, StoreManager>();
}
```

The options that are available are as follows:

- `AddTransient`
- `AddScoped`
- `AddInstance`
- `AddSingleton`

If you are new to **dependency injection (DI)**, the following should give you a better understanding:

- **Transient**: A new object is created each time it is needed. This is best for stateless objects.
- **Scope**: A new object is created for each request.
- **Singleton**: This is similar to the singleton pattern. The very first time the object is needed, a new object is created and every subsequent dependency of this object will use this one.
- **Instance**: The best way to describe this is that it behaves like a singleton, except that a singleton is lazy loaded.

Now that the manager has been included in our DI, let's incorporate it in the controller.

GET by ID

The StoreController class is injected with the IStoreManager interface as a dependency in its constructor:

```
private readonly IStoreManager _storeManager;

public StoresController(IStoreManager storeManager)
{
    _storeManager = storeManager;
}
```

Now for Get on our controller, we are going to refactor it, so don't be too concerned about the implementation:

```
[HttpGet("{id}")]
public StoreModel Get(Guid id)
{
    BaseModel model = _storeManager.Get(id).Model;
    StoreModel storeModel = model as StoreModel;
    return storeModel;
}
```

Take note of the route; we are using ID, and our ID is Guid, which is our unique identifier. Then, we have storemanager, and we pass the ID to our store manager and get back a model, which is returned from the controller.

Pretty easy; what does this look like in an actual call, and how do we call it?

I have created a simple implementation that will return a model with what was requested.

The Fiddler request is as follows:

The Fiddler response is as follows:

```
⊟ JSON
    Description=The best cheeses of the North Island
    DisplayName=Puhoi Cheese
    Id=0609fa16-9f49-4302-9f55-2d7016cd9e8c
    Name=CheeseStore
    NumberOfProducts=25
```

We get a Status Code of 200, which is a success. The result is great as we have data flowing. Consider the scenario where the result is not found. Returning an empty model is not ideal, as we will be returning an empty model with 200. We would want to return something more intuitive.

If we change our implementation to the following, where we check the model from the manager and return null, our response is 204, which doesn't tell the consumer that a particular resource does not exist:

```
[HttpGet("{id}")]
public StoreModel Get(Guid id)
{
    BaseModel model = _storeManager.Get(id).
    if( model == null)
    {
        return null;
    }
}
```

Using an `IAction` result type is more flexible and gives the desired result:

```
[HttpGet("{id}")]
public IActionResult Get(Guid id)
{
    HttpModelResult modelResult = _storeManager.Get(id);
    if (modelResult.HttpStatus == HttpStatusCode.OK)
    {
        StoreModel storeModel = modelResult.Model as StoreModel;
        return Ok(storeModel);
    }

    switch (modelResult.HttpStatus)
    {
        case HttpStatusCode.NotFound:
            return HttpNotFound();
    }
    return HttpBadRequest();
}
```

We can test our model coming back from the manager and notice our returns. There are three different returns. One is OK with the model. The second is NotFound; if the manager did not find the ID that we queried against, we can return a not found status. This is more intuitive to a consumer, and inspecting a result code is far cheaper than parsing data.

At the end, we assume that the request we received was bad and return a bad request.

It is important to note that this is just an example and a pattern of how you can structure your controller; you can add more cases in the switch statement.

You can also change BadRequest to be a bit more intelligent rather than just returning BadRequest; the point here was to show the use of IActionResult and how it gels from a consumer point of view.

Now you can see the desired result in Fiddler:

```
404     HTTP      localhost:52...   /api/stores/0609FA16-9F49-4302-9F55-2D7016CD9E1C
```

This is how the logic is implemented in the Get method of the StoreManager class:

```
public HttpModelResult Get(Guid id)
{
    HttpModelResult result = new HttpModelResult();
    BaseDto dto = _dataStore.Get(id);
    if( dto == null )
    {
        result.HttpStatus = HttpStatusCode.NotFound;
    }
    else
    {
        result.HttpStatus = HttpStatusCode.OK;
        result.Model = _mapper.Map<StoreModel>(dto);
    }
    return result;
}
```

We ask DataStore for the object by the ID. If the result is null, we return Not Found. If we have an object coming back from our data store, then we use a mapper to map between the object from the database and our object that is exposed by the API. Essentially, we map between dto and model. Then, we set our status to OK and wait for our model result.

Mapping

We use AutoMapper to map between **Model** and **Dto** and vice versa. The following diagram shows you how **AutoMapper** fits into our solution:

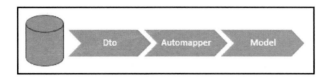

Add a NuGet reference to `AutoMapper` for the API project and the project that will do the mapping.

In the API project, I created a new class to set up the maps. This class inherits from the `AutoMappers` profile class.

This is the simplest set up:

```
public class AutoMapperProfileConfiguration : Profile
{
    public AutoMapperProfileConfiguration()
    {
        CreateMap<StoreModel, StoreDto>()
            .AfterMap((model, dto) => dto.UId = model.Id);
```

It says that you should create a map between `dto` as the source and `model` as the target. However, we know it's not that simple. This is what it ends up being like:

```
public class AutoMapperProfileConfiguration : Profile
{
    public AutoMapperProfileConfiguration()
    {
        CreateMap<StoreModel, StoreDto>()
            .AfterMap((model, dto) => dto.UId = model.Id);

        CreateMap<StoreDto, StoreModel>().
            ForSourceMember("StoreId", s => s.Ignore()).
            ForSourceMember("UId", s => s.Ignore()).
            ForMember("Id", s => s.Ignore()).
            AfterMap((dto, model) => model.Id = dto.UId);
    }

}
```

For `dto`, we ignore `StoreId` and `UId`, and for `model`, we ignore `Id`. Then, after the mapping is done, map `UId` from `dto` to `Id` from `model`.

The set up in the pipe is done with the following in `Startup.cs`:

```
private readonly MapperConfiguration _mapperConfiguration;

public Startup(IHostingEnvironment env)
{
    // Set up configuration sources.
    var builder = new ConfigurationBuilder()
        .AddJsonFile("appsettings.json")
        .AddEnvironmentVariables();

    _mapperConfiguration = new MapperConfiguration(cfg =>
    {
        cfg.AddProfile(new AutoMapperProfileConfiguration());
    });
```

Create a member variable for the mapper configuration. Then, in the `Startup` constructor, we set up a new `MapperConfiguration` variable and add the profile that contains our maps.

We're almost done hooking this up. In `ConfigureService`, we need to add this to the service:

```
public void ConfigureServices(IServiceCollection services)
{
    // Add framework services.
    services.AddTransient<IStoreManager, StoreManager>();
    services.AddTransient<IDataStore, DataStore>();
    services.AddSingleton(sp => _mapperConfiguration.CreateMapper());
    services.AddMvc();
}
```

`IMapper` is created as a singleton as the mapping done will not change, and they contain no state.

Post

Start off with the controller, implementing Post and returning 201 if the object is created, or if it returns what our internal manager sends to us.

```csharp
[Route("")]
[HttpPost]
public IActionResult Post([FromBody] StoreModel model)
{
    HttpModelResult modelResult = _storeManager.Add(model);
    if (modelResult.HttpStatus == HttpStatusCode.Created)
    {
        return new CreatedResult(
            string.Format("/api/stores/{0}",
            modelResult.Model.Id),
            modelResult.Model);
    }
    return new HttpStatusCodeResult((int)modelResult.HttpStatus);
}
```

We have no special routing, but we declare the default route to be clear. Decorate the method with `HttpPost`. As with `Get`, we return `IActionResult`. The model is retrieved from the request body. If you look at the code in this method, we delegate all the work to the manager. Then, we get back a result; if the manager sends us `HttpStatusCode`, we know that the object has been created and we return 201, created with the location of the newly created resource. Any other result is translated back as `HttpStatusCodeResult`. This is my result on Fiddler:

The request body JSON is as follows:

```
Request Body
{
"Name":"CheeseStore",
"NumberOfProducts":251,
"DisplayName":"Puhoi Cheese",
"Description":"The best cheeses of the North Island"
}
```

The response from the server is as follows:

```
HTTP/1.1 201 Created
Content-Type: application/json; charset=utf-8
Location: /api/stores/38475388-f4f6-4750-a053-549bc2b1dda0
```

The manager's work is to get the model from the controller and pass it to this data store:

```
public HttpModelResult Add(StoreModel model)
{
    HttpModelResult result = new HttpModelResult();
    if( _dataStore.Get(model.Name) == null)
    {
        StoreDto dto = _mapper.Map<StoreDto>(model);
        try
        {
            dto = (StoreDto)_dataStore.AddorUpdate(dto);
            if (dto != null)
            {
                StoreModel createdModel = _mapper.Map<StoreModel>(dto);
                result.Model = createdModel;
                result.HttpStatus = HttpStatusCode.Created;
            }
        }
```

However it has a bit more responsibility than that. It needs to tell the manager if the object was created, and if not, then it needs to specify what the problem was. Before the data store can insert the object, the manager checks whether the store has this object. Note that the responsibility to check whether the existing object lies with the manager, not data store. As the name says, it's a store. If the object exists, then the manager returns a conflict to the controller. This is the else block in the manager:

```
else
{
    result.HttpStatus = HttpStatusCode.Conflict;
    return result;
}
return result;
```

We make use of `AutoMapper` to flip between `model` and `dto` and back to a model. You will have to make changes in `AutoMapperProfileConfiguration` for this to work:

```
CreateMap<StoreModel, StoreDto>().
    ForMember("UId", s => s.Ignore()).
    AfterMap((model, dto) => model.Id = dto.UId);
```

Put

We use `Put` to update a store or create a new store. The signature of `Put` is different from `Post`:

```
[HttpPut("{id}")]
public IActionResult Put(Guid id, [FromBody]StoreModel model)
{
    HttpModelResult modelResult = _storeManager.Update(model,id);
    if (modelResult.HttpStatus == HttpStatusCode.Created)
    {
        return new CreatedResult(
            string.Format("/api/stores/{0}",
            modelResult.Model.Id),
            modelResult.Model);
    }
    return new HttpStatusCodeResult((int)modelResult.HttpStatus);
}
```

We have the ID and model in the signature of the controller class. The route has the ID, and the model is in the body of the request. You will notice that the Post has no ID. We ask the store manager to update our model; if we get back a created one from the store manager, then we publish this location of the new resource. Any other state, including OK, is returned as HttpStatusCodeResult.

```
public HttpModelResult Update(StoreModel model, Guid id)
{
    if( _dataStore.Get(id) == null )
    {
        return Add(model);
    }
    else
    {
        model.Id = id;
        StoreDto dto = _mapper.Map<StoreDto>(model);
        dto = (StoreDto)_dataStore.AddorUpdate(dto);
        return new HttpModelResult
        {
            HttpStatus = HttpStatusCode.OK,
            Model = _mapper.Map<StoreModel>(dto)
        };
    }
}
```

I have done some refactoring to our store manager, as one would normally do. If we don't find the ID that we were supplied with, then we add the model to our data store. In the normal flow, the model is updated and 200 is returned.

```
PUT http://localhost:52476/api/stores/4d2edb93-7368-4738-8f7d-2a95448c841f
HTTP/1.1
User-Agent: Fiddler
Host: localhost:52476
Content-Type: application/json
Content-Length: 125

{"Name":"CheeseStore","NumberOfProducts":0,"DisplayName":"Puhoi
Cheese","Description":"The best cheeses of the North Island"}
```

I ran this through Fiddler; note the action, `Put`, and the model in the body.

```
JSON
    Description=The best cheeses of the North Island
    DisplayName=Puhoi Cheese
    Id=4d2edb93-7368-4738-8f7d-2a95448c841f
    Name=CheeseStore
    NumberOfProducts=0
```

The steps prior to this were to create a model using `Post`, update the model with `Put`, and then call get on the resource in order to check whether the update has been performed.

Delete

`Delete` is pretty straight forward. We are going ahead with the principle we set in `Chapter 1`, *Introduction to Microservices and Service-Oriented Architecture*, around the REST principles for Delete. When we delete a representation for the first time, we can return 200, but when we make the same request, the representation does not exist any more, so we should return 404. Let's take a look at this code:

```
[HttpDelete("{id}")]
public IActionResult Delete(Guid id)
{
    HttpModelResult modelResult = _storeManager.Delete(id);
    return new HttpStatusCodeResult((int) modelResult.HttpStatus);
}
```

Ask the store manager to delete the object with a certain ID, and we return whatever we get back from our manager. Let's look at the manager:

```
public HttpModelResult Delete(Guid id)
{
    HttpModelResult result = new HttpModelResult();
    BaseDto dto = _dataStore.Delete(id);
    result.HttpStatus = dto == null ?
        HttpStatusCode.NotFound : HttpStatusCode.OK;
    return result;
}
```

This is simple as well; based on what we get back from the data store, we return 200 or Not found.

I will not display the Fiddler request and the response for the different flows, as I feel it's very basic for what we have covered in the chapter until now. This is just the request for delete:

| DELETE | ⌄ | http://localhost:52476/api/stores/F1C4B685-38AB-4F63-B9EC-B9C67E82AB39 |

Note that our action is `Delete`.

GetAll

Our `GetAll` operation looks simpler than `Delete`:

```
[HttpGet]
public IActionResult Get()
{
    HttpModelResult modelResult = _storeManager.GetAll();
    return Ok(modelResult.Models);

}
```

We ask our manager for all the stores and return this with 200:

```
public HttpModelResult GetAll()
{
    HttpModelResult result = new HttpModelResult();
    IEnumerable<BaseDto> dtos = _dataStore.GetAll();
    List<StoreModel> models = dtos.Select(baseDto =>
                    _mapper.Map<StoreModel>(baseDto)).ToList();
    result.Models = models.AsEnumerable();
    result.HttpStatus = HttpStatusCode.OK;
    return result;
}
```

All we do in the manager is, ask our data store for all the dtos and then map them to a model and return them as `IEnumerable`. Just before that, we set our status to 200.

What's the route looking like? It's looking similar to `GetById`, except that you don't need to set an ID.

Summary

In this chapter, we developed a full CRUD endpoint and looked at some of the new features with ASP.Net core 2.0, like the built-in dependency injection.

We explored the `HttpGet`, `HttpPost`, `HttpPut`, and `HttpDelete` actions, along with some basic routing.

We established a clean pattern to break up the responsibility of the classes and make it easier to extend the given functionality.

The objects are loosely coupled, which makes them easier to test; this was promoted with the inbuilt dependency injection. We also used Fiddler to demonstrate how our API works.

In the next chapter, we will discuss in depth about route mechanism, route builder, attribute routes, constraints, and much more.

5

Implementing Routing

We use **URLs (Uniform Resource Locators)** to access code resources on the web. For example, when you see a request for `www.dummysite.com/pages/profile.aspx`, it's very easy to infer that `profile.aspx` physically exists in the pages folder on the website, dummysite.com.

Notice that the URL and the physical file in our example have a direct relationship--when a request is received by the web server for this file, the code gets executed, and the response is returned to be displayed on the browser.

When working with MVC-based frameworks like ASP.NET Core, the URL maps to controller classes and its action methods using an approach known as Routing.

In this chapter, we will look at the following topics:

- Introducing Routing
- Routing middleware
- Route Builder
- Convention-based and template-based Routing
- Attribute-based routes
- Route constraints
- Link generation
- Best practices for Routing

Introducing Routing

In Chapter 4, *Controller, Actions and Models*, we learnt a lot about Controllers and Actions. Any ASP.NET Web API project will have one or more controllers with many action methods based on HTTP Verbs like GET, POST, PUT, and DELETE.

When we created a basic ASP.NET Core Web API in `Chapter 3`, *Anatomy of ASP.NET Core Web API*, and run the application, we saw the URL in the browser as `http://localhost:5000/api/values`--it displayed the JSON response from the Values Controllers.

A few questions like the following arise here:

- How does the project know it should load a particular controller and action method?
- What if I have many controllers and action methods in a real-world scenario? How do we point to a particular controller?
- What is the mechanism to properly serve the HTTP request?

The mechanism to map incoming HTTP requests to its corresponding controller's action methods is known as Routing. It is one of the key components of the ASP.NET Core MVC/ Web API. Without the Routing mechanism, ASP.NET (MVC/ Web API) will fail to run applications and serve requests. Routing solves all the aforementioned questions.

Routing middleware

In the world of ASP.NET Core, every HTTP request and response has to pass through various middleware. The `Configure` method of the `Startup` class configures the pipeline which processes requests and takes appropriate action on them.

ASP.NET Core provides Routing middleware to perform the tasks of mapping a request to the corresponding controllers and action methods. Let's learn about this middleware.

Create an Empty ASP.NET Core project, add `Microsoft.AspNetCore.All` to it by manually editing either `*.csproj` or NuGet. Add the following package details in the dependencies so that it gets restored and is ready to be used:

```
> " Microsoft.AspNetCore.All ": "2.0.0-preview2-final"
```

Open the `Startup` class to add the following code to see the Router middleware in action:

```csharp
using Microsoft.AspNetCore.Builder;
using Microsoft.AspNetCore.Hosting;
using Microsoft.AspNetCore.Http;
using Microsoft.Extensions.DependencyInjection;
using Microsoft.AspNetCore.Routing;

namespace BasicRoutes
{
  public class Startup
  {
    public void ConfigureServices(IServiceCollection services)
    {
      // Adding Router Middleware
      services.AddRouting();
    }
    public void Configure(IApplicationBuilder app,
      IHostingEnvironment env, ILoggerFactory loggerFactory)
    {
      //HTTP pipeline now handles routing
      app.UseRouter(new RouteHandler(
        context => context.Response.WriteAsync("Mastering Web API!!")
      ));
    }
  }
}
```

You can break down the preceding code as follows:

- `Services.AddRouting()` adds the Routing middleware to be used.
- `app.UseRouter` handles routing for HTTP requests. It takes in `RouteHandler` to process the request. Here we are just writing the response with a string.

For any request that comes in, the pipeline needs someone to process it. This is done by `RouteHandler`; every route should have a handler.

When you run the application (press *F5*), the browser displays the string **Mastering Web API**, as seen in this screenshot:

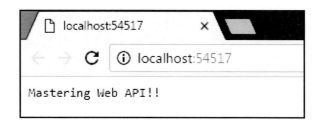

Basic example of routing middleware

This is most basic example of routing in ASP.NET Core. As the pipeline is only routing it, accessing the application with any URL will give the same response.

The RouteBuilder class

The `RouteBuilder` class helps us to build custom routes and handle them on request arrival. The MVC also uses this class to build its default routing mechanism of the controller, actions.

In the last example, we created a basic route that serves on any route. Now we will create custom routes with different HTTP verbs like GET and POST.

Copy the following code in the `Configure` method of `Startup.cs` for custom route builder:

```
public void Configure(IApplicationBuilder app, IHostingEnvironment env,
ILoggerFactory loggerFactory)
{
  var routes = new RouteBuilder(app)
  .MapGet("greeting", context => context.Response.WriteAsync("Good
morning!!
    Packt readers."))
  .MapGet("review/{msg}", context => context.Response.WriteAsync(
    $"This book is , {context.GetRouteValue("msg")}"))
  .MapPost("packtpost", context => context.Response.WriteAsync(
    "Glad you did Post !"))
  .Build();
  app.UseRouter(routes);
}
```

You can break down the preceding code as follows:

- Instantiate a new `RouteBuilder` class.
- Using `MapGet`, we set the greeting path to handle client requests with the HTTP verb GET.
- Using `MapGet`, we set the review path to handle client requests with `RouteData` or `RouteValue`. The Request handler delegate reads the message.
- Using `MapPost`, we get the `packtpost` path to handle the client POST requests.

Route Builder using MapGet

MapRoute

`MapRoute` is an extension method to add a route to `IRouteBuilder` with a specified name and template. A `DefaultHandler` needs to be added for route handling.

The following code shows how to define `defaultHandler` to be used with `MapRoute`:

```
var routeHandler = new RouteHandler(context =>
{
  var data = context.GetRouteData().Values;
  return context.Response.WriteAsync("Controller Name is " +
    data["controller"].ToString());
});

var routes = new RouteBuilder(app, routeHandler)
.MapRoute("packt", "{controller}/{action}")
.Build();
app.UseRouter(routes);
```

ASP.NET Core Web API and Routing

Until now, we saw the basics of Routing without MVC or web API involved in the form of Middleware Router, RouteBuilder, and MapRoute. It was essential to understand how these concepts work together.

When we create an ASP.NET Core app as a web API, there are certain routing-related functionalities which are essential to know about.

In `Chapter 3`, *Anatomy of ASP.NET Core Web API*, we created a simple web API project; looking at the `Configure` and `ConfigureServices` methods of the `Startup` class, only the MVC middleware and service got added. There is no reference to the Routing middleware.

The question that now arises is how does the web API project do all the Routing that is required. The answer lies in the MVC middleware, `app.UseMvc()`, added in the `Configure` method.

`UseMvc()` is a middleware for both MVC and web API projects written by Microsoft's ASP.NET Core team. This middleware confirms MVC and web API work through the same codebase.

The following code is part of the ASP.NET MVC open source project on GitHub (`https://github.com/aspnet/Mvc`):

```
public static IApplicationBuilder UseMvc(
  this IApplicationBuilder app,
  Action<IRouteBuilder> configureRoutes)
  {
    if (app == null)
    {
      throw new ArgumentNullException(nameof(app));
    }
    if (configureRoutes == null)
    {
      throw new ArgumentNullException(nameof(configureRoutes));
    }
    if (app.ApplicationServices.GetService(typeof(MvcMarkerService))
      == null)
    {
      throw new InvalidOperationException(
        Resources.FormatUnableToFindServices(
          nameof(IServiceCollection),
        "AddMvc",
        "ConfigureServices(...)"));
```

```
}
var middlewarePipelineBuilder =
  app.ApplicationServices.GetRequiredService
  <MiddlewareFilterBuilder>();
middlewarePipelineBuilder.ApplicationBuilder = app.New();
var routes = new RouteBuilder(app)
{
  DefaultHandler =
    app.ApplicationServices.GetRequiredService<MvcRouteHandler>(),
};
configureRoutes(routes);
routes.Routes.Insert(0,
  AttributeRouting.CreateAttributeMegaRoute(
    app.ApplicationServices));
return app.UseRouter(routes.Build()); }
```

You can break down the preceding code as follows:

- The `UseMvc` method creates an instance of RouteBuilder.
- `RouteBuilder` requires `DefaultHandler` for processing the routes; this is provided by the `MvcRouteHandler` class.
- The class `MvcRouteHandler` implements `IRouter`, which does the work of URL pattern matching and generating the URL.
- `configureRoutes` is the action method to get the routes configured. We did this same task in the previous examples.
- `AttributeRouting` is added as the first entry to the collection of `IRouter`.
- The `CreateAttributeMegaRoute` method scans through all the controller actions and builds routes automatically. This is one of significant lines of `UseMvc`.
- At the end routes are build and added to the Router middleware using `UseRouter`. This is similar to tasks performed at the beginning of this chapter.

`AttributeRouting.CreateAttributeMegaRoute` in `UseMvc` provides Attribute Routing by default in both ASP.NET Core MVC and web API applications.

Convention-based Routing

In the first release of the ASP.NET Web API, the routing mechanism was convention-based. This type of routing has definition for one or more route templates in terms of parameterized strings.

This style of routing is still supported in ASP.NET Core; the following code snippet shows how to achieve this:

```
public void Configure(IApplicationBuilder app)
{
  //Rest of code removed for brevity
  app.UseMvc(routes =>
  {
    // route1
    routes.MapRoute(
      name: "packtroute1",
      template: "api/{controller}/{id}"
    );
    // route2
    routes.MapRoute(
      name: "packtroute1",
      template: "testpackt",
      defaults: new { controller = "Books", action = "Index" }
    );
  });
}
```

The convention-based style of routing is not popular, because of the following reasons:

- It does not support certain types of URL patterns common to the web API world
- Resources having child resources are very difficult to create. For example, /products/1/orders/2/reviews
- It's not scalable when web APIs have many controllers and actions

Template-based Routing

When working with web APIs, you would have come across many varieties of URIs such as /product/12, /product/12/orders, /departments/, /books, and so on.

In the web API world, they are known as Route--a string describing a URI template. For example, a sample route can be formed on this URI pattern: /products/{id}/orders.

There are few points to observe here:

- A URI template consists of literals and parameters
- Products and orders are literals in the preceding sample example

- Anything in curly braces { } is known as parameters--{id} is one such example
- A path separator (/) has to be a part of a route template--The URIs understand / as path separators
- The combination of literals, path separator, and parameters should match the URI pattern

When working with a web API, literals will either be controllers or methods. The route parameters play a significant role in making a route template multipurpose. Parameters in curly braces can play multipurpose roles as follows:

- Even though route templates have parameters, they can be made optional by placing '?' in the template. For example, /books/chapters/{numb?}--here, if we don't provide numb, then it loads all the chapters, and if we provide numb, then the relevant chapter is loaded.
- A route template can have more than one route parameters.
- A route parameter can have * as a prefix so that it binds to the rest of the URI. This kind of parameter is called as a catch-all parameter.
- A default value can be provided to a route parameter. This default value will come into effect when the route parameter is not supplied for it. For example, "{controller=Home}/{action=Index}" will load the Index action method in the Home controller.
- Route parameters can have constraints to ensure the routes are generated in the proper way. For example, /customers/{id:int}/services/. The {id:int} parameter indicates that id has to be an integer, otherwise, the web API responds with a 404 response type.

The following are a few sample route templates defined in the Configure method of the Startup class:

```
public void Configure(IApplicationBuilder app)
{
  app.UseMvc(routes =>
  {
    // Route Template with default values and optional parameter
    routes.MapRoute(
      name: "default",
      template: "{controller=Home}/{action=Index}/{id?}");

    //Route Template with default value, parameter constrainst
    routes.MapRoute(
      name: "alternate_route",
      template: "{controller}/{action}/{id:int}/{guid:string}",
```

```
        defaults: new { controller = "Dashboard" });

    // Route Template with no default values or parameters
    routes.MapRoute(
      name: "simple_route",
      template: "{controller}/{action}");
  });
}
```

Attribute-based Routing

In the world of .NET programming, the tag that adds the declaration information of the various elements such as classes, methods, and enum to programs are called as attributes.

ASP.NET Web API 2 introduced the concept of Attribute-based Routing, giving more control over the URIs in a web API. This helps us to easily build URIs that have hierarchies of resources.

In ASP.NET Core apps, Attribute-based Routing is provided by default. In the `Configure` method of the `Startup` class, the line `app.UseMvc()` indicates to include the MVC middleware in the request processing pipeline.

In the section *ASP.NET Core Web API and Routing*, we explained how Attribute-based Routing is implemented by default unlike ASP.NET Web API 2, where it had to be explicitly enabled in the configuration.

`AttributeRouting.CreateAttributeMegaRoute` does this heavy work of iterating through all the MVC Controller actions and build routes automatically.

When we created the demo project in Chapter 3, *Anatomy of ASP.NET Core Web API*, it was created using the web API template that comes with the ASP.NET Core tooling.

Let's understand attribute routes from `ValuesController.cs` in the demo project:

```
using System.Collections.Generic;
using Microsoft.AspNetCore.Mvc;

namespace MyFirstCoreAPI.Controllers
{
  [Route("api/[controller]")]
  public class ValuesController : Controller
  {
    // GET api/values
    [HttpGet]
```

```
public IEnumerable<string> Get()
{
  return new string[] { "value1", "value2" };
}

// GET api/values/5
[HttpGet("{id}")]
public string Get(int id)
{
  return "value is " + id;
}

// POST api/values
[HttpPost]
public void Post([FromBody]string value)
{
}

// PUT api/values/5
[HttpPut("{id}")]
public void Put(int id, [FromBody]string value)
{
}

// DELETE api/values/5
[HttpDelete("{id}")]
public void Delete(int id)
{
}
    }
  }
```

The ValuesController class is decorated with the Route attribute as
[Route("api/[controller]")].

On running the application, you can see the results when we navigate to
`http://localhost:5000/api/values/`, as seen in the following screenshot:

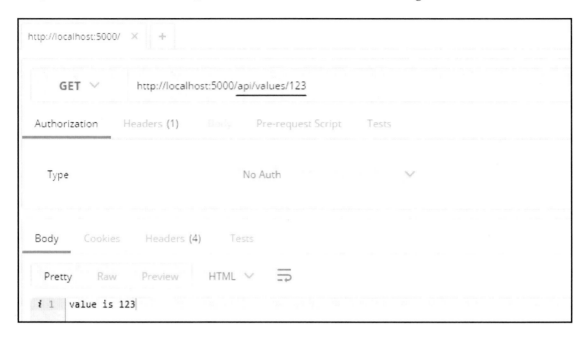

Attribute Route in action

Attribute Routes are defined on the controller; we need to access the URL, as shown in the
preceding screenshot. `/values` is the controller name, the actions `Get` and `Get(int id)`
are executed based on the `HttpGet` verb while testing.

Attribute routes for RESTful applications

Syntactically, attribute routes are defined as follows:

```
[HttpMethod("Template URI", Name?, Order?)]
```

- Based on HttpVerbs, ASP.NET Core provides these HttpMethods to be used for
  attribute routes--`HttpDeleteAttribute`, `HttpGetAttribute`,
  `HttpHeadAttribute`, `HttpOptionsAttribute`, `HttpPatchAttribute`,
  `HttpPostAttribute`, and `HttpPutAttribute`.
- `Template URI` is string that describes routes.

- Name--it's the optional name given to the attribute route. It is usually used when actions seem to be overloaded methods.
- Orders help to take precedence in the execution of overloaded HTTP methods in the controller. Orders depend on literals, parameters, constraints, and also Order. This is an optional parameter.

With these syntax in mind, let's create a new web API controller, PacktController, add action methods, and attribute routes to them:

```
using Microsoft.AspNetCore.Mvc;
using System.Collections.Generic;

namespace MyFirstCoreAPI.Controllers
{
  [Route("api/[controller]")]
  public class PacktController : Controller
  {
    // Get: api/packt/show
    [HttpGet("Show")]
    public string Show()
    {
      return "I am Packt Show !!";
    }

    // GET api/packt
    [HttpGet]
    public IEnumerable<string> Get()
    {
      return new string[] { "Packt 1", "Packt 2" };
    }

    // GET: /api/packt/13
    [HttpGet("{id:int}", Name = "GetPacktById", Order = 0)]
    public string Get(int id)
    {
      return "Response from GetPacktById" + id;
    }

    // POST: /api/packt
    [HttpPost]
    public IActionResult Post()
    {
      return Content("Created Post !!");
    }

    // POST: /api/packt/packtpost
    [HttpPost("packtpost")]
```

```
        public IActionResult Post([FromBody]string chapterName)
        {
          return Content("You invoked packt post");
        }

        // PUT api/packt/5
        [HttpPut("{id}")]
        public void Put(int id, [FromBody]string value)
        {
        }

        // DELETE api/packt/15
        [HttpDelete("{id}")]
        public void Delete(int id)
        {
        }
    }
}
```

You can break down the preceding code as follows:

The PacktController class has the following seven action methods:

- Show(): Gets invoked using the HttpGet request on route /api/packt/show.
- Get(): Gets invoked using the HttpGet request on route /api/packt.
- Get(int id): Gets invoked using the HttpGet request on route /api/packt/13. The route name is provided here.
- Post(): Gets invoked using the HttpPost request on route /api/packt/.
- Post([FromBody]string chapterName): Gets invoked using the HttpPost request on route /api/packt/packtpost.
- Put(): Gets invoked using the HttpPut request on route api/packt/12. The route parameter ID is provided, because PUT corresponds to updating functions, and updates are performed on existing records.
- Delete(): Gets invoked using the HttpDelete request on route api/packt/12. To delete any record, we need to pass its unique identity; so, the ID route parameter needs to be passed.

Multiple Routes

Sometimes, we might get routing requirements like different routes applied to the same controller or action methods. At first, it seems to be very surprising, but in large projects, we might need this kind of routing.

Multiple Routes can be achieved by putting multiple route attributes on the controller as shown in this code snippet:

```
[Route("Stocks")]
[Route("[controller]")]
public class PacktsController : Controller
{
  [HttpGet("Check")]
  [HttpGet("Available")]
  public string GetStock()
  {
     return "Its multiple route";
  }
}
```

Run the application to see the multiple routes in action. You would verify the multiple routes are working by accessing the endpoints on the browser as `/api/stocks/check or /api/packts/available`.

Routing constraints

ASP.NET Core, either as an MVC or a web API application, supports both attribute and centralized routing mechanism. The routes can either be directly set on the controller and actions using the Route attribute, or by creating and mapping all the routes in one place.

We have seen that different route templates can be created with or without route parameters. When route templates have parameters in them, it helps to build excellent routing patterns. But the presence of route parameters can cause issues too; let's see an example for this:

```
public void Configure(IApplicationBuilder app, IHostingEnvironment env,
  ILoggerFactory loggerFactory)
{
  var routeBuilder = new RouteBuilder(app);
  routeBuilder.MapGet("employee/{id}", context =>
  {
    var idValue = context.GetRouteValue("id");
    return context.Response.WriteAsync($"The number is - {idValue}");
```

```
    });

    var routes = routeBuilder.Build();
    app.UseRouter(routes);
}
```

You can break down the preceding code as follows:

- A basic route with the template `employee/{id}`, where `{id}` is the route parameter, is supplied
- The routes template is designed to GET the employees list by passing the ID
- `GetRouteValue` reads the `{id}` parameter, and returns a response

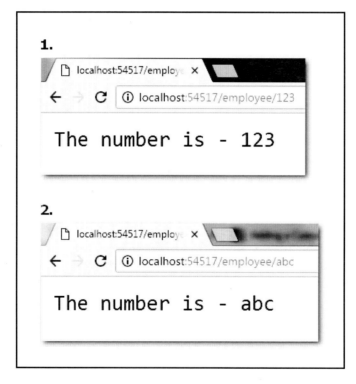

Route Parameters without constraints

Run the application to see the different ways the route parameters are supplied. It seems everything is working--in fact, it is working perfectly, but an issue still exists.

Here, we are assuming that the employees are storing their ID as an integer, as most organisations use integers for employee IDs, like John's employee ID is 23, or Sarah has the employee ID 45. When the route parameter ID is passed as an integer, everything works well, but what if {id} is passed as a string, as shown in the preceding image?

The application does accept a parameter, and responds back well. But when working on a real project dealing with a database source, the ID provided as a string will break the application, and result in an exception or error.

An obvious question is how can we restrict request processing on such kind of a route parameter if wrong data is passed in the route parameters. The answer is Route constraints.

Route constraints help us restrict request processing if the parameters fail the constraint conditions applied to them.

Parameter constraints can be added by using : on the parameter. For example, "employee/{id:int}"

When a request with route parameter constraints sends an invalid type, the HTTP response returned is 404 (Not Found). Yes, ASP.NET Core responds the failing HTTP request because of route constraints as 404 (Not Found). The request processing doesn't hit the controller processing the request.

Let's apply Integer constraint on the {id} parameter from the preceding code, and run the application, as follows:

```
public void Configure(IApplicationBuilder app, IHostingEnvironment env,
  ILoggerFactory loggerFactory)
{
  var routeBuilder = new RouteBuilder(app);

  // Id parameter should be Integer now
  routeBuilder.MapGet("employee/{id:int}", context =>
  {
    var idValue = context.GetRouteValue("id");
    return context.Response.WriteAsync($"The number is - {idValue}");
  });

  // Name parameter should be length 8
  routeBuilder.MapGet("product/{name:length(8)}", context =>
  {
    var nameValue = context.GetRouteValue("id");
    return context.Response.WriteAsync($"The Name is - {nameValue}");
```

```
    });

    var routes = routeBuilder.Build();
    app.UseRouter(routes);
}
```

You can break down the preceding code as follows:

- Route template `employee/{id:int}` takes parameter ID as integer only
- Route template `product/{name:length(8)}` takes only length of 8 as parameter

Run the application to see that the routes are now disciplined in the request processing. Route constraints are the first line of defence.

The following figure shows that when the length of the route parameter name was 8, it returned the response properly. But when name length is not 8, it responded back with a 404 error:

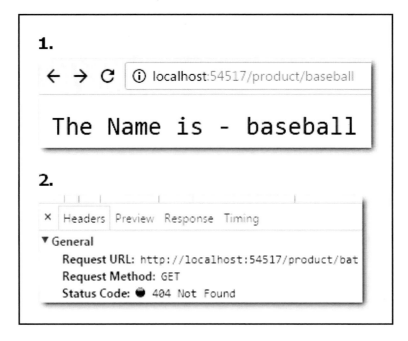

Route Constraints in action

Route constraints can be applied on Attribute routes as well. Here is an example of it:

```
using Microsoft.AspNetCore.Mvc;
namespace MyFirstCoreAPI.Controllers
{
  [Route("api/[controller]")]
  public class PacktController : Controller
  {
    // GET: /api/packt/13
    [HttpGet("{id:int}")]
    public string Get(int id)
    {
      return "Response from " + id;
    }
  }
}
```

Types of route constraints

The ASP.NET Core team has created a bunch of widely used route constraint scenarios based on different data types. The following table lists different route constraints:

Constraint Name	Usage	Remark
Int	{id:int}	The parameter should be an integer
Bool	{isExists:bool}	The parameter should be either TRUE or FALSE
Datetime	{eventdate:datetime}	Accepts only date time as a parameter
Decimal	{amount:decimal}	Accepts only decimal as a parameter
Double	{weight:double}	Accepts only double as a parameter
Float	{distance:float}	Matches only float as a parameter
Guid	{id:guid}	Accepts only GUID as a parameter

Long	`{ticks:long}`	The parameter should be long type
Minlength	`{username:minlength(8)}`	The minimum length of the parameter should be 8
Maxlength	`{filename:maxlength(5)}`	The maximum length of the parameter should be 5
Length(min, max)	`{name:length(4,16)}`	The minimum length of the parameter can be 4 and maximum length 16
Min(value)	`{age:min(18)}`	The minimum value of the parameter age should be 18
Max(value)	`{weight:max(90)}`	The maximum value of the parameter weight should be 90
Range(min, max)	`{age:range(18,100)}`	The age parameter should be between 18 - 100
Alpha	`{name:alpha}`	Only alphabets allowed as parameters
Regex(expression)	`{email:regex(/\S+@\S+\.\S+/}`	Uses regular expression to match the parameter; e-mail is one such example
Required	`{productId:required}`	Parameter must be provided

We can combine different route constraints to parameters based on the requirements. For example, if `tableno` is an integer, and is available between 18 and 30, then we can define routes as follows:

```
[Route("api/[controller]")]
  public class HotelController : Controller
{
  [HttpGet("{tableno:int}/{tableno:range(18, 30)}")]
  public string Get()
  {
    return "Table Range is 18 - 30";
  }
}
```

Writing custom route constraints

Till now, we used the inbuilt route constraints; they serve a large number of use cases, but different business requirements could lead to the need to write custom constraints. Writing custom Route constraints is achieved using the `IRouteConstraint` interface present in the `Microsoft.AspNetCore.Routing` namespace.

The interface has a `Match` method, which takes in `HttpContext`, `IRoute`, `routeKey`, `values`, and `RouteDirection`. When the `Match` method is implemented, if the condition for the constraint matches with the parameter value, it returns TRUE, else FALSE.

For example, let's take a business use case for custom route constraints which specifies that the parameter should contain the domain name as `@packt.com`, else it should respond with 404 error.

1. Create a C# class `DomainConstraint` by copying the following code. We implement the `IRouteConstraint` interface and the `Match` method in this code:

```
public class DomainConstraint : IRouteConstraint
{
  public bool Match(HttpContext httpContext, IRouter route,
    string routeKey, RouteValueDictionary values,
      RouteDirection routeDirection)
  {
    var isMatch = false;
    if (values["domName"].ToString().Contains("@packt.com"))
    {
      isMatch = true;
    }
    return isMatch;
  }
}
```

2. Open `Startup.cs`, add this constraint as `RouteOption` in the `ConfigureServices` method.

3. In `Startup.cs`, use the **DomainConstraint** domain in the route template in the `Configure` method, as follows:

```
using Microsoft.AspNetCore.Builder;
using Microsoft.AspNetCore.Hosting;
using Microsoft.AspNetCore.Http;
using Microsoft.Extensions.DependencyInjection;
using Microsoft.Extensions.Logging;
using Microsoft.AspNetCore.Routing;
```

```
namespace BasicRoutes
{
  public class Startup
  {
    public void ConfigureServices(IServiceCollection services)
    {
      // Adding Router Middleware
      services.AddRouting();

      services.Configure<RouteOptions>(options =>
      options.ConstraintMap.Add("domain",
        typeof(DomainConstraint)));
    }

    public void Configure(IApplicationBuilder app,
      IHostingEnvironment env, ILoggerFactory loggerFactory)
    {
      var routeBuilder = new RouteBuilder(app);

      // domName parameter should have @packt.com
      routeBuilder.MapGet("api/employee/{domName:domain}",
        context =>
      {
        var domName = context.GetRouteValue("domName");
        return context.Response.WriteAsync(
          $"Domain Name Constraint Passed - {domName}");
      });

      var routes = routeBuilder.Build();
      app.UseRouter(routes);
    }
  }
}
```

Running the preceding application will show responses as follows.

Since the route parameter contains the @packt.com domain, as per the custom constraint, this works well, as shown in this screenshot:

Domain Constraint returns response

Now let's pass the parameter without @packt.com; this would throw the 404 Not Found error as follows:

▼ General
   Request URL: http://localhost:54517/api/employee/mm@packtr.com
   Request Method: GET
   Status Code: ● 404 Not Found

Domain Constraint returns 404 error

Link generation

The routing mechanism provides enough to link to the routes in the application, however, at times, generating links pointing to specific routes becomes essential. We can achieve custom links using the link generation concept.

ASP.NET Core provides the UrlHelper class, an implementation of the IUrlHelper interface to build URLs for an ASP.NET Core application (MVC or web API). The methods CreatedAtRoute and CreatedAtAction are two inbuilt methods for link generation. Let's use them in an example:

```
using Microsoft.AspNetCore.Mvc;
using System.Collections.Generic;
using System.Linq;

namespace BasicRoute.Controllers
{
  public class TodoController : Controller
  {
    // List containing Todo Items
    List<TodoTasks> TodoList = new List<TodoTasks>();

    // Gets Todo item details based on Id
    [Route("api/todos/{id}", Name = "GetTodoById")]
    public IActionResult GetTodo(int id)
    {
      var taskitem = TodoList.FirstOrDefault(x => x.Id == id);
      if (taskitem == null)
      {
         return NotFound();
      }
      return Ok(taskitem);
    }
```

```
    // Adds or POST a todo item to list
    [Route("api/todos")]
    public IActionResult PostTodo([FromBody]TodoTasks todoItems)
    {
      TodoList.Add(todoItems);
      // CreatedAtRoute generators link
      return CreatedAtRoute("GetTodoById", new {
        Controller = "Todo", id = todoItems.Id }, todoItems);
    }
  }

  public class TodoTasks
  {
    public int Id { get; set; }
    public string Name { get; set; }
  }
}
```

You can break down the preceding code as follows:

- The `TodoTasks` class is the basic C# class having `id` and `Name` for Todo tasks
- `TodoController` defines two action methods, `GetTodo` and `PostTodo`, with appropriate attribute routing.
- The `CreatedAtRoute` method generates a link, and adds it to the header of the response with link generated so that clients can access it.

A similar `CreatedAtRoute` can be written to have a more focused link generation. When we run the application using the Postman client, the Location Header is added explicitly with the URL pointing to the `GetTodo` method with `id`, as shown in the following screenshot:

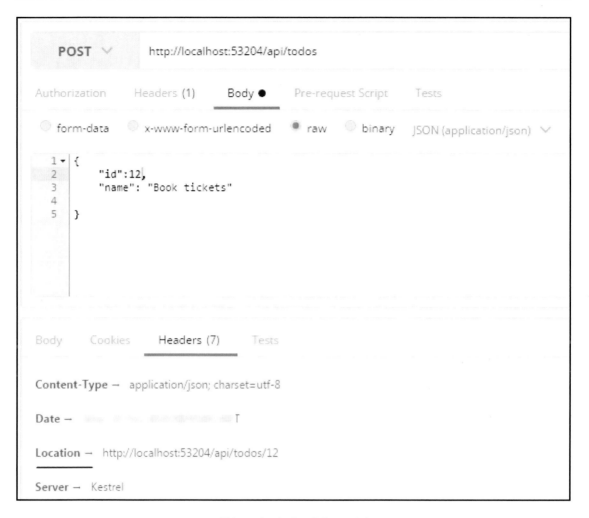

Link generation using CreatedAtRoute method

Routing best practices

ASP.NET Core provides a lightweight, completely configurable Routing mechanism in the form of middleware, Convention-based routing, direct or Attribute Routing, constraints, and so on. Proper usage of these routing features is necessary for optimal performance of the application.

Some of the best practices that need to be considered are summarized next; these practices will evolve as more applications are built with various use cases. These lists may or may not apply to your application depending on your application's needs:

- Use the inbuilt `UseMvc` middleware which sits on top of the Routing middleware for achieving Routing strategy.
- Conventional routing is sufficient a CRUD style of web API is being developed. It reduces the overhead of writing direct routes for all the actions in various controllers.
- Try avoiding the catch-all route parameters, that is, `{*empId}`. When used in conventional (centralised) routing, there are chances that unwanted routes may match this catch-all resulting in unexpected behaviors.
- When working with an ASP.NET Core Web API, it's better to use HTTP-verb-based routing, that is, attribute routing with HTTP verbs like GET, POST, PUT, and DELETE. The clients can consume these web APIs with ease.
- Order on the attributes routes should be avoided, instead, use Route Names for different API methods.
- Multiple routes can point to the same controllers/ actions, but using this on a large scale might result in combining actions' implementation with many conditional cases.
- Route parameter constraints are a powerful feature, but they should not be used for model validation.
- Designing web APIs with both conventional and attribute routing should be minimized.

Summary

The ASP.NET Core routing functionality is powerful, and highly configurable. In this chapter, you learned how the routing middleware works with the HTTP pipeline. We used RouteBuilder to create route tables and navigated between them. You also learned about the `UseMvc` middleware implementing routing middleware internally.

Routing can be either conventional or Attribute-based, we discussed and implemented route parameters using custom constraints. The Link generation feature can be used for generating links to specific routes. You also learnt some best practices for web API routing.

The upcoming chapter focuses on the middleware concept of ASP.NET Core--you will learn the basics of middleware, writing some custom middleware, and about Filters in ASP.NET Core applications.

6

Middleware and Filters

Any web application development framework's success depends on its abilities to handle HTTP request and response efficiently. Any HTTP request has to undergo a series of verification and validation before it can access the requested resource.

When numerous simultaneous requests hit the web server, serving them quickly without breaking down under load is a key factor for well-designed web applications. This involves designing framework based on a modular approach, where we can use features only if required.

ASP.NET Core is a completely modular way of developing modern web applications; it's designed on the concept of including what you need instead of including all features, which makes it heavy to process requests.

Middleware and filters are such features of ASP.NET Core, and they play an important role in the processing of HTTP requests. You will learn about these two features in depth in this chapter.

In this chapter, we will cover the following topics:

- Introducing middleware
- HTTP request pipeline and middleware
- Order of middleware
- Built-in middleware
- Creating custom middleware
- Migrating HTTP modules to middleware
- Introducing filters
- Action filters
- Authentication and authorization filters
- Exception filters

Introducing middleware

Let's assume that you created the ASP.NET Core application (MVC or web API), controllers, and action methods connected to the database to fetch records and then added authentication; everything runs smoothly.

Just for fun, comment on the code inside the `Configure` method of `Startup` class and run the application. Surprisingly, there won't be any build errors and a blank browser window shows up.

Navigating to any route, pages, or assets always returns a blank screen. Taking a deep dive into this, we can infer the following:

- The `Configure` method is one of the starting points when an HTTP request arrives
- When a request arrives, someone has to process the request and return a response
- An HTTP request has to undergo various operations, such as authentication, CORS, and so on, before they access the resource

The `Configure` method of the `Startup` class is the centre of an HTTP request pipeline; any software-component part of this pipeline is called middleware in ASP.NET Core. They are responsible for request and response processing, based on their placement order in the pipeline.

Each middleware can be designed to pass the request onto the next middleware or end the request processing pipeline. The request pipeline is built using request delegates. The request delegates handle each HTTP request.

 Without middleware components, ASP.NET Core does nothing.

The `Configure` method takes in one of the parameters as `IApplicationBuilder`. This interface provides the mechanism to configure an application's request pipeline. The request delegates are configured using these four extension methods of the `IApplicationBuilder` interface:

- The `Use()` method adds the middleware request delegate to the application pipeline. The request delegate handler can be in-line as an anonymous method or a reusable class.

- The `Run()` method is also known as the terminal middleware delegate in the application pipeline. Nothing is processed after this.
- The `Map()` method branches the request pipeline based on the matches of request path.
- The `Mapwhen()` method branches the request pipeline based on the result of the given predicate or condition.

Let's understand how various middleware components work together with `IApplicationBuilder`.

HTTP request pipeline and middleware

The ASP.NET Core request pipeline processing is completely rewritten from the traditional ASP.NET request processing. Every request is processed through a sequence of request delegates to return a response.

ASP.NET Core documentation depicts HTTP request processing, as shown in the following screenshot:

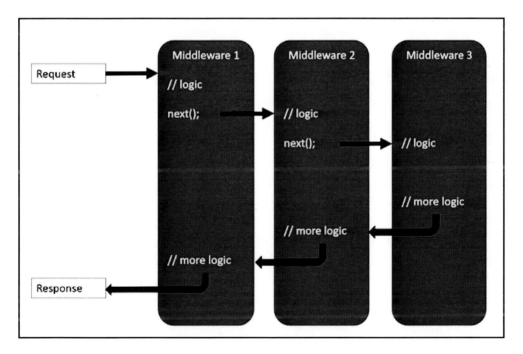

HTTP request processing in ASP.NET Core

The blue bars indicate that the middleware components (either built-in or custom built), once an HTTP request arrives on pipeline (the `Configure` method), encounters **Middleware 1** component. The processing of request takes place in **//logic**, then request is passed on the next middleware in the sequence using `next()`.

The request processing reaches **Middleware 2** components, does the processing, and passes onto the next **Middleware 3** using `next()`. Here, after the request is processed, it does not encounter `next()`, indicating that the sequence ends here and starts returning a response.

The response is processed in a reverse order--**Middleware 3**, **Middleware 2**, and **Middleware 1**, as the end response is returned back to client.

`IApplicationBuilder` keeps track of the request processing pipeline in sequence; this way, it's easy for processing request and response smoothly.

The request delegates should be designed with a specific focus instead of combining several delegates to make them a single component. Middleware should be as lean as possible to make them reusable.

Middleware can either pass the request for further processing or stop passing to process request on its own. Some examples are authentication, CORS, Developer Exception page, and so on.

Middleware in action

In the previous section, we looked into a pictorial representation of the middleware request pipeline processing. In this section, you will learn the role of middleware in the request pipeline by writing a code.

Create an Empty ASP.NET Core application and comment out/remove the default code in the `Configure` method of the `Startup` class.

We will write a code to understand the four extension methods from the previous section: `Use()`, `Run()`, `Map()`, and `MapWhen()` of `IApplicationBuilder`.

The middleware components accept the `RequestDelegate` method. They are the functions that process the HTTP request with a signature as follows:

```
public delegate Task RequestDelegate(HttpContext context);
```

It takes in one parameter of `HttpContext` and returns `Task`, working asynchronously.

Use()

When middleware is written as `app.Use(...)`, a middleware delegate is added to the application's request pipeline. It can be written as an inline delegate or in a class.

It can pass the processing onto next middleware or end pipeline processing it. The `Use` extension method has delegates taking two parameters, the first parameter being `HttpContext` and the second, a `RequestDelegate`.

A very basic middleware can be written as shown in the following code snippet:

```
app.Use(async (context, next) =>
{
  await context.Response.WriteAsync("Middleware 1");
});
```

Running this code will show `Middleware 1` on the browser.

This middleware component does have some logic of writing content on response, but it won't call any other middleware because the second parameter of the request delegate is missing.

To call the next middleware, we will need to call the `Invoke()` method of the request delegate `next`, as shown in the following piece of code:

```
public void Configure(IApplicationBuilder app, IHostingEnvironment
  env, ILoggerFactory loggerFactory)
{
  app.Use(async (context, next) =>
  {
    await context.Response.WriteAsync("Middleware 1<br/>");
    // Calls next middleware in pipeline
    await next.Invoke();
  });

  app.Use(async (context, next) =>
  {
    await context.Response.WriteAsync("Middleware 2<br/>");
    // Calls next middleware in pipeline
    await next.Invoke();
  });

  app.Use(async (context, next) =>
  {
    await context.Response.WriteAsync("Middleware 3<br/>");
    // No invoke method to pass next middleware
  });
```

```
      app.Use(async (context, next) =>
      {
        await context.Response.WriteAsync("Middleware 4<br/>");
        // Calls next middleware in pipeline
        await next.Invoke();
      });
    }
```

We can break down the preceding code as follows:

- `Middleware 1`, `Middleware 2`, `Middleware 3`, and `Middleware 4` are the simple inline middleware examples.
- `Middleware 1` and `Middleware 2` have request delegates invoking the `next` middleware in pipeline.
- `Middleware 3` does not have the `next` invoking code, and the pipeline will infer that this is last request delegate and stops further processing. It's known as **short circuiting**.
- Even though `Middleware 4` is written with the `next` invoke, it doesn't get called as `Middleware 3`, which has not passed request processing.

Run the application to see the middleware response in the browser. The response from `Middleware 4` is not written because the pipeline has treated that `Middleware 3` is last and ends processing further, that is, end of pipeline processing:

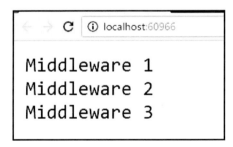

Middleware using app.Use (...)

Run()

The `Run()` method adds a `RequestDelegate` that is terminal to the pipeline. Any middleware components written after `Run` will not be processed as ASP.NET Core treats it as an end of the pipeline processing.

Copy the following code snippet in the beginning of the `Configure` method before the middleware written using `Use()`:

```
app.Run(async context => {
    await context.Response.WriteAsync("Run() - a Terminal Middleware
    <br/>");
});
```

Running the application, you will only see the `Run()` middleware executed with the rest of the middleware (1,2,3,4) not executed at all.

Some of the middleware do expose this method for treated as terminal middleware. It shouldn't be used in code to terminate the request processing.

> Adopt the `Use()` method for request processing because it can either pass or short circuit requests.

Map()

The `Map()` method provides the ability to branch the middleware pipeline processing based on the matches of request path. The `Map()` method takes two parameters: `PathString` and the delegated named `Configuration`.

The following code snippet shows `Map()` in action; copy this in the `Configure` method and run the application:

```
public void Configure(IApplicationBuilder app,
  IHostingEnvironment env, ILoggerFactory loggerFactory)
{
    app.Use(async (context, next) =>
    {
        await context.Response.WriteAsync("Middleware 1 without Map
        <br/>");
        await next();
    });
```

```
    // Get executed only on "/packtchap2"
    app.Map(new PathString("/packtchap2"), branch =>
    {
      branch.Run(async context => { await
      context.Response.WriteAsync("packtchap2 - Middleware 1
      <br/>"); });
    });

    // Get executed only on "/packtchap5"
    app.Map(new PathString("/packtchap5"), branch =>
    {
      branch.Run(async context => { await context.Response.WriteAsync(
        "packtchap5 - Middleware 2 <br/>"); });
    });
    app.Run(async context => { await context.Response.WriteAsync("
      Middleware 2 without Map <br/>"); });
}
```

Run the application to see it in action. Navigate to
`http://localhost:60966/packtChap3` and `http://localhost:60966/packtChap5`.

 The port number 60966 will be different when it is run on your machine.

We can break down the code as follows:

- The `packtchap2` and `packtchap5` middleware get executed only when they are branched out.
- `Middleware 1 without Map` gets executed, irrespective of map branching.
- `Middleware 2 without Map` will not get executed when any of the preceding branching is applied. It's obvious because the pipeline processing has changed course.

Branched middleware can contain as many middleware components as it likes. The following screenshot shows `Map()` in action:

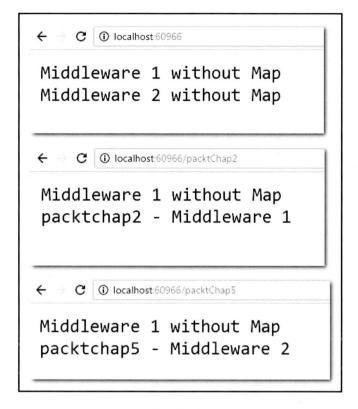

Map (...) in action

MapWhen()

Works similarly to the `Map()` method, but with more control over URL, request headers, query strings, and so on. The `MapWhen()` method returns Boolean after checking any condition from the `HttpContext` as parameter.

Copy the following code snippet in the `Configure` method of the `Startup` class:

```
public void Configure(IApplicationBuilder app, IHostingEnvironment env,
  ILoggerFactory loggerFactory)
{
  app.Use(async (context, next) =>
  {
    await context.Response.WriteAsync("Middleware 1 - Map When <br/>");
    await next();
  });
```

```
app.MapWhen(context =>
  context.Request.Query.ContainsKey("packtquery"), (appbuilder) =>
{
  appbuilder.Run(async (context) =>
  {
    await context.Response.WriteAsync("In side Map When <br/>");
  });
});
}
```

Running this example will show the following result:

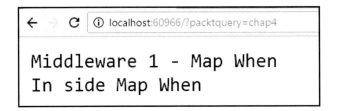

MapWhen in action

When the URL maps the query string to `packtquery`, the request pipeline processing gets branched and execute `MapWhen()` based middleware.

Order of middleware

The ASP.NET Core request pipeline processing works by running middleware components as per the sequence they are placed in the `Configure` method of the `Startup` class.

The pictorial representation of request processing describes the execution order of middleware. The sequence order is created by placement of the `Use`, `Run`, `Map`, and `MapWhen` extension method code placements. Invoking of next middleware decides the order of the middleware execution.

The following are some of the real-world scenarios where middleware order plays an important role:

- Authentication middleware should handle requests initially. Only authenticated requests are allowed to access application.

- In case of web API projects, CORS middleware fits well as initial middleware and then authentication middleware.
- Custom middleware can perform some custom processing before accessing resources, even though the request is authenticated.
- A web API response needs to be modified before it is returned to the client.

The following code snippet shows the importance of the middleware order:

```
public void Configure(IApplicationBuilder app, IHostingEnvironment env,
   ILoggerFactory loggerFactory)
{
   app.Use(async (context, next) =>
   {
     await context.Response.WriteAsync("Middleware 1<br/>");
     // Calls next middleware in pipeline
     await next.Invoke();
     await context.Response.WriteAsync("Middleware 1
        while return<br/>");
   });

   app.Map(new PathString("/packtchap2"), branch =>
   {
     branch.Run(async context => { await context.Response.WriteAsync("
        packtchap2 - Middleware 1<br/>"); });
   });

   app.Run(async context => {
     await context.Response.WriteAsync("Run() - a Terminal
        Middleware <br/>");
   });

   app.Use(async (context, next) =>
   {
     await context.Response.WriteAsync("Middleware 2<br/>");
     // Calls next middleware in pipeline
     await next.Invoke();
   });
}
```

Run the application to see the result in the browser, as shown in the following screenshot:

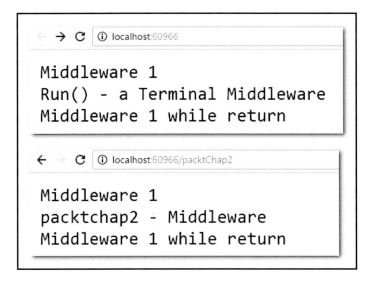

Middleware order in action

We can break down the code as follows:

- Middleware written using Use(...) does processing before passing onto the next middleware using the Invoke() method
- Middleware 1 gets executed and the response is returned
- Middleware written using Run gets processed and starts reverse execution of middleware because Run() is terminal (end)
- Middleware 2 never gets called because of the presence of Run() before it
- Middleware using Map() gets executed only when the packtchap2 path string is valid

Built-in middleware

The ASP.NET Core team has written a number of built-in middleware to work for wide variety of requirements. Some of the built-in middleware are as follows:

- **Authentication**: This is used for authentication support, such as login, logout, and so on.

- **CORS**: This configures Cross-Origin Resource Sharing that is used for web API projects.
- **Routing**: This defines and constrains request routes. Chapter 5, *Implementing Routing*, is dedicated to routing.
- **Session**: This provides support for managing user sessions.
- **Static Files**: This supports to serve static files and directory browsing as part of wwwroot.

Using StaticFiles middleware

Static files (HTML, CSS, images, JS files) are served from the wwwroot folder in ASP.NET Core applications. In this section, let's add a built-in static file serving middleware loading all the assets from the wwwroot folder.

Create an empty ASP.NET Core project, or you can continue from the preceding middleware code examples. The NuGet package of Microsoft.AspNetCore.StaticFiles used for serving static contents is already part of Microsoft.AspNetCore.All.

Open the Startup class and add the following code in the Configure method to use this StaticFiles middleware:

```
app.UseStaticFiles();
```

Create an HTML file, index.html, in wwwroot; this is the static file that will be served when the application runs:

```
<!DOCTYPE html>
<html>
  <head>
    <meta charset="utf-8" />
    <title>Mastering Web API</title>
  </head>
  <body>
    <h3>Served by StaticFile middleware.</h3>
  </body>
</html>
```

Running the application, you will see `index.html` being served on browser, as shown in the following screenshot:

Index.html served by StaticFile middleware

Writing custom middleware

Every project has its own business or domain-specific requirements for the request pipeline processing. The built-in middleware is good enough, but writing custom middleware gives us more control over the request processing strategy.

In this section, we will write the custom middleware component with respect to web API projects. A custom middleware can be written by considering these points:

- A C# class with a middleware name
- A `RequestDelegate` variable--_next--to invoke the next middleware in the pipeline
- The class constructor taking in a request delegate object that is injected using DI
- An `Invoke` method accepting `HttpContext` as parameter and returning `Task` asynchronously

We will write a custom middleware with a business scenario, as every request should contain the `packt-book` header, whose value should be `Mastering Web API`. If the header value is missing or incorrect, then HTTP response should be a bad request, and if it matches properly, then web API should return the request resource.

Create a C# class with the name `PacktHeaderValidator` and copy the following code in it:

```
using Microsoft.AspNetCore.Builder;
using Microsoft.AspNetCore.Http;
using System.Threading.Tasks;
```

```
namespace custom_middleware
{
  // Custom ASP.NET Core Middleware
  public class PacktHeaderValidator
  {
    private RequestDelegate _next;

    public PacktHeaderValidator(RequestDelegate next)
    {
      _next = next;
    }

    public async Task Invoke(HttpContext context)
    {
      //If matches pipeline processing continues
      if (context.Request.Headers["packt-book"].Equals(
        "Mastering Web API"))
      {
        await _next.Invoke(context);
      }
      else
      {
        // Pipeline processing ends
        context.Response.StatusCode = 400; //Bad request
      }
    }
  }

  #region ExtensionMethod
  //Extension Method to give friendly name for custom middleware
  public static class PacktHeaderValidatorExtension
  {
    public static IApplicationBuilder
      UsePacktHeaderValidator(this IApplicationBuilder app)
    {
      app.UseMiddleware<PacktHeaderValidator>();
      return app;
    }
  }
  #endregion
}
```

Use this newly created custom middleware in the `Configure` method of the `Startup` class as follows:

```
public void Configure(IApplicationBuilder app, IHostingEnvironment env,
  ILoggerFactory loggerFactory)
{
  //Custom middleware added to pipeline
  app.UsePacktHeaderValidator();
  app.UseMvc();
}
```

We can break down the code as follows:

- The `PacktHeaderValidator` class looks for the `packt-book` header value.
- If `packt-book` values match, the pipeline process continues. It returns the web API controller data.
- If `packt-book` values do not match, the pipeline processing ends.
- Middleware `PacktHeaderValidator` is added to the `Configure` method. The `UseMvc()` middleware action executes only if the header values match.

To test this code example, we will use the Postman tool for testing. We can pass header values, view status codes, and also API responses:

- Run (*F5*) the web API projected where custom middleware is written
- Open the Postman tool and access the URL, `http://localhost:55643/api/values`, using `GET`
- Test with valid and invalid header values to see the result, as shown in the following screenshot:

Custom middleware in action

Migrating HTTP modules to middleware

Prior to ASP.NET Core, the ASP.NET world had concepts of HTTP Handlers and HTTP Modules. They were part for request pipeline, having access to life cycle events throughout the request.

They are similar to the concept of Middleware in ASP.NET Core. In this section, we will migrate the HTTP module to ASP.NET Core middleware.

Writing HTTP modules and registering them in `web.config` is out of the scope of this book; we will refer to this MSDN article, *Walkthrough: Creating and Registering a Custom HTTP Module* (`https://msdn.microsoft.com/en-us/library/ms227673.aspx`), and migrate to ASP.NET Core middleware.

To summarize the article--the HTTP module appends a string to the start and end of response when request of file extension is `.aspx`.

Create C# class `AspxMiddleware` that does look for the request that contains the PATH which contains `.aspx`. If present, then it responds with appropriate text as part of the code. An extension method is also written to use in the `Configure` method in the `Startup` class, as follows:

```
using Microsoft.AspNetCore.Builder;
using Microsoft.AspNetCore.Http;
using System.Threading.Tasks;

namespace httpmodule_to_middleware
{
  public class AspxMiddleware
  {
    private RequestDelegate _next;
    public AspxMiddleware(RequestDelegate next)
    {
      _next = next;
    }

    public async Task Invoke(HttpContext context)
    {
      if (context.Request.Path.ToString().EndsWith(".aspx"))
      {
        await context.Response.WriteAsync("<h2><font color=red>" +
          "AspxMiddleware: Beginning of Request" +
          "</font></h2><hr>");
      }

      await _next.Invoke(context);

      if (context.Request.Path.ToString().EndsWith(".aspx"))
      {
        await context.Response.WriteAsync("<hr><h2><font color=red>" +
          "AspxMiddleware: End of Request</font></h2>");
      }
    }
  }

  #region ExtensionMethod
  //Extension Method to give friendly name for custom middleware
  public static class AspxMiddlewareExtension
  {
    public static IApplicationBuilder UseAspxMiddleware(this
      IApplicationBuilder app)
    {
      app.UseMiddleware<AspxMiddleware>();
      return app;
```

```
        }
    }
    #endregion
}
```

Call the middleware in the `Configure` method of the `Startup` class as follows:

```
public void Configure(IApplicationBuilder app, IHostingEnvironment env,
    ILoggerFactory loggerFactory)
{
    // Calling HTTP module migrated to middleware
    app.UseAspxMiddleware();
    app.Run(async (context) =>
    {
        await context.Response.WriteAsync("Hello World!");
    });
}
```

Running the application to view the middleware response, we have converted `BeingRequest` and `EndRequest` of the HTTP module into the middleware class, as shown in the following screenshot:

HTTP modules into Middleware in action

Introducing filters

Middleware is a powerful concept in ASP.NET Core; properly designed middleware can reduce the burden of request processing in the application. ASP.NET Core applications, either in the form of MVC or web API, work on MVC middleware, dealing with Authentication, Authorization, Routing, Localization, Model binding, and so on.

ASP.NET MVC apps contain Controllers and Actions, and controlling their execution would be great if required.

Filters help us to run code before or after a particular stage in the execution pipeline. They can be configured to run globally, per-controller, or per-action.

Filter pipeline

Filters run within the MVC context; it runs along with the MVC Action Invocation pipeline, which is also known as the **Filter pipeline**.

Filter pipeline gets executed in the following way:

- Starts only when MVC middleware takes over. This is the reason filters are not part of other middleware.
- Authorization filters are the first to run; if it's not authorized, then it short-circuits the pipeline immediately.
- Resource filters come into action for authorized request. They can run at the very beginning of the request as well as at the end, before leaving the MVC pipeline.
- Actions are an essential part of MVC. The Action filters run just before or after the actions of controllers get executed. They have access to model-bound parameters.
- Every Action returns results; the Result filter comes into play with results (before or after).
- Uncaught exceptions are bound to happen in an application, and handling them is crucial. For these kinds of Exceptions, custom written filters can be applied globally to keep track of them.

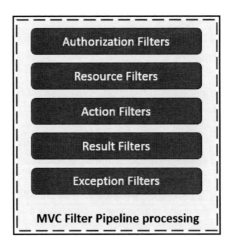

MVC Filter pipeline

Filter scoping

A filter's ability to scope it into three levels makes it a powerful feature in ASP.NET MVC applications.

Filters can be applied globally or per-controller or per-action level:

- A filter's written attributes can be applied at any level. A global filter gets applied on every controller or every action if it's not really necessary.
- Controller attribute filters get applied to controller and all its action methods.
- Action attribute filters get applied to particular actions only. This gives more flexibility to apply filters.
- Multiple filters on action execution are determined by the order property. If the same orders arise, execution starts at global level, then controller, and finally at action level.
- When action runs, the order of filters is reversed, that is, from action to controller to global filter.

Action filters

An Action filter is an attribute that can be applied to a controller or a particular action method.

Action filters implement either the `IActionFilter` or `IAsyncActionFilter` interface. They can view and directly modify the result of an action method.

Let's create a simple action filter using the `IActionFilter` interface. It checks for Header entry `publiser-name`; if its value does not match `Packt`, then it returns an action result as `BadRequestObjectResult`.

Add the `CheckPubliserNameAttribute` class in ASP.NET Core Web API project. Copy the following code snippet:

```
using Microsoft.AspNetCore.Mvc;
using Microsoft.AspNetCore.Mvc.Filters;

namespace filters_demo
{
  //Action Filter example
  public class CheckPubliserNameAttribute : TypeFilterAttribute
  {
    public CheckPubliserNameAttribute() : base(typeof
```

```
        (CheckPubliserName))
      {
      }
   }
   public class CheckPubliserName : IActionFilter
   {
      public void OnActionExecuted(ActionExecutedContext context)
      {
         // You can work with Action Result
      }

      public void OnActionExecuting(ActionExecutingContext context)
      {
         var headerValue = context.HttpContext.Request.Headers[
           "publiser-name"];
         if (!headerValue.Equals("Packt"))
         {
            context.Result = new BadRequestObjectResult("Invalid Header");
         }
      }
   }
}
```

Open `ValuesController` and add the `Action` filter created in the preceding code to the `Get()` method, as shown in the following code:

```
[HttpGet]
[CheckPubliserName]
public IEnumerable<string> Get()
{
   return new string[] { "value1", "value2" };
}
```

We can break down the code as follows:

- The `CheckPubliserName` class implements `IActionFilter` and checks the header value in the `OnActionExecuting` method.
- In the `ValuesController` class, the `Get` method is added with the action filter `CheckPubliserName`. This method returns data only when a valid header is passed.

Run the application with valid header to see response.

In this example, we can see the difference between middleware and filter, as filter can be applied to the `Action` method or `Controller`.

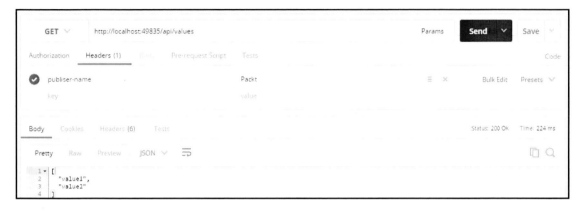

Action Filter in returns response

Authorization filter

These filters control the access to action methods or controllers. They are the first to get executed in the filter pipeline. Once the `Authorization` filter is authorized, other filters get executed.

Create `ProductsController` in the web API project, the following code snippet added the `Authorize` attribute at controller level. It indicates that any action methods cannot be accessed unless authorized.

The `Get()` method is decorated with the `AllowAnonymous` attribute; it allows to access the action method:

```
using Microsoft.AspNetCore.Authorization;
using Microsoft.AspNetCore.Mvc;
using System;

namespace filters_demo.Controllers
{
  [Route("api/[controller]")]
  [Authorize]
  public class ProductsController : Controller
  {
```

```
      // GET: api/values
      [HttpGet]
      [AllowAnonymous]
      public string Get()
      {
        return "Year is " + DateTime.Now.Year.ToString();
      }

      // GET api/values/5
      [HttpGet("{id}")]
      public string Get(int id)
      {
        return "value is " + id;
      }
    }
}
```

Run the application and access the products API using Postman.

Exception filter

In ASP.NET Core, exceptions can be handled in two ways: by UseExceptionHandler middleware or writing our own exception handler using the IExceptionFilter interface.

We will write a custom exception handler using the IExceptionFilter interface, register it globally in MVC services, and test it.

Create the PacktExceptionFilter class and implement the IExceptionFilter interface and the OnException method. This filter reads the exception and prepares to send it to the client, as follows:

```
using Microsoft.AspNetCore.Http;
using Microsoft.AspNetCore.Mvc.Filters;
using System;
using System.Net;

namespace filters_demo
{
  // Exception Filter example
  public class PacktExceptionFilter : IExceptionFilter
  {
    public void OnException(ExceptionContext context)
    {
      HttpStatusCode status = HttpStatusCode.InternalServerError;
      String message = String.Empty;
```

```
    var exceptionType = context.Exception.GetType();
    if (exceptionType == typeof(ZeroValueException))
    {
        message = context.Exception.Message;
        status = HttpStatusCode.InternalServerError;
    }
    HttpResponse response = context.HttpContext.Response;
    response.StatusCode = (int)status;
    var err = message;
    response.WriteAsync(err);
        }
    }
}
```

Create the `ZeroValueException` class as the `Exception` class:

```
using System;
namespace filters_demo
{
  public class ZeroValueException : Exception
  {
    public ZeroValueException(){}

    public ZeroValueException(string message)
    : base(message)
    { }

    public ZeroValueException(string message, Exception innerException)
    : base(message, innerException)
    { }
  }
}
```

Open the `Startup` class and modify the `ConfigureServices` method to include MVC service with exception filter options:

```
public void ConfigureServices(IServiceCollection services)
{
  // Exception global filter added
  services.AddMvc(config => {
    config.Filters.Add(typeof(PacktExceptionFilter));
  });
}
```

Create the `EmployeeController` web API controller. The following code snippet shows that the `Get()` method throws an exception if `id` is 0:

```
using System;
using Microsoft.AspNetCore.Mvc;

namespace filters_demo.Controllers
{
  [Route("api/[controller]")]
  public class EmployeeController : Controller
  {
    // GET api/values/5
    [HttpGet("{id}")]
    public string Get(int id)
    {
      if (id == 0)
      {
          throw new ZeroValueException("Employee Id Cannot be Zero");
      }
      return "value is " + id;
    }
  }
}
```

Running the application, access `Employee` API by passing id as zero (0). The application responds to us with an exception message:

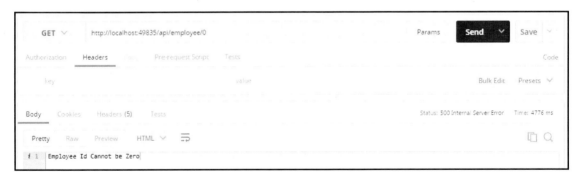

Exception filter in action

Summary

In this chapter, you learned a great deal about middleware, the request pipeline, and understood the middleware and its order. We wrote custom middleware and migrated HttpModule to middleware. The concept of middleware is the heart of request processing.

You learned about filters, its pipeline, ordering, and created Action filters and Exception filters in depth, and also learned about Authorization filter.

In the next chapter, we will focus on writing unit tests and integration tests.

7

Perform Unit and Integration Testing

There is no system that is 100% correct. Every system or procedure has bugs. Know that everything you write is not correct--it is subject to change, and will need correction. Some of the best systems in the world are modelled around this fact.

One, in particular, is the airline industry, and we know there have been very few accidents, except of late. Their risk is modelled around systemic failure or the Swiss cheese model, represented in this diagram:

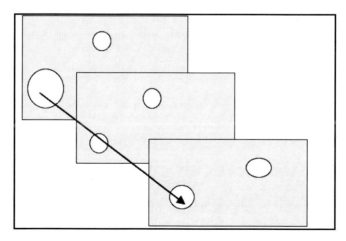

Each component of your system can have bugs, which is expected. The problem comes into being when the holes line up and a flaw is exposed. Having an adequate set of tests along the way can help with this problem.

In this chapter, we will cover the following topics:

- Test-driven development
- Integration API testing
- xUnit

Uncle Bob's three rules of test-driven development

Here are some guidelines to **Test-Driven development (TDD)**:

- Only write code to make a test pass
- When writing a test, write the minimal to make a test fail; this includes your code not compiling
- Write the minimal amount of code to make a test pass

With that said, the other rule of thumb is Red-Green-Refactor.

Red-Green-Refactor

Write a test; if that doesn't compile, this is red. Make it pass, that is your green. Then refactor the code, not the unit test, to your heart's content, that is your refactor.

So red, green, refactor, that should be your mantra.

I know I have already started the production code in the preceding chapters. If this was a book about TDD, then I would have started with the test. Our aim has been to introduce ASP.NET Core 2.0.

We will go back to our example that we started off with, Puhoi cheese, and I will recap that we are storing and can retrieve a few stores that we have. A store has a description and the number of products that it has, among other data.

Let's say we want to expand on that, and provide some information about the products.

A product will have a name, some description, price, the number in stock, and the size (for now, we will keep the size simple). Let's get cracking.

First create a test project--we will start with our models, and work our way up:

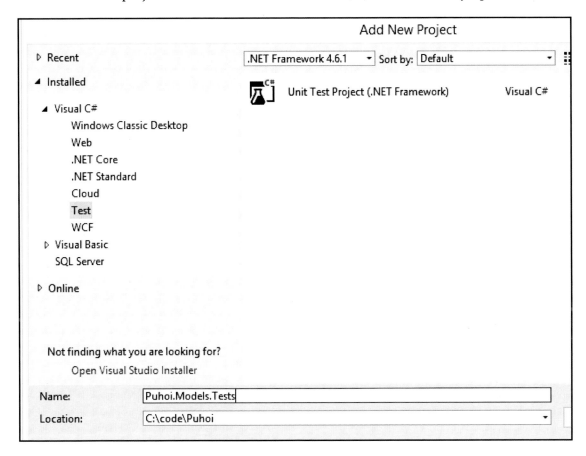

I create a new class for our `ProductModel` test, as follows:

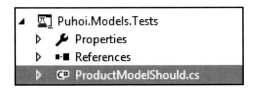

Let us write the first test thinking about Red-Green-Refactor and the three rules of TDD.

By creating a new `ProductModel` class which does not exist, we have compilation errors, which is our red as shown next:

```
[TestMethod]
public void BeABaseModel()
{
  // arrange
  ProductModel model = new ProductModel();
```

To make this test pass thus far, we need to create a `ProductModel` class:

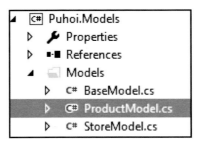

Add a reference to the test project, and we can now build our test project. Let us complete the test:

```
[TestMethod]
public void BeABaseModel()
{
  // arrange
  ProductModel model = new ProductModel();

  // act
  BaseModel baseModel = (BaseModel) model;

  // assert
  baseModel.Should().NotBeNull();
}
```

I use `FluentAssertions` for a more behavior-driven syntax; add a NuGet reference to `FluentAssertions`.

Fix the `ProductModel` class as follows:

```
public class ProductModel : BaseModel
```

Flick back to the test class, and give it a run. It should pass; we have green:

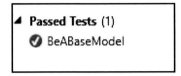

There is nothing to refactor, so we will continue to our next test. Hope you enjoyed the first test unit.

Let's start adding tests for our model attributes; I will begin with `Description`, as follows:

```
[TestMethod]
public void HaveADescriptionProperty()
{
  //arrange
  const string testDescription = "Test Description";

  // act
  ProductModel model = new ProductModel { Description =
    testDescription };
```

We have red.

Add `Description` to the `ProductModel` class, like this:

```
public class ProductModel : BaseModel
{
  public string Description { get; set;}
```

Then I complete the test for `Description` by adding the assertion as follows:

```
[TestMethod]
public void HaveADescriptionProperty()
{
  //arrange
  const string testDescription = "Test Description";

  // act
  ProductModel model = new ProductModel { Description =
  testDescription };

  // assert
  model.Description.Should().Be(testDescription);
}
```

This is the pattern that can be applied to be our model to a full set of requirements that we need to use TDD.

The following screenshot shows the complete set of passing tests:

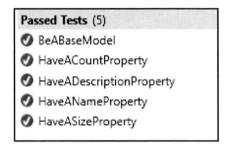

The resulting model is as follows:

```
public class ProductModel : BaseModel
{
    public string Description { get; set; }
    public string Name { get; set; }
    public int Count { get; set; }
    public string Size { get; set; }
}
```

Next, we move on to the validators; as before, we will use Fluent Validation to assist our validation cases.

I created a Valid model, and called this a Green model, as follows:

```
public static class GreenProductModel
{
  public static ProductModel Model()
  {
    return new ProductModel
    {
      Id = Guid.NewGuid(),
      Name = "Gold Strong Blue Cheese",
      Description = "Award winning Blue Cheese from Puhoi Valley",
      Count = 10000,
      Size = "Small"
    };
  }
}
```

Then we'll create a test to say that when we have a Green model, I expect the validation count to be zero:

```
[TestMethod]
public void ReturnNoValidationErrorsForAGreenModel()
{
  // arrange
  ProductModel model = GreenProductModel.Model();

  // act
  IEnumerable<ValidationResult> validationResult =
    model.Validate(new ValidationContext(this));
```

Nice, we have red. Now let us get our model to have a validator:

```
public class ProductModel : BaseModel, IValidatableObject
{
  public string Description { get; set; }
  public string Name { get; set; }
  public int Count { get; set; }
  public string Size { get; set; }

  public IEnumerable<ValidationResult> Validate(ValidationContext
   validationContext)
  {
    yield return new ValidationResult(string.Empty);
  }
}
[TestMethod]
public void ReturnNoValidationErrorsForAGreenModel()
{
  // arrange
  ProductModel model = GreenProductModel.Model();

  // act
  IEnumerable<ValidationResult> validationResult =
    model.Validate(new ValidationContext(this));

  // assert
  validationResult.Should().HaveCount(0);
}
```

My test result is red, as seen in the following screenshot:

```
◢ Failed Tests (1)
   ✖ ReturnNoValidationErrorsForAGreenModel
```

Now we have to make this test pass.

I used our implementation of validate from the `StoreModel` class on the `ProductModel` class, which led me to create a validator for the `ProductModel` class, as follows:

```
public class ProductModelValidator : BaseValidator<ProductModel>
{
  public ProductModelValidator()
  {
  }
}
```

With no real validators, which is fine, this was the least amount of code I needed to get my test to pass:

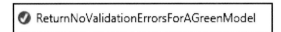

Now I will take the Green model, make some changes to get it to a Red model, and then test the validation to get a validation result. In this case, we want something which is not equal to zero, and we know that we are testing our model:

```
[TestMethod]
public void ReturnInValidWhenNameIsEmpty()
{
  // arrange
  ProductModel model = GreenProductModel.Model();
  model.Name = string.Empty;

  //act
  IEnumerable<ValidationResult> validationResult =
    model.Validate(new ValidationContext(this));

  //assert
  validationResult.Should().HaveCount(1);
}
```

This preceding code is our red test. I have used the Green model and set the `Name` property to an empty string. Calling validate, I expect the validator to return one invalidation.

Now the code to make the test pass is as follows:

```
public class ProductModelValidator : BaseValidator<ProductModel>
{
  public ProductModelValidator()
  {
    RuleFor(p => p.Name).NotEmpty();
```

```
      }
   }
```

This will make our test pass, and establish the pattern for the rest of the validation for the attributes.

I encourage you to complete the rest of the validation.

After writing the test code, I ended up with these validators:

```
public ProductModelValidator()
{
   RuleFor(p => p.Name).NotEmpty();
   RuleFor(p => p.Description).NotEmpty();
   RuleFor(p => p.Size).NotEmpty();
}
```

All the tests pass this time, as seen in this screenshot:

Running the API test

Open a command line to the API project, and using the tools for .NET core, run the following command:

```
dotnet run
```

So we have our API running on port 5000, or you can get the API to run on IIS--I choose this, as it's simpler, and allows me to quickly have the server running the API, and to run some tests against it. The first test is as follows:

```
[TestMethod]
public async Task ReturnOkForHealthCheck()
{
  // arrange
  using (HttpClient client = new HttpClient())
  {
    client.BaseAddress = new Uri(_baseUri);

    //act
    HttpResponseMessage response = await
client.GetAsync("stores/healthcheck");

    // assert
    response.Should().NotBeNull();
    response.StatusCode.Should().Be(HttpStatusCode.OK);
  }
}
```

In the preceding test code, we call the healthcheck endpoint on the controller, and check that it is not null, and then that we can get back a OK (200) response.

Nothing fancy, but there's at least some test in place to start off with.

To set up the base address, I set this in app.config, and get this value at the test initialize:

```
private string _baseUri;
private const string _configurationBaseUri = "baseUri";

[TestInitialize]
public void TestInit()
{
    _baseUri =
ConfigurationManager.AppSettings.Get(_configurationBaseUri);
}
```

Lastly, the value is set in the app.config file, as follows:

```
<appSettings>
  <add key="baseUri" value="http://localhost:5000/api/"/>
</appSettings>
```

The Post Created test

```
[TestMethod]
public async Task ReturnCreatedForAPost()
{
    // arrange
    using (HttpClient client = new HttpClient())
    {
        client.BaseAddress = new Uri(_baseUri);
        //act
        StoreModel storeModel = GreenStoreModel();
        HttpResponseMessage response = await client.PostAsJsonAsync(
            "stores", storeModel);
        // assert
        response.Should().NotBeNull();
        response.StatusCode.Should().Be(HttpStatusCode.Created);

        // clean up
        await DeleteStore(client, storeModel.Id);
    }
}
```

We use the standard `HttpClient` wrapping this in a using statement, so the client can be cleaned up when we exit the test. The common pattern here is used with the other actions as well.

Setting the base URI

We use our Green model, and then use the client's `PostAsJsonAsync` notice that we don't need to do anything with our model, just point to the client to request the URI, which we build up in the test.

We assert that the response should not be empty. Also, we expect that the status code should be created.

The Post Conflict test

With this test, we check if our service responds with a status of `Conflict`. How can we do this?

Send the same data twice, and this is what we do.

We get our Green model as before. Call `post` using our `HttpClient`, and although this is an act, in this context of this particular test, it is part of our setup. Now call `post` again, which is where we act. We then assert that we get back a conflict:

```
[TestMethod]
public async Task ReturnConflictForAPost()
{
  // arrange
  using (HttpClient client = new HttpClient())
  {
     client.BaseAddress = new Uri(_baseUri);
     //arrange
     StoreModel storeModel = GreenStoreModel();
     storeModel.Name = "ConflictStore";
     HttpResponseMessage response = await client.PostAsJsonAsync("
        stores", storeModel);
     response = await client.PostAsJsonAsync("stores", storeModel);

     // act
     response = await client.PostAsJsonAsync("stores", storeModel);

     // assert
     response.StatusCode.Should().Be(HttpStatusCode.Conflict);
  }
}
```

The Put tests

In the `Put` tests, we execute a post request to have our resource created. Then use the same model, which is our green model, and change the name for the model. This is where we do this:

```
storeModel.Name = "Creamy Cheese";
```

Now we are ready to call the `put` method using our `HttpClient`, thereafter asserting that our response is an okay:

```
[TestMethod]
public async Task ReturnOkForAPut()
{
  // arrange
  using (HttpClient client = new HttpClient())
  {
     client.BaseAddress = new Uri(_baseUri);
     //arrange
     StoreModel storeModel = GreenStoreModel();
```

```
        storeModel.Id = Guid.NewGuid();
        HttpResponseMessage response = await
client.PostAsJsonAsync("stores",
        storeModel);
        storeModel.Name = "Creamy Cheese";
        // act
        string putUri = string.Format("stores/{0}", storeModel.Id);
        response = await client.PutAsJsonAsync(putUri, storeModel);

        // assert
        response.StatusCode.Should().Be(HttpStatusCode.OK);
    }
}
```

The Delete tests

In the `Delete` tests , we use the same pattern as the preceding test. We create our resource as we did before. Then use `HttpClient` to call `Delete`, and assert that the response we get back is an okay:

```
[TestMethod]
public async Task ReturnOkForDelete()
{
  // arrange
  using (HttpClient client = new HttpClient())
  {
    client.BaseAddress = new Uri(_baseUri);
    //arrange
    StoreModel storeModel = GreenStoreModel();
    storeModel.Id = Guid.NewGuid();
    HttpResponseMessage response = await
        client.PostAsJsonAsync("stores", storeModel);
    // act
    string deleteUri = string.Format("stores/{0}", storeModel.Id);
    response = await client.DeleteAsync(deleteUri);

    // assert
    response.StatusCode.Should().Be(HttpStatusCode.OK);
  }
}
```

The xUnit tests

An alternative to MS-Test is xUnit, an open source unit testing framework. Those of you familiar with nUnit and xUnit will love having this in .NET Core and Visual Studio.

Microsoft has packed xUnit with .NET core SDK, so you don't have to install xUnit as a separate package.

The Models tests

Create a new project; this will be the class library for .NET Core.

I named this `Puhoi.Models.xUnit.Tests`. I will be writing the same test that we created earlier on in the chapter for the models, but as a xUnit test, and then we'll look at the differences:

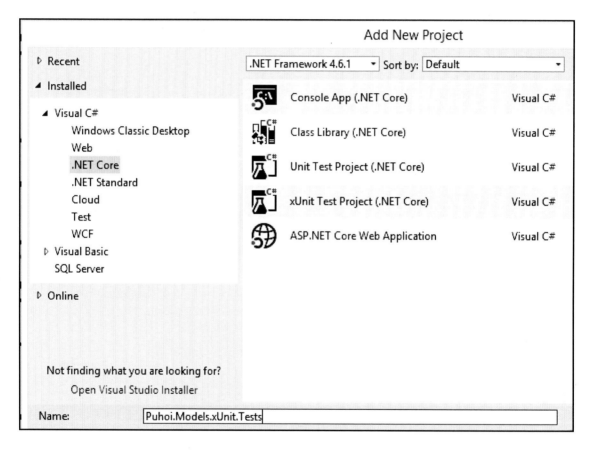

I copied `GreenProductModel` into the project; you can do this, or add the file as a shortcut.

To be able to use the models project and common library, which are .NET assemblies, I had to recreate them as .NET Core assemblies. You will find copies of these in the repository.

You should now see this in your solution explorer:

So, add a reference to `Puhoi.Models.Core`.

Now that we have our internal core assemblies, we now need our external assemblies. If you recall, we have used `FluentAssertions` for our assertions in the test.

`FluentAssertions` is prerelease, so you have to remember to tick the prerelease box:

Create a new class, `ProductModelShould`, and add the following test:

```
[Fact]
public void BeABaseModel()
{
    // arrange
    ProductModel model = new ProductModel();

    // act
    BaseModel baseModel = (BaseModel)model;

    // assert
    baseModel.Should().NotBeNull();
}
```

Notice the `Fact` attribute above our test method. Also, the class is not decorated with `TestClass`.

Open a command window, go to where the test project is, that is, `..\Puhoi.Models.xUnit.Tests`, and run the following commands:

- `dotnet restore`
- `dotnet build`
- `dotnet test`

We restore the packages in `project.json`, compiling the test project, and lastly, running the test, all from the command line. You can see the benefit of having this, which can be a batch take on your environment, and ultimately, running on your continuous build and deploy.

The results of the test will be outputted to console:

```
[TestMethod]
public void BeABaseModel()
{
    // arrange
    ProductModel model = new ProductModel();

    // act
    BaseModel baseModel = (BaseModel) model;

    // assert
    baseModel.Should().NotBeNull();
}
```

If we compare the test that we had written in our MS test, it is the same except that the `TestMethod` attribute is substituted with `Fact`.

This is not to say that you can take your MS test and swap the attributes, and you have a xUnit test. Let's explore some more of the tests that we have written, and what it takes to convert them to xUnit as well as demonstrate that xUnit can be used with .NET Core assemblies.

The validator class

This class validates the `model` object we are using in project:

```
[Fact]
public void ReturnNoValidationErrorsForAGreenModel()
{
```

```
// arrange
ProductModel model = GreenProductModel.Model();

// act
IEnumerable<ValidationResult> validationResult =
  model.Validate(new ValidationContext(this));

// assert
validationResult.Should().HaveCount(0);
}
```

This preceding test looks very similar to our MS test, nothing too exciting.

API Test

Let's try and replicate our API test. Create a new .Net Core project named
`PuhoiAPI.xUnit.Tests`, and change the `project.json` file as follows.

Add an `appsettings.json` file with the following entry:

```
{
   "baseUri": "http://localhost:5000/api/"
}
```

Add a class named `StoresControllerShould` as done previously. Copy `RedStoreModel`
and `GreenStoreModel` as previously set out.

This the constructor:

```
      public StoresControllerShould()
      {
          var builder = new
  ConfigurationBuilder().AddJsonFile("appsettings.json");
          var config = builder.Build();
          _baseUri = config[_configurationBaseUri];
          _jsonSerializer = new JsonSerializer();
      }
```

We use the `ConfigurationBuilder` class to read our `appsettings` file, which is in a
JSON format.

This is different from what we have in the MS test. As we write our first test, it will become
apparent why we need the `JsonSerializer` method.

Our `healthcheck` test is as follows:

```
[Fact]
public async void ReturnOkForHealthCheck()
{
  // arrange
  using (HttpClient client = new HttpClient())
  {
    client.BaseAddress = new Uri(_baseUri);

    //act
    HttpResponseMessage response = await
client.GetAsync("stores/healthcheck");

    // assert
    response.Should().NotBeNull();
    response.StatusCode.Should().Be(HttpStatusCode.OK);
  }
}
```

Open the command line to the API project, and type `dotnet run`. This will start up the web server hosting our API. Either run the test from within Visual Studio, or from the command line with the following commands:

- `dotnet restore`
- `dotnet build`
- `dotnet test`

The test will pass. Next, let us write a test to post some data to our API:

```
[Fact]
public async Task ReturnCreatedForAPost()
{
  // arrange
  using (HttpClient client = new HttpClient())
  {
    client.BaseAddress = new Uri(_baseUri);
    StoreModel storeModel = GreenStoreModel();
    HttpContent httpContent = SerializeModelToHttpContent(
      storeModel);

    //act
    HttpResponseMessage response = await client.PostAsync(
      "stores", httpContent);

    // assert
    response.Should().NotBeNull();
```

```
            response.StatusCode.Should().Be(HttpStatusCode.Created);
            await DeleteStore(client,storeModel.Id);
        }
    }
```

So there are a few things that are different in this preceding test as compared to our MS test. We get the model, which is what we need, but then we have to serialize the model to `HttpContent`. Why ? Our `HttpClient` in .NET Core is different from the plain .NET library. The `PostSync` method takes a URI and `HttpContent`. After this, our assertions are the same:

```
    private HttpContent SerializeModelToHttpContent(object obj)
    {
        string storeModelJSon = _jsonSerializer.Serialize(obj);
        HttpContent stringContent = new StringContent(
            storeModelJSon,
            Encoding.UTF8,
            "application/json");

        return stringContent;
    }
```

We use `JsonSerializer` to serialize the object to a string. This is an example of the conversion:

```
    {
        "NumberOfProducts":5,
        "DisplayName":"API ",
        "Description":"Green Model",
        "Id":"036c4610-c9c2-47ea-9aff-39e2341916e1",
        "Name":"Test"
    }
```

This is the only difference compared to the MS test, and the same is done with PUT.

```
    string putUri = string.Format("stores/{0}", storeModel.Id);
    response = await client.PutAsync(putUri, httpContent);
```

Get remains the same, as we do not send any data as part of the payload.

Summary

In this chapter, we covered Test-driven development using Uncle Bob's three laws along with saying Red-Green-Refactor to help us along the way.

We created some assertions using more of behavior-driven assertions. We then applied all of this to testing our API as if we were running integration tests. All of this is in the context if you have set up an automatic deployment, and you need some certainty that your API is fully functional.

Then we introduced the xUnit test for when we need to create some of our assemblies as pure .NET Core assemblies. We validated the theory that what we created with our MS test could be created with xUnit as well.

In the next chapter we will focus on implementing different security mechanisms for web API.

8
Web API Security

Web APIs serve requests with data and respond with processed data over the HTTP, that is, the internet. Web API does the necessary work of dealing with data, either confidential, personal, or business related, in the form of CRUD operations. Any layman would understand that CRUD operations on data shouldn't be performed by everyone.

With positive or negative intentions, web API designs will be exposed to the outside world to sneak in without permission. The security of web API should be our foremost priority, and the focus should be on who will access it, what they will access, and how safe is the data that is communicated.

In this heterogeneous world of web applications, mobile apps, server-server communication, desktop apps, and so on, the security of web API should be seamless across them to avoid hassles in switching the clients. It should be designed on the lines of authentication and authorization concepts.

In this chapter, we will cover the following topics:

- Understanding Threat Model and OWASP
- Applying SSL
- CORS
- Data Protection API
- Protecting web API
- Implementing JWT
- Claims-based authorizations
- Identity management in web API

Understanding Threat Model and OWASP

Right from the start, until the application is being used in production, it's exposed to different kinds of threats. These different kinds of threats can break the application from being successfully used. Therefore, it is important to address the threats.

Threat Model

The approach to identify and classify, and the process of addressing the threats is called **Threat Modelling**. The outcome of this process is a **Threat Model**. This process is not merely related to code review, following coding standards, or deployment processes.

Threat Modelling comprises more of analyzing the security of an application, and it's more result-oriented when it starts in the early stages of SDLC. The threats rise from written code, deployment strategy, environment, other applications, and hardware failure.

Broadly, the threats can be grouped in three categories based on their nature: decomposing the application, ranking the threats, and strategies counter measures and mitigation.

Decomposing the application is the most essential part as it helps in better understanding the application. This involves creating the use cases in which application is used, its interaction with external entities, such as software, patches, other applications, services, and so on.

The extensive documentation helps us stay updated and help any new joiners learn about the application soon. Various kind of information can be documented, such as the application name, version, owner, list of external dependencies, entry points of user data inputs, various assets used, and different levels of trusts given to various dependencies that directly affect the application.

Ranking of threats will provide us with a list of prioritized threats. The list will ensure the constant focus on the top categories of threats, which may reduce the chances of threats being affecting again and again.

A *DREAD (Damage + Reproducibility + Exploitability + Affected Users + Discoverability)* score can be calculated for a threat to determine its priority, and the Microsoft DREAD threat-risk ranking model is one of best ways to categorize the threats.

When threats strike, we can't sit idle and ponder over what to do. For that, counter measures and mitigations need to build up so that, in minimum downtime, the application is up and running.

Some of the counter measures that comprise of general basis are authentication, authorization, configuration management, backup of application data, error handling, validation of data, and logging. Denial of service and elevated privilege can also be considered based on application sensitivity.

More about threat modelling can be read at `https://www.owasp.org/index.php/Applicat ion_Threat_Modelin`.

OWASP

Over the years of the internet growing rapidly, it's usage has been positive as well as negative. The negative aspect is more challenging as web applications are used in almost all types of industries.

Web applications are constantly being targeted for vulnerability, providing too much information to explore, and no secure connection.

OWASP, also known as the **Open Web Application Security Project** foundation, has collated a number of steps to maintain healthy, secured, and efficient web applications without being exposed to threats.

As we are exploring web API (REST-based services), we will briefly explore few of those threats here:

- Passwords, session tokens, and API keys (any sensitive information) should not appear in URL. As the URLs can be captured in server logs, it's like willingly giving information.
- Using OAuth 2.0 or OpenID Connect as protocols for authentication and authorization.
- Protect HTTP methods for appropriate methods. Sometimes, protecting every HTTP (`Get`, `Post`, `Put`, and `Delete`) is not advisable. RESTful APIs need endpoints such as products to be fetched without authentication; however, to add, update, or delete, we need to protect those methods.
- Use Authorization properly. In any given application, just being an authenticated user should not have liberty to delete a resource. Check if the user has an appropriate role, or else respond back with 403 Forbidden.

- Input validation plays an important role since web API doesn't have a UI of its own. The request model validation should be strict, to ensure that proper data is stored.

- API rate limits should be set to restrict the number of requests. This is especially important during a brute force attack to take the service down.
- Response data should be as appropriate as necessary. A Product class may have 30 properties, but it does not return all of them to clients.
- Validating the content type should be done so that unwanted requests are not processed.
- Parameterized values should be passed to a data access layer to avoid SQL injection. Use of ORMs can solve this problem.

There are many other factors that can be considered while designing web API. Read through `https://www.owasp.org/index.php/REST_Security_Cheat_Sheet` for more information.

Applying SSL

When the web API requests and responses are transmitted over the internet (HTTP), we may encrypt the password, but the rest of the application data is exposed to the internet. The man in the middle can place an in-between client application and web API application to read those values.

It is very likely to see data being transmitted when the connection is unsecured; to overcome this, we can encrypt the connection using **SSL (Secured Sockets Layer)** using HTTPS. When this is applied, the communication with web API should take place using HTTPS instead of HTTP.

In ASP.NET Core, SSL can be enforced using the `RequireHttps` attribute, or enabled globally by applying a filter to `IServiceCollection`. As our intention is to make an entire application secured, we should be applying the global filter to use HTTPS.

Open the `Startup.cs` class and configure the services to use HTTPS if the non-development environment is used. We can enable HTTPS in non-development environment as shown in the following code snippet:

```
public void ConfigureServices(IServiceCollection services)
{
  // Add framework services.
  services.AddMvc();
```

```
//Checks if non Development environment, then enables HTTPS attribute
if (!env.IsDevelopment())
{
  services.Configure<MvcOptions>(o => o.Filters.Add(new
    RequireHttpsAttribute()));
}
}
```

You can change the ASP.NET Core Environment Variable `ASPNETCORE_ENVIRONMENT` to production or staging to see the HTTPS in action.

> First-time users need to at least enable a self-signed certificate to work with HTTPS. Creating, procuring, and enabling SSL on ASP.NET Core on IIS or Nginx is beyond the scope of this book, but plenty of resources exist on internet. Check out the following links for your reference: `https://www.digicert.com/ssl-certificate-installation-microsoft-iis-7.htm` and `https://www.digicert.com/ssl-certificate-installation-nginx.htm`

CORS

Cross Origin Resource Sharing (CORS) allows cross origin apps to access the application. In case of web API, it's a faceless application that receives a request and returns a response; however, when this web API is consumed in another web application (using AJAX in JavaScript to call APIs), the client would be on a different domain.

Consider an example, the web API is hosted as `www.packtdemo.com/api` and the web application is hosted as `www.packtdemoweb.com`. When the web app calls, the API responds with *No Access-Control-Allow-Origin header is present on the requested resource*. This means your domain is not allowed to access API resources.

This CORS concept can also be used to limit any unwanted web applications to access the web API. The idea behind this is to add the CORS policy in ASP.NET Core Startup processing and apply them either globally or as per controller.

In this chapter, we will build a demo ASP.NET Core Web API project, `PersonalBudget`, to keep a track of personal expenditure. Add the web API controller with `BudgetCategoryController` as its name.

Create two simple web apps with an index.html page, and use XMLHttpRequest to call the preceding web API controller, BudgetCategoryController, using the GET method. You will see a similar error in the browser console, as shown in the following screenshot:

```
✖ XMLHttpRequest cannot load                                     (index):1
  http://localhost:50854/api/BudgetCategory/. No 'Access-Control-Allow-Origin'
  header is present on the requested resource. Origin 'http://localhost:3000' is
  therefore not allowed access.

  >
```

CORS error on browser console

Now, let's add the CORS policy to a web API project. Open the Startup class and update it with the following code:

```
public void ConfigureServices(IServiceCollection services)
{
    // Add framework services.
    services.AddMvc();

    //Code removed for brevity
    services.AddCors(options =>
    {
        options.AddPolicy("DemoCorsPolicy",
        c => c.WithOrigins("http://localhost:3000/"));
    });
}
public void Configure(IApplicationBuilder app, IHostingEnvironment env,
    ILoggerFactory loggerFactory)
{
    //Code removed for brevity
    app.UseMvc();
    app.UseCors("DemoCorsPolicy");
}
```

You can break down the preceding code as follows:

- Adding a CORS policy with its name as DemoCorsPolicy
- This policy will only allow requests with the localhost:3000 origin
- The policy is then placed in an HTTP pipeline processing in the Configure method

- To allow every web application to access web API, use * instead of the domain name

Run the web API and web applications; the demo web API 1 could successfully receive a response and the demo web API 2 will receive an error, as shown in the preceding code related to CORS.

> The CORS policy can include varieties of combinations, such as Origins, Methods, Headers, and so on, making them more flexible.

Data Protection API

ASP.NET Core uses `Microsoft.AspNetCore.DataProtection` to handle the encryption keys used to protect state values that get posted between the app and the client.

The `Machine.config` keys are no longer used for data protection in ASP.NET Core. Data Protection is quite an extensive topic; you can refer to the Microsoft documentation (`https://docs.microsoft.com/en-us/aspnet/core/security/data-protection/`) to know more about this.

> The Cookie generation takes places using Data Protection APIs.

We will take a simple example of encrypting the ID values for a given entity.

Consider the `BudgetCategory` class having various properties that are uniquely identified by the ID. When we retrieve a list of budget categories or single objects, the ID passed should also be included. As this ID will be sensitive information to the business, we don't have to pass the real ID that is saved in the database.

For these kinds of requirement, we can encrypt while responding, and decrypt while receiving the request. We can achieve this behavior with the Data Protection API.

Continuing with the preceding project, create two classes `BudgetCategory` and `BudgetCategoryDTO`, the later class having `EncryptId` as a string, which is the encrypted version of ID. `BudgetCategoryDTO` is used for request and response operations and object mapping is done using `AutoMapper`.

The Data Protection APIs are added to services using `services.AddDataProtection()` in the `Startup` class in the `ConfigureServices` method. Create a `StringConstants` class with a property to hold the key used for encryption and decryption; this is called the purpose key:

```
public class StringConstants
    {
        public string IdQryStr => "AppIdString";
//Name can be anything.
    }
```

As we are using `AutoMapper` for object mapping, we need to convert the integer ID to String ID with the help of the Data Protection API, the `IDataProtectionProvider` interface, and the purpose key.

A custom `IdProtectorConverter` type converter is used to map from integer ID to String ID. This needs to be configured in the HTTP pipeline processing in the `Configure` method, as shown in the following piece of code:

```
public void Configure(IApplicationBuilder app, IHostingEnvironment env,
    ILoggerFactory loggerFactory,
    IDataProtectionProvider dataprovider, StringConstants strconsts)
{
    loggerFactory.AddConsole();
    AutoMapper.Mapper.Initialize(cfg =>
    {
      cfg.ConstructServicesUsing(type => new
        IdProtectorConverter(dataprovider, strconsts));
      cfg.CreateMap<BudgetCategoryDTO, BudgetCategory>();
      cfg.CreateMap<BudgetCategory, BudgetCategoryDTO>
        ().ConvertUsing<IdProtectorConverter>();
    });
}
```

The custom type converter, `IdProtectorConverter`, is used by `AutoMapper`, and it is written as follows:

```
namespace PersonalBudget
{
  public class IdProtectorConverter : ITypeConverter<BudgetCategory,
    BudgetCategoryDTO>
  {
    private readonly IDataProtector protector;
    public IdProtectorConverter(IDataProtectionProvider
      protectionprovider, StringConstants strconsts)
    {
      this.protector = protectionprovider.CreateProtector
```

```
                (strconsts.IdQryStr);
          }
        public BudgetCategoryDTO Convert(BudgetCategory source,
            BudgetCategoryDTO destination, ResolutionContext context)
        {
            return new BudgetCategoryDTO
            {
                Name = source.Name,
                Amount = source.Amount,
                EncryptId = this.protector.Protect(source.Id.ToString())
            };
        }
    }
}
```

You can break down the preceding code as follows:

- `BudgetCategory` is the source, and `BudgetCategoryDTO` is the destination that is passed to a client calling the web API
- `IDataProtectionProvider` and `StringConstants` are DI into the constructor to create `IDataProtector`
- In the `Convert` method, the encryption of the ID value takes place using `this.protector.Protect(source.Id.ToString())`

Now that the client receives an encrypted ID, they will send this ID to fetch a particular record. At this point of time, we need to decrypt this ID to pass on data source to fetch the record.

We need to call the `Unprotect` method of `IDataProtector` to convert it back to the integer ID; the following piece of code snippet performs this task:

```
[Route("api/[controller]")]
public class BudgetCategoryController : Controller
{
    private readonly PersonalBudgetContext _context;
    private readonly IDataProtector protector;

    public BudgetCategoryController(PersonalBudgetContext context,
        IDataProtectionProvider protectionprovider,
        StringConstants strconsts)
    {
        this.protector = protectionprovider.CreateProtector(
            strconsts.IdQryStr);
        _context = context;
    }
```

```
[HttpGet("{id}")]
public IActionResult Get(string id)
{
    var decryptId = int.Parse(protector.Unprotect(id));
    var item = _context.BudgetCategories.Find(decryptId);
    if (item == null)
    {
        return NotFound();
    }
    var results = Mapper.Map<BudgetCategoryDTO>(item);
    return Ok(results);
}
}
```

Run the application to add few `BudgetCategory` element and retrieve its list using Postman . The following screenshot shows the encrypted ID:

Data Protection API in action

Protecting web API

APIs Controller classes are the heart of web API applications performing the most essential work of fulfilling business requirements. We need to protect them from unauthorized access.

The web APIs (controllers) are protected using the `Authorize` attribute that is applied on controller. Until and unless the client calling is identified, the access to the controller action methods are not given.

The following code snippet shows that the `Authorize` attribute applied to `BudgetCategoryController` accesses this API endpoint and will result in an unauthorized response (HTTP 401 Status code):

```
using Microsoft.AspNetCore.Authorization;

namespace PersonalBudget.Controllers
{
  [Authorize]
  [Route("api/[controller]")]
  public class BudgetCategoryController : Controller
  {
    ...
  }
}
```

Trying to access this endpoint on the browser or Postman will result in an unauthorized access, as shown in the following screenshot:

Shows Unauthorized response on protected API endpoint

Implementing JWT

JWT are also called **JSON Web Tokens**; they are industry standards for security token used in securely transmitting information between client and server as JSON objects.

They are widely used for being self-contained, small, and complete. Being small in size, they can be sent through URL, POST parameters, or inside HTTP Headers.

JSON Web tokens contain credentials, claims, and other information. To know more about JWT, I recommend reading `https://jwt.io/introduction/`.

One of the reasons for JWT to be so popular is that, when it is used with web API, the clients consuming them can work with ease, be they mobile app, hybrid app, web app, or any programming language based on Desktop apps or services too.

A sample JWT is an encrypted string containing information for secure communication, as shown in the following screenshot:

```
eyJhbGciOiJIUzI1NiIsInR5cCI6IkpXVCJ9.eyJz
dWIiOiIxMjM0NTY3ODkwIiwibmFtZSI6IkpvaG4gR
G9lIiwiYWRtaW4iOnRydWV9.TJVA95OrM7E2cBab3
0RMHrHDcEfxjoYZgeFONFh7HgQ
```

JSON web token sample

The workflow for secured communication using JWT on web API can be illustrated in the following diagram taken from the jwt.io website. The steps are self-explanatory.

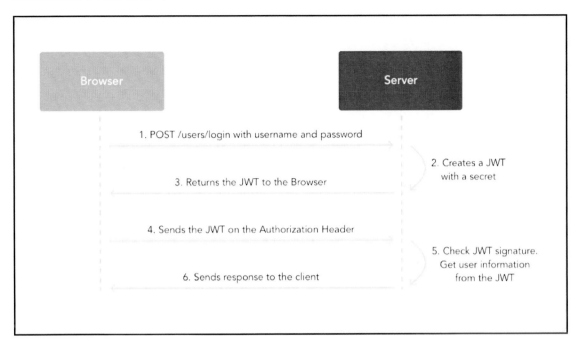

JWT and web API in action (Image Credit - jwt.io)

Generating JWTs

The first step is to generate JSON web tokens in the ASP.NET Core Web API project. For this, let's create a web API Controller--`AuthController`.

In this `AuthController`, we will use `CredentialsModel` containing a username and password to check against `AppUsers`. If the users exist, then we generate a JWT token that is passed as a response.

We will use the Entity Framework Core In-Memory provider to generate database context and tables and seed data to it. Refer to `Chapter 9`, *Integration with Database*, on working with different databases using EF 6, EF Core, and Dapper ORMs.

The `AuthController` code will use `PersonalBudgetContext`, which is the EF Core database context, and `IConfigurationRoot`, which reads the `appsettings.json` file and contains the `config` entries for the JWT generation:

```
namespace PersonalBudget.Controllers
{
  public class AuthController : Controller
  {
    private readonly PersonalBudgetContext _context;
    private readonly IConfigurationRoot _config;
    public AuthController(PersonalBudgetContext context,
      IConfigurationRoot config)
    {
        _context = context;
        _config = config;
    }

    [HttpPost("api/auth/token")]
    public IActionResult CreateToken([FromBody] CredentialsModel model)
    {
        if (model == null)
        {
            return BadRequest("Request is Null");
        }
        var findusr = _context.AppUsers.First(m => m.UserName.Equals(
          model.Username) && m.Password.Equals(model.Password));
        if(findusr != null)
        {
          var claims = new[]
          {
            new Claim(JwtRegisteredClaimNames.Sub, findusr.UserName),
            new Claim(JwtRegisteredClaimNames.Jti,
              Guid.NewGuid().ToString()),
          };

          var key = new SymmetricSecurityKey(
            Encoding.UTF8.GetBytes(_config["Tokens:Key"]));
          var creds = new SigningCredentials(key,
            SecurityAlgorithms.HmacSha256);

          var token = new JwtSecurityToken(
            issuer: _config["Tokens:Issuer"],
            audience: _config["Tokens:Audience"],
            claims: claims,
            expires: DateTime.UtcNow.AddMinutes(12),
            signingCredentials: creds
          );
```

```
        return Ok(new
        {
            token = new JwtSecurityTokenHandler().WriteToken(token),
            expiration = token.ValidTo
        });
    }
    return BadRequest("Failed to generate Token");
    }
  }
}
```

You can break down the preceding code as follows:

- The constructor takes database context and configuration entries using DI. The context and configuration should be registered in a `Startup` class-- `ConfigureServices`.
- `CreateToken` is the HTTP POST Action method that generates the JWT token, taking `CredentialsModel`.
- It checks if the username and password exists in the `AppUsers` table; if so, then it returns the object.
- A JWT token has to have these details before generating issuer, audience, claims, expires, and signingCredentials.
- Issuer is one who generates JWT; in our case, it's the web API. Best practice is to keep these entries in a configuration file.
- Claims will help us generate JWT with proper claims, that is, username, unique keys, or any other information included.
- Expires is the time validity of the generated JWT.
- SigningCredentials are most important aspects as they contain a strong key (place them in configuration files) and have security algorithms used. It's recommend to use a pretty strong key for a better JWT.
- At the end, it uses the preceding information to generate JWT and returns it as a response.

Running the application and calling the API endpoint with proper credentials will result in a response as shown here:

API endpoint generates JWT

Validating JWT

From the figure, *JSON web token sample*, we achieved the generation of JSON Web Token and returned it as a response. Now, when any client (web, mobile, or desktop) calls the web API endpoint with the preceding generated token, we need to validate if this valid JWT is generated by our application.

If it validates successfully, then allow it to access the requested resource, that is, the user is authenticated now. If we don't validate it, then we are bound to get an unauthorized response.

Since this will be the first step when the API request reaches the HTTP pipeline, we need to add validation functionality in the `Configure` method of the `Startup` class using the `UseJwtBearerAuthentication` middleware.

Add the following piece of code in the HTTP pipeline processing so that validation of JWT takes place:

```
public void Configure(IApplicationBuilder app, IHostingEnvironment env,
    ILoggerFactory loggerFactory)
{
    //Rest of code for brevity
    //JWT Validation
    app.AddJwtBearerAuthentication( "PacktAuthentication",new
JwtBearerOptions()
    {
        options.ClaimsIssuer = Configuration["Tokens:Issuer"];
        options.Audience = Configuration["Tokens:Audience"];
        TokenValidationParameters = new TokenValidationParameters()
        {
          ValidIssuer = Configuration["Tokens:Issuer"],
          ValidAudience = Configuration["Tokens:Audience"],
          ValidateIssuerSigningKey = true,
          IssuerSigningKey = new SymmetricSecurityKey(
              Encoding.UTF8.GetBytes(Configuration["Tokens:Key"])),
          ValidateLifetime = true
        }
    });
}
```

You can break down the preceding code as follows:

- `AddJwtBearerAuthentication` service takes in the options parameter `JwtBearerOptions` to validate JWT.
- While generating the JWT token, we used some parameters; now, the same parameters are needed to check the validity of a token in request.
- The parameters data is read from the configuration files. Some of the parameters are `ValidIssuer`, `ValidAudience`, and `IssuerSigningKey`.
- Any changes in the preceding parameters will fail in validating the JWT, that is, a tampered token will not be validated.
- Once this succeeds, the request resource is accessible.

Run the application and use Postman to call the API endpoint with a token in the header, as shown in the following screenshot:

JWT validation in action

OAuth

OAuth is an industry-standard protocol for authorization; it focuses on client development by providing specific authorization flows for web applications, desktop, mobiles, and so no.

The usage of OAuth needs a UI for flow-based authentication. The steps to integrate it with ASP.NET Core Web API are much simpler than thought. Refer to `https://auth0.com/auth enticate/aspnet-core-webapi/oauth2`, and follow the steps shown there.

Claims-based Authorizations

In the previous sections, we saw how to achieve authentication using JWT, that is, identify a user against the data stored and allow them access to the web API resources.

In most of the applications, we need to allow only certain authenticated users to perform tasks. This also known as authorization.

In ASP.NET Core, the authorization technique can be used to achieve claims. Instead of traditional roles used for authorization, we use claims with JWT to perform authorization.

Modify `AppUsers` to include the `IsSuperUser` property. This property will indicate if the login user is a super user or not. The `AppUsers` class now includes the `IsSuperUser` property:

```
namespace PersonalBudget.Models
{
  public class AppUser
  {
    public int Id { get; set; }
    public string UserName { get; set; }
    public string Password { get; set; }
    public bool IsSuperUser { get; set; }
  }
}
```

Modify the `AuthController CreateToken` action method to include `IsSuperUser` as claim. This will get added to the generating token:

```
var claims = new[]
{
    new Claim(JwtRegisteredClaimNames.Sub, findusr.UserName),
    new Claim(JwtRegisteredClaimNames.Jti, Guid.NewGuid().ToString()),
    new Claim("SuperUser", findusr.IsSuperUser.ToString())
};
```

Now, run the application and call the token generation endpoint as shown in the preceding code. The new token with the `SuperUser` claims will be added. You can verify the token contents on the jwt.io website.

Authorization using the claims policy

We were successfully able to generate a token with claims; now, it's time to add the claim policy.

The claim policy model consists of three main concepts: policy name, requirements, and handlers.

- A policy name is used to identify the claims requirements
- A requirement contains a list of data parameters used by the policy name to evaluate the user identity
- A handler evaluates the properties of the requirements to check if the user is authorized to access an API resource or not

The first step is to register the `SuperUser` policy in the `ConfigureServices` method of the `Startup` class using `AddAuthorization`. For that, the requirement is to check if the `SuperUser` policy is set to `TRUE` or not:

```
public void ConfigureServices(IServiceCollection services)
{
  //Claim Authorization Policy
  services.AddAuthorization(cfg =>
  {
    cfg.AddPolicy("SuperUsers", p => p.RequireClaim(
      "SuperUser", "True"));
  });

  //Code removed for brevity
}
```

The claim policy should be used with the `Authorize` attribute on either controller level or action method level. Here, we want only the authenticated user with the `SuperUser` claim in their JWT to access the `POST` method to create `BudgetCategory`:

```
[HttpPost]
[Authorize(Policy = "SuperUsers")]
public IActionResult Post([FromBody]BudgetCategoryDTO value)
{
    if (value == null)
    {
        return BadRequest();
    }
    if (!ModelState.IsValid)
    {
        return BadRequest(ModelState);
    }
    var mappeditem = Mapper.Map<BudgetCategory>(value);
    var newItem = _context.BudgetCategories.Add(mappeditem);
    Save();
    var dtomapped = Mapper.Map<BudgetCategoryDTO>(mappeditem);
    return Ok(dtomapped);
}
```

Run the application and use Postman or Fiddler to call the token generation API endpoint, as shown in the preceding code.

Use a non-super user credentials, then use the generated token to call the POST method of BudgetCategory

This will be bound to fail; however, interestingly, it doesn't give a 401 unauthorized response, but it gives a much more clear 403 Forbidden response.

 The 403 Forbidden response says that you're authenticated but not allowed to perform this operation; that is, you're authenticated but not authorized.

Now, try the same scenario with SuperUser as TRUE and call the POST method with a newly generated token. Everything works well and it adds the record with an OK response. The following screenshots show the claim-based authorization in action:

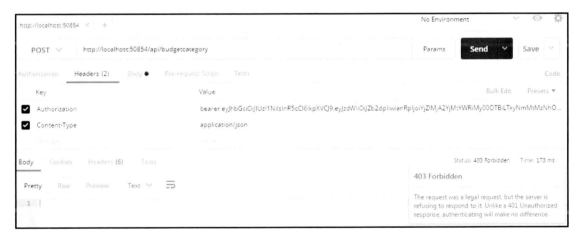

Claims fail and return Forbidden response

A super user with a valid authentication and authorization token was able to access the resource, as shown here:

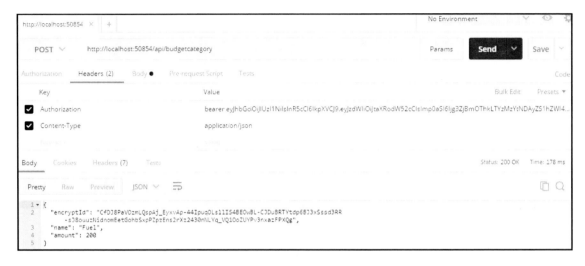

Claims work and return Ok response

Identity management in web API

ASP.NET Core Identity is a membership system to add the login functionality along with creation, updating, and deleting application users. The identity system also provides the role management to assign specific roles to the users to provide authorization.

Identity management is one of the primary tasks in web security. The ASP.NET Core Identity package provides all the features for complete working.

It also provides external authentication with Google, Facebook, Twitter, and so on. It's highly recommended that you refer to the following link for a better understanding of Identity:

https://docs.microsoft.com/en-us/aspnet/core/security/authentica
tion/identity

We will add the Identity framework for the ASP.NET Core Web API project, authenticate it using application users, and also look into **2FA (Two Factor Authentication)**.

Adding the Identity package

Create a new ASP.NET Core application with a web API template, or use any existing application. The following packages will be a part of the .NET Core SDK:

```
Microsoft.AspNetCore.Identity
Microsoft.AspNetCore.Identity.EntityFrameworkCore
```

Configuring the Startup class

Once the packages are restored, include Identity in the `ConfigureServices` and `Configure` methods of the `Startup` class, as shown in the following piece of code:

```
public void ConfigureServices(IServiceCollection services)
{
    services.AddTransient<IdentityDbSeeder>();
    services.AddDbContext<IdentityDbContext>(options =>
options.UseSqlServer(Configuration.GetConnectionString("BudgetConnStr"),
        sqlopt => sqlopt.MigrationsAssembly("BudegetIdentityDemo")));

    services.AddIdentity<IdentityUser, IdentityRole>()
        .AddEntityFrameworkStores<IdentityDbContext>();

    // Add framework services.
    services.AddMvc();
}
public void Configure(IApplicationBuilder app, IHostingEnvironment env,
    ILoggerFactory loggerFactory, IdentityDbSeeder identitySeeder)
{
    app.UseIdentity();
    app.UseMvc();
    identitySeeder.Seed().Wait();
}
```

ASP.NET Core Identity is undergoing breaking changes, and with the final changes of ASP.NET Core 2.0, most of this becomes obsolete. However, a modified code, post release, will be available in the code bundles. Watch out!!

You can break down the preceding code as follows:

- `IdentityDbContext` is a default database context used for Identity to use EF Core to work with databases. Setting up a connection string, it's read from `appsettings.json`.

- The `AddIdentity` method gets added to services. The `IdentityUser` and `IdentityRole` methods are added to services as well. They are the actual users and their roles.
- The `app.UseIdentity` method in the HTTP pipeline indicates that processing should pass through Identity.
- The `IdentityDbSeeder` class helps create a sample user when the application runs. In a real-world scenario, we would have a separate API endpoint to add users.

Creating identity-related database

Using the EF command tools, we will run migration and create an identity database, and then we are ready with the identity-related classes and database. To create database using the EF command tools, refer to the EF Core section in `Chapter 9`, *Integration with Database*.

Cookie-based authentication

Once the Identity tables are created in the database, run the application once to seed a default user. (This is an optional step, for demo purpose we seed the database).

Create `AuthController`, copy the following piece of code to read the username and password, validate against the identity database, and return cookie:

```
using Microsoft.AspNetCore.Identity;
using Microsoft.AspNetCore.Identity.EntityFrameworkCore;
using Microsoft.AspNetCore.Mvc;
using System.Threading.Tasks;

namespace BudegetIdentityDemo.Controllers
{
  public class AuthController : Controller
  {
    private readonly SignInManager<IdentityUser> _signInMgr;

    public AuthController(SignInManager<IdentityUser> signInMgr)
    {
      _signInMgr = signInMgr;
    }

    [HttpPost("api/auth/login")]
    public async Task<IActionResult> Login([FromBody]
      CredentialModel model)
```

```
    {
        var result = await _signInMgr.PasswordSignInAsync(model.UserName,
            model.Password, false, false);
        if (result.Succeeded)
        {
            return Ok();
        }
        return BadRequest("Failed to login");
    }
  }
}
```

You can break down the preceding code as follows:

- `SignInManager` contains the necessary methods for login, so its DI into **AuthController**
- The `Login` action method takes in `CredentialModel` (username and password) for authenticating against the `Identity` database
- The `PassSignInAsync` method, using the credentials model properties, verifies the account and returns an `OK` response, but, in turn, it sets the cookie in the browser to be used for further API calls

Run the application and use Postman to make an endpoint call once the credentials match. An `OK` response is returned with the cookie, as shown in the following screenshot:

Cookie authentication using Identity

Now, keep the Postman window as it is and make another call to `BudgetCategoryController` (refer to the code samples), even though it has the `Authorize` attribute. The cookie does get validated to return a response, as shown in the following screenshot:

API response with Cookie authentication

Two-factor authentication

The usual way of authentication, that is, username with password, works in most cases, but when the need for additional security arises, such as a phone number or email verification, then we need to use the **two-factor authentication (2FA)**.

We will still use the good old username and password authentication; however, along with that, if 2FA is enabled for users, then we will send a security code via SMS or email, and only when the code is entered, the actual sign in takes place.

Note that either the SMS or email needs to be confirmed along with 2FA enabled.

We will create `TwoFactorAuthController` with the following piece of code:

```
namespace BudegetIdentityDemo.Controllers
{
  public class TwoFactorAuthController : Controller
  {
    private readonly SignInManager<IdentityUser> _signInMgr;
    private readonly UserManager<IdentityUser> _usrMgr;
```

```
private IPasswordHasher<IdentityUser> _hasher;

public TwoFactorAuthController(SignInManager<IdentityUser>
  signInMgr,
  IPasswordHasher<IdentityUser> hasher,
UserManager<IdentityUser> usrMgr)
{
  _signInMgr = signInMgr;
  _usrMgr = usrMgr;
  _hasher = hasher;
}

[HttpGet("api/twofactorauth/login")]
public async Task<IActionResult> Login([FromBody]
  CredentialModel model)
{
  var user = await _usrMgr.FindByNameAsync(model.UserName);
  if (user != null)
  {
    if (_hasher.VerifyHashedPassword(user, user.PasswordHash,
      model.Password) == PasswordVerificationResult.Success)
    {
      if (user.TwoFactorEnabled && user.PhoneNumberConfirmed)
      {
        var code = await
          _usrMgr.GenerateChangePhoneNumberTokenAsync(
          user, user.PhoneNumber);
        await SendSmsAsync(user.PhoneNumber, "Use OTP " + code);
      }
    }
  }
  return BadRequest("Failed to login");
}

[HttpPost]
public async Task<IActionResult> VerifyCode(
  VerifyCodeViewModel model)
{
  if (!ModelState.IsValid)
  {
    return BadRequest();
  }
  var result = await _signInMgr.TwoFactorSignInAsync(
    model.Provider, model.Code, model.RememberMe,
    model.RememberBrowser);
  if (result.Succeeded)
  {
    return Ok();
```

```
        }
        return BadRequest("Failed to Login");
    }

    private Task SendSmsAsync(string number, string message)
    {
        // Plug in your SMS service here to send a text message.
        // Use Twilio or clickatell for related docs
        return Task.FromResult(0);
    }
  }
}
```

You can break down the preceding code as follows:

- The `SiginManager`, `UserManager`, and `IPasswordHasher` classes are needed for login, fetching user details, and password matching respectively. They are DI into the controller.
- The `Login` action method checks if the user exists, 2FA is enabled, and phone number is confirmed.
- If so, then an SMS is sent through a third-party SMS provider such as Twilio or Clickatell.
- `VerifyCode` checks if the SMS code matches. If it does, then the actual login takes place, returning a cookie.

This example involves multiple endpoints; the clients consuming this endpoint can refer to ASP.NET Core (MVC apps) with Individual User Accounts to check how the UI flow is done.

ASP.NET Core with Identity and JWT can work.

Summary

Web API security should be a priority right from the beginning. Even though the business needs it or not, the developer should focus on providing the right kind of security to the web API in the form of SSL and CORS, and the authentication using a token.

Authorization also plays an important role in API usage, as application users may have different levels of credentials; we looked into this with a claims-based authorization. ASP.NET Core security can be extended with Identity management using Identity Server 4, OpenId Connect mechanism, and so on.

In the next chapter, we will learn about integration with database using popular ORMs in the market.

9
Integration with Database

Data is king in the world of software applications, either in the form of databases, files, streams, and so on. It's very hard to find applications that don't interact with the database. In the previous chapter, you learnt a great deal about the ASP.NET Core handling requests in the form of routes, middleware, and filters, and its security mechanism; they form the faceless frontend of the application.

Until now, we haven't talked about ASP.NET Core dealing with the backend (a popular term for storage of data), that is, with databases. Any ASP.NET Core (Web API) will definitely have to integrate with databases at some point of time during application development or right from the beginning.

Microsoft SQL Server was often considered the go-to database for ASP.NET apps. Now with ASP.NET Core, integration with different kinds of database is more interesting than ever. In different database systems, such as Oracle, MySQL, PostgreSQL, SQLite, and so on, integration is more cross-platform in nature now.

With the help of ORMs, integration with database is quick, scalable, and efficient as well. We will explore ORMs by Microsoft, known as **Entity Framework** (EF 6.x and EF Core) and **Dapper** (Micro ORM) for the existing and new database.

In this chapter, we will cover the following topics:

- A brief introduction to Object Relational Mapper
- Integrating using Entity Framework 6.x
- Integrating using Dapper
- Integrating using EF Core

Brief introduction to Object Relational Mapper

Integrating with the database deals with lots of groundwork to perform simple **CRUD** (**create**, **read**, **update**, and **delete** operations. Some of the ground work is connecting to the database, releasing the connection, pooling, querying the database, dealing with single or multiple records, connection resiliency, bulk update, and so on.

Writing up the code for this ground work is a huge task, often ending with lots of handwritten code, duplication of code, erroneous results, and maintenance issues.

Object Relational Mapper (ORM) offers a better way to integrate with the database in the form of class-object mapping to a relational database table.

ORM provides the necessary ground work as mentioned above and also uses object orient concepts to map class objects to a relational database table.

For example, the widely used learning database for Microsoft SQL Server is Adventure Works. The relational table, `Production.Product` maps to the `Product` class in .NET-based applications. ORM is not confined to the tables; they deal with stored procedures, views, schema migration, and so on.

Some of the popular ORMs are Entity Framework (6.x and core), NHibernate, Dapper, and so on.

In this chapter, we will focus on using the Entity Framework and Dapper ORM for integration of database with ASP.NET Core Web API.

Integrating ASP.NET Core Web API and an existing database using Entity Framework 6.x

Entity Framework (EF) is ORM for .NET world. EF, just like other ORM, can be used to create new databases and tables or use it against an existing database.

We will be building ASP.NET Core Web API integrating against existing database using Entity Framework 6.1. We will use the Microsoft SQL Server learning database **AdventureWorks2014**.

EF 6.1 is an ORM built with full .NET framework, meaning it works with full .NET apps only. To achieve this, we will need to create ASP.NET Core for full .NET Framework instead of .NET Core.

We will create `AdvWorksAPI` (ASP.NET Core Web API) integrated with the AdventureWorks2014 database using EF 6.1, by following these steps.

Restoring the AdventureWorks2014 database

Download and restore the AdventureWorks2014 database backup (`https://msftdbprodsamples.codeplex.com/releases/view/125550`). Microsoft SQL Server 2014 is used in this example.

This will act as an existing database for us to use EF 6.1. You can use any existing database.

EF6 data access library

As mentioned in the preceding section, EF6 works only on full .NET Framework; so, we can't directly use them in an ASP.NET Core application. For this, we will need a class library and we will perform reverse engineering on the existing database, AdventureWorks2014 is our example.

Reverse engineering is a process in the Entity Framework (ORM) to generate the classes/models (they correspond to tables) and build a database context to work with the database.

Create a blank Visual Studio solution, `AdvWorksAPI`, and add class library `AdvWorksAPI.DataAccess` to it. This will act as data access layer and will be referenced in ASP.NET Core app.

To generate classes/models using reverse engineering, right-click on the project name to add a new ADO.NET Entity Data Model and follow the steps to connect to a database, select the appropriate tables, stored procedure, and other database items using the **Entity Data Model** wizard.

For more visual steps, please refer to `https://msdn.microsoft.com/en-us/data/jj200620`.

During this process, we have selected the `Production.Product` table only; this will result in the `Product` class, `AdvWorksContext` class containing `DbSet` of `Product` to work with. In EF terms, we performed the reverse engineer code, the first process of the AdventureWorks2014 database.

In the real world, existing database schema will surely contain many tables, SPs, and so on. Web API's are usually built targeting only relevant tables. By reverse engineering only the relevant tables, we are reducing the in-memory database snapshot generated when EF runs in the application.

It's one of the recommended approaches to use required tables when working with the existing database for EF.

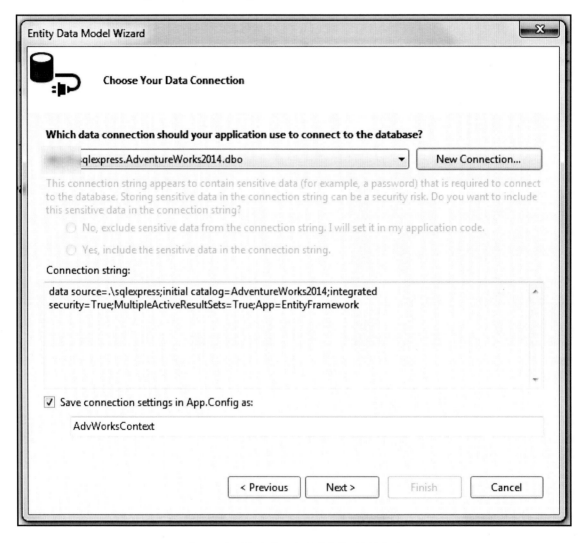

Connect to the existing database using the Entity Data Model wizard

Creating an ASP.NET Core app for the full .NET Framework

As mentioned earlier in this chapter, EF6 is built on a full .NET Framework, so we can't create an ASP.NET Core app under .NET Core, instead, we should be creating it targeting the full .NET Framework.

Every ASP.NET Core feature can be used, but it cannot be deployed on a non-Windows machine. Most of the existing enterprise still use a full .NET Framework on deployed machines, so leveraging it won't be an issue.

In the blank solution, create `AdvWorks.WebAPI`, an ASP.NET Core Web Application (.NET Framework) with web API template. This will be our ASP.NET Core Web API for integration with the AdventureWorks2014 database.

As we have the data access class library ready, include it in the web API project using **Add Reference**. Ensure that the EntityFramework (6.1.3) library you add is either using NuGet or Package Manager Console.

> On the target project, right-click the project name and click **Add Reference** to open a folder dialog window, navigate to the `bin` folder and select **AdvWorksAPI.DataAccess** to add it web API project.

Using IProductRepository to access the database

Generally, when accessing databases using ORM, a repository pattern is used to access EF DataContext. There are many purposes of using it, the prominent ones among them being are:

- It separates the logic to retrieve data
- The mapping of entities to the business model irrespective of data source
- It helps in unit testing as well as integration tests

Create an interface `IProductRepository` and its implementation `ProductRepository` in the `Service` folder as follows:

```
namespace AdvWorks.WebAPI.Services
{
  public class ProductRepository : IProductRepository
  {
    private AdvWorksContext _context;
```

```
public ProductRepository(AdvWorksContext context)
{
    _context = context;
}
public void AddProduct(Product proddetails)
{
    _context.Products.Add(proddetails);
}
public void DeleteProduct(Product proddetails)
{
    _context.Products.Remove(proddetails);
}
public Product GetProduct(int productId)
{
    return _context.Products.Where(c => c.ProductID ==
        productId).FirstOrDefault();
}
public IEnumerable<Product> GetProducts()
{
    return _context.Products.Take(10).ToList();
}
public bool ProductExists(int productId)
{
    return _context.Products.Any(c => c.ProductID == productId);
}
public bool Save()
{
    return (_context.SaveChanges() >= 0);
}
    }
}
```

You can break down the preceding code as follows:

- It's an implementation of the `IProductRepository` interface.
- `AdvWorksContext` is dependency injected from the `Startup` class, which helps in the unit test.
- `AddProduct` takes in the `Product` object and adds it to `AdvWorksContext`. It's not saved in the database yet.
- `DeleteProduct` takes in the `Product` object and gets removed from `AdvWorksContext`. It's not saved in the database yet.
- `GetProduct` takes in `ProductId` to retrieve the product details.
- `GetProducts` returns the first 10 products stored in the database. As the table has many records, it takes the first 10 records.

- `ProductExists` returns a Boolean based on the existing product.
- The `Save` method persists all `AdvWorksContext` changes done.

Connection strings and IProductRepository in startup

A connection string is a must when working with database; it contains the location of the database server, database name, credentials to access the database, and other information.

ASP.NET Core stores all configuration/connection data in JSON files known as `appsettings.json`. Copy the following connection string in the `appsettings.json` file:

```
{
  //Others removed for brevity
  "connectionStrings": {
    "AdvWorksDbConnection": "Server=.\\sqlexpress;initial
    catalog=AdventureWorks2014;Trusted_Connection=True;
    MultipleActiveResultSets=true"
  }
}
```

Now that we have provided the connection string (`AdvWorksDbConnection`) and wrote `IProductRepository` to access the database, we will need to configure (participate in dependency injection) them to be across the application.

For this, we will need to add them in services in the `ConfigureServices` method, as shown in the following code:

```
public void ConfigureServices(IServiceCollection services)
{
  services.AddMvc();
  services.AddScoped<AdvWorksContext>(_ => new
    AdvWorksContext(Configuration.GetConnectionString(
    "AdvWorksDbConnection")));
  services.AddScoped<IProductRepository, ProductRepository>();
}
```

Using AutoMapper

Any existing database would have many columns in tables. Sometimes, the web API response or request object does not need all properties in line with table columns.

We can write a trimmed down version of the `Product` class in the data access layer as the `ProductDTO` class in the `Models` folder. With many columns, manual mapping becomes difficult to maintain. The `Product` class should be transformed to `ProductDTO` and vice versa; this transformation can be eased using `AutoMapper`.

`AutoMapper` is a convention-based object-object mapper for .NET. Install this using NuGet.

First, let's create `ProductDTO`, a trimmed version of the `Product` class in the `Models` folder, as follows:

```
using System.ComponentModel.DataAnnotations;
namespace AdvWorks.WebAPI.Models
{
  public class ProductDTO
  {
     public int ProductID { get; set; }
     [Required]
     [StringLength(50)]
     public string Name { get; set; }
     [Required]
     [StringLength(25)]
     public string ProductNumber { get; set; }
     [StringLength(15)]
     public string Color { get; set; }
     public short ReorderPoint { get; set; }
     public decimal StandardCost { get; set; }
     public decimal ListPrice { get; set; }
     public decimal? Weight { get; set; }
     public int DaysToManufacture { get; set; }
  }
}
```

 Using `AutoMapper` is optional, using it would help keep objects lean.

We will need to initialize `Mapper` in the pipeline processing so that request and response are mapped accordingly:

```
public void Configure(IApplicationBuilder app,
  IHostingEnvironment env, ILoggerFactory loggerFactory)
{
  AutoMapper.Mapper.Initialize(cfg =>
  {
    cfg.CreateMap<Product, ProductDTO>();
```

```
        cfg.CreateMap<ProductDetailsDTO, Product>();
    });
    app.UseMvc();
}
```

Now that we have an interface to talk to the database using `DbContext`, an initialized mapper to object transformation, it's time to write the web API controller.

Writing ProductController to access the database

Right-click on the `Controllers` folder to add the `Web API Controller` class, and name it as `ProductController`. Copy the following piece of code to perform CRUD operations on the `Product` table:

```
public class ProductController : Controller
{
    private readonly IProductRepository _productRepository;

    public ProductController(IProductRepository productRepository)
    {
        _productRepository = productRepository;
    }
    // GET: api/values
    [HttpGet]
    public IActionResult Get()
    {
        var prodlist = _productRepository.GetProducts();
        var results = Mapper.Map<IEnumerable<ProductDTO>>(prodlist);
        return Ok(results);
    }
    // GET api/values/5
    [HttpGet("{id}")]
    public IActionResult Get(int id)
    {
        if (!_productRepository.ProductExists(id))
        {
            return NotFound();
        }
        var prod = _productRepository.GetProduct(id);
        var results = Mapper.Map<ProductDTO>(prod);
        return Ok(results);
    }
    //Complete code part of source code bundle
}
```

Complete source code is available in the code bundle.

We can break down the preceding code as follows:

- IProductRepository is dependency injected in the constructor; we registered this in the Startup class.
- The Get() method returns a list of products from the database via the IProductRepository interface. AutoMapper comes into action for object transformation, Product to ProductDTO.
- The Get(int id) method returns the matching product based on ProductID, else returns the NotFound(404) HTTP response. AutoMapper also does transforms to ProductDTO.
- The Post() method receives ProductDetailsDTO (an object similar to ProductDTO) using FromBody of request. It checks for null and model validation, and, if any, returns BadRequest. It also maps back to the Product object and adds it to DbContext of EF6. The Save method is called to persist the entry in the Production.Product table of the AdventureWorks2014 database.
- The Put() method also performs a similar operation as post, the only difference being is update, not create.
- The Delete() method checks if the products exists, then deletes it from the database by calling the Save() method.

Build and run the project; use PostMan to perform CRUD operations on ProductController, as shown in the following screenshot:

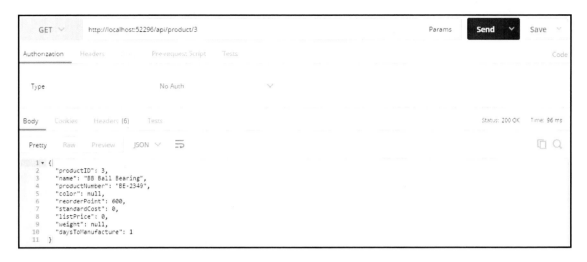

Get product from the database using EF 6

Integrating using Dapper

Dapper is an open source simple object mapper for .NET-based applications. It's also referred to as **Micro ORM** when compared with Entity Framework or NHibernate.

It extends the `IDbConnection` interface and does not depend on any specific DB implementation; this makes it work with almost all relational databases, such as SQLite, SQL CE, Firebird, Oracle, MySQL, PostgreSQL, and SQL Server.

It's considered as the king of ORM for being lightweight, high performance among other ORM. I recommend reading their GitHub repo at `https://github.com/StackExchange/dapper-dot-net`.

As Dapper is used with an existing database, we will use the same AdventureWorks2014 database for it. In this section, we will work with the `HumanResources.Department` table.

Let's create an ASP.NET Core Web API application integrating with the AdventureWorks2014 database using Dapper ORM.

Creating AdvWrksDapper Web API and adding Dapper library

Dapper can be used with the full .NET Framework as well as .NET Core Framework, so let's create the ASP.NET Core (.NET Core) application with web API and name it as `AdvWrksDapper`. Use the NuGet manager to add Dapper library.

Using IDepartmentRepository and department model to access the database

Create the `Department` class in the `Models` folder to participate in accessing the database. Remember, property names should be in accordance with table column names:

```
using System.ComponentModel.DataAnnotations;

namespace AdvWrksDapper.Models
{
  /// <summary>
  /// HR.Department Table of Adventure Works Database
  /// </summary>
  public class Department
  {
    [Key]
    public int DepartmentID { get; set; }
    [Required]
    [StringLength(50)]
    public string Name { get; set; }
    [Required]
    [StringLength(50)]
    public string GroupName { get; set; }
  }
}
```

Just like we did in the previous example, we will create `IDepartmentRepository` for performing CRUD operations, which are as follows:

```
public class DepartmentRepository : IDepartmentRepository
{
  private readonly AdvWorksConfig _advConfig;
  public DepartmentRepository(IOptions<AdvWorksConfig> advconfig)
  {
    _advConfig = advconfig.Value;
  }
```

```
public IDbConnection Connection
{
  get
  {
    return new SqlConnection(_advConfig.DbConnectionString);
  }
}

public bool AddDepartment(Department deptdetails)
{
  bool isSuccess = false;
  using (IDbConnection dbConnection = Connection)
  {
    dbConnection.Open();
    var rows = dbConnection.Execute("INSERT INTO
      HumanResources.Department (name,groupname)
      VALUES(@Name,@GroupName)", deptdetails);
    if (rows == 1)
    {
      isSuccess = true;
    }
  }
  return isSuccess;
}
public IEnumerable<Department> GetDepartments()
{
  using (IDbConnection dbConnection = Connection)
  {
    dbConnection.Open();
    return dbConnection.Query<Department>("SELECT * FROM
      HumanResources.Department");
  }
}
//Complete code part of source code bundle
}
```

We can break down the preceding code as follows:

- Reading the connection string `appsettings.json` configured in the `Startup` class using ASP.NET Core options pattern.
- The `Connection` property is used to access the SQL database using the connection string.
- The `AddDepartment` method adds the department by opening the connection and executing the `INSERT SQL` statement and returns `TRUE` on success. This is quite different from the EF6 example seen in the previous section.
- The `DeleteDepartment` method deletes the record from the database table based on `DepartmentId` and returns `TRUE` on success.
- The `DepartmentExists` method checks the record exists.
- The `GetDepartment` method returns the department record based on `DepartmentId`.
- The `GetDepartments` method returns a list of the departments present in the table.
- The `UpdateDepartment` method performs an update SQL operation and returns `TRUE` on success.

Connection string and IOptions in ASP.NET Core

Any database can be accessed by the connection string containing its location, database name, access credentials, and so on. This information can be placed in `appsettings.json`, as shown in the following piece of code:

```
{
  "ApiConfig": {
    "DbConnectionString": "Server=.\\sqlexpress;initial
      catalog=AdventureWorks2014;Trusted_Connection=True;
      MultipleActiveResultSets=true"
  }
}
```

We can access this configuration or the connection string details in the application and use it as a strongly typed configuration class across application eliminating magic strings.

To do this, let's create the `AdvWorksConfig` class in the `Models` folder, as shown in the following lines of code:

```
namespace AdvWrksDapper.Models
{
  public class AdvWorksConfig
  {
    public string DbConnectionString { get; set; }
  }
}
```

In the `Startup` class, the `ConfigureServices` method modifies the code to read the configuration section and also registers `IDepartmentRepository` to be a dependency injected in the application:

```
public void ConfigureServices(IServiceCollection services)
{
  // Add framework services.
  services.AddMvc();
  services.Configure<AdvWorksConfig>(Configuration.GetSection(
    "ApiConfig"));   services.AddScoped<IDepartmentRepository,
    DepartmentRepository>();
}
```

Adding the DeparmentController Web API

Add a new web API controller class in the `Controllers` folder, naming it as `DepartmentController` and add the following code to perform CRUD operations using HTTP verbs:

```
[Route("api/[controller]")]
public class DepartmentController : Controller
{
  private readonly IDepartmentRepository _deptrepo;
  public DepartmentController(IDepartmentRepository deptrepo)
  {
    _deptrepo = deptrepo;
  }
  // GET: api/values
  [HttpGet]
  public IActionResult Get()
  {
    var results = _deptrepo.GetDepartments();
```

```
     return Ok(results);
   }

   // GET api/values/5
   [HttpGet("{id}")]
   public IActionResult Get(int id)
   {
     if (!_deptrepo.DepartmentExists(id))
     {
        return NotFound();
     }
     var dept = _deptrepo.GetDepartment(id);
     return Ok(dept);
   }

   // POST api/values
   [HttpPost]
   public IActionResult Post([FromBody]Department dept)
   {
     if (dept == null)
     {
       return BadRequest();
     }
     if (!ModelState.IsValid)
     {
       return BadRequest(ModelState);
     }

     if (!_deptrepo.AddDepartment(dept))
     {
       return StatusCode(500, "A problem happened while handling
         your request.");
     }
     else
     {
       return StatusCode(201, "Created Successfully");
     }
     //Complete code part of source code bundle
   }
}
```

You can break down the preceding code as follows:

- Dependency injecting `IDepartmentRepository` in the constructor.
- The `Get()` method fetches all departments and returns as a list.
- The `Get(int id)` method fetches the department record based on the ID.
- The `Post()` method checks if the request is not null and is valid, else it returns a `BadRequest` response. If everything is fine, it saves the record into the database.
- The `Put()` method updates the records of an individual department.
- The `Delete()` method checks if the department exists, deletes if it exists, or returns a `NotFound` response.

Build and run the application; use Postman (or Fiddler) to test the web API. We will test the POST method in this scenario by passing the JSON object corresponding to the `Department` object:

```
{
    "name":"Cafeteria",
    "groupName": "Housekeeping Department"
}
```

Pass this JSON in the body of the HTTP request and set content type as application/JSON.

Upon sending the request, it goes through the POST method, then to `IDepartmentRepository`, and performs the INSERT operation to add the new department.

Similarly, perform other operations such as GET, PUT, and DELETE using Postman.

> Note that we didn't use AutoMapper here; you can use it by referring to the EF6 demo.

Post department data to web API using Dapper

Integrating with EF Core

Entity Framework Core (**EF Core**) is the latest ORM from Microsoft for the .NET Core framework in line with the ASP.NET Core roadmap. Now, ASP.NET Core and EF Core provide a great platform to build cross-platform web applications.

EF Core is a complete rewrite of EF 6 into more focused packages to make it leaner. The EF team plans to support both relational and non-relational databases. At the time of writing this book, EF 1.1 was released and will take a while to develop as a mature ORM. To learn more about EF Core, visit https://docs.microsoft.com/en-us/ef/.

In this section, we will create the PacktContactsCore web API project to integrate with the database using EF Core. We will use the MS SQL Server 2014 Express Edition as the database server; however, at present, you can also work with SQLite, MySQL, and PostgreSQL.

Creating PacktContactsCore ASP.NET Core project

We are completely dealing with .NET Core framework for ASP.NET and EF ORM, so let's create an ASP.NET Core project with a web API template with its name as `PacktContactsCore`.

You can either use the Yeoman generators or .NET CLI to create a project.

Adding the EF Core package and tooling

This step is very important because we are adding EF Core using NuGet packages and EF Core Tooling. The EF tooling provides CLI support to work with EF migrations and perform database updates.

Use the NuGet Package Manager or PMC (CLI) to the add EF Core SQL Server package:

```
"Microsoft.EntityFrameworkCore.SqlServer": "2.0.0-preview2-final"
"Microsoft.EntityFrameworkCore.Tools": "2.0.0-preview2-final",
```

 To work with other databases, install appropriate NuGet packages by referring to the provider list in this link: `https://docs.efproject.net/en/latest/providers/index.html`.

Contacts model class and DbContext

Create a `Contacts` class in the `Models` folder that corresponds to the `Contacts` table in the database, as follows:

```
using System;
using System.ComponentModel.DataAnnotations;
namespace PacktContactsCore.Model
{
  public class Contacts
  {
    [Key]
    public int Id { get; set; }
    [Required]
    [MinLength(4)]
    public string FirstName { get; set; }
    public string LastName { get; set; }
```

```
    [Required]
    public string Email { get; set; }
    public DateTime DateOfBirth { get; set; }
  }
}
```

With EF, we will need `ContactsContext`-a `DbContext` class-acting as a bridge between the database and the application to perform database-related operations:

```
using Microsoft.EntityFrameworkCore;
using PacktContactsCore.Model;
namespace PacktContactsCore.Context
{
  public class ContactsContext : DbContext
  {
    public ContactsContext(DbContextOptions<ContactsContext>
     options)
    : base(options) { }
    public ContactsContext() {
    }
    public DbSet<Contacts> Contacts { get; set; }
  }
}
```

Configuring services to use the SQL Server database

To connect to a database application, one needs a connection string; just like the preceding examples of EF6 and Dapper, add connection string details in the `appsettings.json` file as follows:

```
{
  "ConnectionStrings": {
    "SqlDbConnStr": "Server=.\\sqlexpress;initial
    catalog=PacktContactsDB;Trusted_Connection=True;"
  }
}
```

The `ContactsContext` method needs to be added to the services collection in the `Startup` class by reading the database connection string:

```
public void ConfigureServices(IServiceCollection services)
{
  // Add framework services.
  services.AddDbContext<ContactsContext>(options =>
```

```
      options.UseSqlServer(Configuration.GetConnectionString(
      "SqlDbConnStr")));
    services.AddMvc();
}
```

EF tools for database migrations and updates

Now that we are ready with the `Contacts` and `ContactsContext` (`DbContext`) class and have registered the SQL Server to services collection with the connection string, it's time to add EF migrations and update the database. (In EF terms, it means creating or updating the database schema.)

While using EF (either 6.x or Core), the first step is to generate a `migration` class based on data model. This step generates a replica of SQL script in C# code-like table creations, adding column constraints, seeding, and more.

Run the following command from the `root` folder of the project to create the EF migrations class:

```
dotnet ef migrations add init
```

Once successfully done with migration command execution, a `Migrations` folder is created in the project containing the first SQL scripts (in code format) and contacts the context snapshot (its replica of schema in code).

In the preceding command, `init` is the step of adding migrations, that is, this is initialization (first step). Suppose any changes are made, then we will need to provide an appropriate name. For example, a new table address gets added, so, make the `migration` class unique by adding `addressAdded` instead of `init`.

Now, run the following command to generate the database along with its schema in the database location provided in the connection string:

```
dotnet ef database update
```

This command will connect to the SQL server database server and create (updates, if it already exists) the database. The database name is present in the connection string, as shown in the following screenshot:

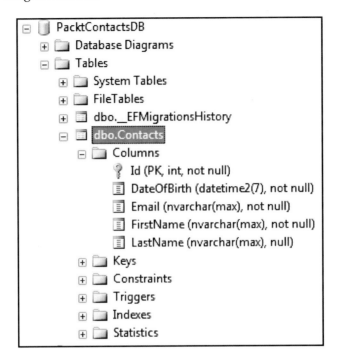

PacktContactsDB created by running EF Core commands

ContactsController for CRUD operations

Add a new web API Controller class, `ContactsController`; it will perform CRUD operations on `PacktContactsDB`. Copy the following code:

```
[Route("api/[controller]")]
public class ContactsController : Controller
{
    private readonly ContactsContext _context;
    public ContactsController(ContactsContext contactContext)
    {
        _context = contactContext;
    }

    // GET api/values/5
```

```
[HttpGet("{id}", Name ="GetContactById")]
public IActionResult Get(int id)
{
  var result = _context.Contacts.Any(c => c.Id == id);
  if (!result)
  {
    return NotFound();
  }
  return Ok(_context.Contacts.Where(c => c.Id == id)
    .FirstOrDefault());
}

// POST api/values
[HttpPost]
public IActionResult Post([FromBody]Contacts reqObj)
{
  if (reqObj == null)
  {
    return BadRequest();
  }
  if (!ModelState.IsValid)
  {
    return BadRequest(ModelState);
  }

  var contextObj = _context.Contacts.Add(reqObj);
  var count = _context.SaveChanges();
  if (count == 1)
  {
    return Ok();
  }
  else
  {
    return StatusCode(500, "A problem happened while handling
      your request.");
  }
}
//Complete code part of source code bundle
}
```

Controller code does not use repository pattern and `AutoMapper`, reader can explore EF 6 example to implement repository pattern and `AutoMapper`.

We can break down the preceding code as follows:

- The constructor takes `ContactsContext` via DI.
- The `Get()` method retrieves a list of contacts from the database.
- The `Get(int id)` method gets contact details to match the ID passed, else returns `NotFound`.
- The `Post()` method inserts the `Contacts` object into the database after a null check and model validation.
- `Put()` updates the `Contacts` object based on ID and updates all properties. `AutoMapper` can be used here for object mapping.
- The `Delete()` method deletes from the database based on ID.

Build and run the application and use Postman to test web API. The following screenshot shows a `PUT` request in action with an appropriate response:

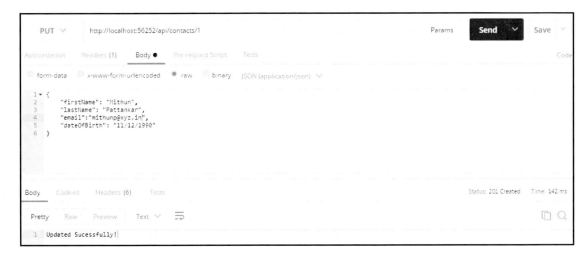

The PUT method in action for EF Core

 Exercise for reader to perform other operations either using Postman or Fiddler.

Summary

In this chapter, you learned a great deal about integrating the ASP.NET Core applications with databases using ORMs, such as EF 6.x, Dapper, and EF Core. With many options to use database providers, it certainly gives great flexibility.

Without using ORMs, we can still use classic ADO.NET to communicate with the database.

In the next chapter, our focus will be to handle errors and exceptions, gracefully inform clients about it, and design tracing and logging mechanisms.

10

Error Handling, Tracing, and Logging

Errors, or exceptions, are bound to occur in any software application, even after extensive testing on various environments. Once the application is in production, the software is exposed to a higher load, proper or erroneous user inputs, system or network crashes, and other occurrences that would lead to an application crash if not handled properly.

The concept of exception management says that the system should continue working in the case of a catastrophic failure, and should log detailed information of the failure in the form of errors or an unhandled exception for further investigation.

As we are building an ASP.NET Core Web API application in this book, which will be mainly consumed by web or mobile clients, any exception should be gracefully handled by the web API so that the clients can continue to work.

In this chapter, we will learn the basics of logging in ASP.NET Core, writing errors or exceptions to various logging providers, and building an exception handler to gracefully return the appropriate response to clients.

In this chapter, we will be looking at the following topics:

- Basics of Logging in ASP.NET Core
- MyWallet--Demo ASP.NET Core project
- Logging errors to a file using NLog
- Logging errors to a database using Serilog
- Exception management in a MyWallet project

Basics of Logging in ASP.NET Core

One of ASP.NET Core's features is its in-built logging using `ILoggerFactory`. Right away, when you create an ASP.NET Core application (empty-, MVC-, or web API-based), you will see that the `IWebHost's CreateDefaultBuilder` method of the program class does the ground-level work for the Logging functionality to work-it reads the `appsettings.json` file for the logging section to provide all the necessary infrastructure to log information to debug or console window.

The use of Logging is greatly simplified by `ILoggerFactory` in two parts--`AddProvider` and `CreateLogger`.

The `AddProvider` method takes in `ILoggerProvider` to write/store the logging information generated by the application. The provider can either be a console, debug window, file, database, cloud-based storage, or third-party log analysis service (Splunk, Raygun, Loggly, and so on).

The `CreateLogger` method takes the name of the class or method that will write the log information through the aforementioned possible providers.

In short, to log all the logging information to a file, we need to use the file provider (NLog, Serilog, or any other provider) and create an instance of `CreateLogger` to send the log information to be stored in the file.

Logging level

The log information that is written will have a different level based on the severity of the information being written. The following table depicts the log level in ASP.NET Core in ascending order:

Log level	Written as	Remarks
Trace = 0	`_logger.LogTrace (...)`	Part of developer debugging. Can include sensitive information.
Debug = 1	`_logger.LogDebug (...)`	Part of developer debugging. Used most of the time.
Information = 2	`_logger.LogInformation(...)`	Flow of application can be logged here. Not meant for debugging.

Warning = 3	`_logger.LogWarning (...)`	For unexpected events. For example, data doesn't match business rules.
Error = 4	`_logger.LogError (...)`	Unhandled events of application; can be errors.
Critical = 5	`_logger.LogCritical (...)`	Events that need immediate action for resolution.

Logging in action

Here, we will look at how to create an ASP.NET Core application with a web API template. The `Microsoft.Extensions.Logging` extension along with the `Debug` and `Console` extensions are already added.

Open the `Startup` class and make the following changes to view the in-built action:

```
public void Configure(IApplicationBuilder app, IHostingEnvironment env,
   ILoggerFactory loggerFactory)
{
   var strtpLogger = loggerFactory.CreateLogger<Startup>();
   strtpLogger.LogTrace("Looking at Trace level ");
   strtpLogger.LogDebug("This is Debug level");
   strtpLogger.LogInformation("You are Startup class - FY Information");
   strtpLogger.LogWarning("Warning - Entered Startup so soon");
   strtpLogger.LogError("This result in Null reference exception");
   strtpLogger.LogCritical("Critical - No Disk space");
   app.UseMvc();
}
```

You can break down the preceding code as follows:

- The logging level and category are read from the `appsettings.json` file's logging section
- The logger factory adds both the console and debug window provider
- We create an instance of the `Startup` class logger as `strtpLogger`
- This logger factory instance logs to the console and debug window according to the log levels

Run the application as a console app (using Kestrel and displaying console window). The console window shows the logs as follows (this is part of the console window):

```
C:\Program Files\dotnet\dotnet.exe
dbug: basic_logging_demo.Startup[0]
      This is Debug level
    : basic_logging_demo.Startup[0]
      You are Startup class - FY Information
warn: basic_logging_demo.Startup[0]
      Warning - Entered Startup so soon
    : basic_logging_demo.Startup[0]
      This result in Null reference exception
crit: basic_logging_demo.Startup[0]
      Critical - No Disk space
```

Logs displayed according to level

Looking at the preceding figure, we can see that it provides information of the origin of the log, namely the `Startup` class, and the different log levels.

Even though we wrote the `Trace` log level in the `Startup` class, it's not written in the console window. This is because of the log category present in `appsettings.json`.

Logging category

In the `Startup` class code snippet, you can see that the `AddConsole` log provider is reading the Logging section of `appsettings.json`. This section contains logging category details such as Default, System, and Microsoft.

The Log Category helps in writing logs that are specific to the application, the framework, or the entire system. Ideally, during development or in production, application level-specific logging is sufficient.

Let's add application level-specific logging instead of the default settings that are currently present. Open `appsettings.json`, remove the existing `LogLevel` details, and make the changes as shown here:

```json
{
  "Logging": {
    "IncludeScopes": false,
    "LogLevel": {
      "basic_logging_demo": "Warning"
    }
  }
}
```

`basic_logging_demo` is the project name (this can be any string), and we are setting the log level as `Warning`. Any logs below the warning level (refer to the log level table) will not be displayed on the console. Run the application again to view only the `Warning`, `Error`, and `Critical` logs displayed on console window.

ILoggerFactory in dependency injection

The dependency injection is baked into ASP.NET Core by default, and we can leverage this by injecting `ILogger` into the controller, middleware, filter, or any other class too.

Open the `ValuesController` web API class (created by default with the web API template), edit the code as follows, and run the application to view the logs on the console window:

```
namespace basic_logging_demo.Controllers
{
  [Route("api/[controller]")]
  public class ValuesController : Controller
  {
    private ILogger<ValuesController> _logger;
    public ValuesController(ILogger<ValuesController> logger)
    {
      _logger = logger;
    }
    // GET api/values
    [HttpGet]
    public IEnumerable<string> Get()
    {
      _logger.LogWarning("Warning from Values Controller ");
      return new string[] { "value1", "value2" };
    }

    // POST api/values
    [HttpPost]
    public void Post([FromBody]string value)
    {
      try
      {
        if(value.Length > 0)
        {
          _logger.LogInformation($"String length is {value.Length}");
        }
      }
      catch (Exception ex)
      {
```

```
            _logger.LogError("Error Occurred while POST ", ex.Message);
            throw;
        }
    }  //Removed code for brevity
    }
}
```

You can break down the preceding code as follows:

- In the same way that we used `CreateLogger` in the previous example, we have another way to create `ILogger` and inject it. Here we are creating a `ILogger` instance of `ValuesController`, and are using constructor to inject it.
- The `GET` method logs a warning and the `POST` method logs the information and error to the console when we hit these API endpoints.

Inject the `ILogger<T>` instance in the same way for middleware, filter, or any other classes to log information.

MyWallet - Demo ASP.NET Core project

To learn more about logging using different providers, we will be creating a demo ASP.NET Core application MyWallet that has the following functionalities:

- It should be able to list all the daily expenses.
- It should be able to get a particular expense by passing the ID.
- It should be able to add/post a single expense to the list. If the movie expense exceeds $300, then it is invalid request data.
- It should be able to edit and delete a particular expense.

In this demo application, we will be using a EF Core InMemory provider. This EF Core package runs the application in memory instead of persisting onto a database. It's ideal for unit testing the data access layer, but is used here to make the example simpler.

You can use any database provider (Sql Server, MySQL, SQLite) by reading `Chapter 09`, *Integration with Databases*.

Using the NuGet package manager, add `Microsoft.EntityFrameworkCore.InMemory` to the latest package. Create the web API controller as `WalletController`, `DailyExpense` as the model class, and `ExpenseContext` as the data context.

Don't forget to inject the `ExpenseContext` data context in the `Startup` class and the `ConfigureServices` method.

The `WalletController` web API controller code is shown here, based on the scenarios chosen:

```
[Route("api/[controller]")]
public class WalletController : Controller
{
    private readonly ExpenseContext _context;
    private readonly ILogger<WalletController> _logger;

    public WalletController(ExpenseContext context,
      ILogger<WalletController>
      logger)
    {
        _context = context;
        _logger = logger;
    }

    // GET api/values/5
    [HttpGet("{id}")]
    public IActionResult Get(int id)
    {
        var spentItem = _context.DailyExpenses.Find(id);
        if (spentItem == null)
        {
            _logger.LogInformation($"Daily Expense for {id} does
                not exists!!");
            return NotFound();
        }
        return Ok(spentItem);
    }

    // POST api/values
    [HttpPost]
    public IActionResult Post([FromBody]DailyExpense value)
    {
      if (value == null)
      {
          _logger.LogError("Request Object was NULL");
          return BadRequest();
      }
```

```
        CheckMovieBudget(value);

        if (!ModelState.IsValid)
        {
            return BadRequest(ModelState);
        }
        var newSpentItem = _context.DailyExpenses.Add(value);
        Save();
        return Ok(newSpentItem.Entity.Id);
    }
}
```

You can break down the preceding code as follows:

- Use DI to inject `ILogger<WalletController>` and `ExpenseContext` (EF Core requires this).
- `Get(int id)` finds the `DailyExpense` item by searching for and returning it. If not found, we log the information, stating that it's not found.
- `Post()` checks whether the request is NULL. If so, it returns `BadRequest` and logs the error. The `CheckMovieBudget` method looks at whether the movie expense is not more than $300 and returns a `Model Validation` error. If everything works well, it saves the daily expense.
- The `Put()` and `Delete()` methods check for the expense item. If it is not found, they log the information. If found, then it either updates or deletes it, depending on what it finds.

Run the application as a console app to view the various log information on the console window by hitting it using Postman or Fiddler.

Until now, we have been using the console window to view the log information in the code because ASP.NET Core provides the Console or Debug Window as the default log provider. In real-world apps, we need to log the information to a file, database, or cloud, and for this we need to use third-party log providers.

Logging errors to a file using NLog

NLog is one of the third-party providers that we can use for logging information in ASP.NET Core. We will be logging to a file in this case. However, we can use NLog to log to a database or cloud as well.

To know more about NLog, refer to `https://github.com/NLog/NLog.Extensions.Logging`.

Using the NuGet package manager, add NLog-related packages:

```
"NLog.Extensions.Logging": "1.0.0-rtm-beta5"
"NLog.Web.AspNetCore": "4.4.1"
```

 At the time of writing this book, NLog is still in beta. Refer to the preceding link for updates.

In the `Configure` method of the `Startup` class, modify the method to include NLog for logging information to the file:

```
public void Configure(IApplicationBuilder app, IHostingEnvironment env,
    ILoggerFactory loggerFactory)
{
    loggerFactory.AddNLog();
    app.AddNLogWeb();
    // Rest of code removed for brevity
    app.UseMvc();
}
```

For NLog, there is a configuration file to work with the different configuration settings, such as the log level, file name, log file location, and so on. Create the `nlog.config` file in the root directory and copy the following code for the most basic configuration:

```
<?xml version="1.0" encoding="utf-8" ?>
<nlog xmlns="http://www.nlog-project.org/schemas/NLog.xsd"
    xmlns:xsi="http://www.w3.org/2001/XMLSchema-instance">

    <extensions>
      <add assembly="NLog.Web.AspNetCore"/>
    </extensions>

    <!-- define various log targets -->
    <targets>
      <target xsi:type="File" name="ownFile-web" fileName="D:\PacktLogs\
        nlog-own-${shortdate}.log" layout="${longdate}|${
        event-
properties:item=EventId.Id}|${logger}|${uppercase:${level}}|
        ${message} ${exception}|url: ${aspnet-request-url}|action: $
        {aspnet-mvc-action}" />

      <target xsi:type="Null" name="blackhole" />
    </targets>
    <rules>
      <!--Skip Microsoft logs and so log only own logs-->
```

```
        <logger name="Microsoft.*" minlevel="Trace" writeTo="blackhole"
          final="true" />
        <logger name="*" minlevel="Trace" writeTo="ownFile-web" />
     </rules>
  </nlog>
```

Once everything is up and running, accessing `WalletController` (either through Postman or Fiddler) results in the creation of a log file with `nlog-own-(date).log` at the location provided in the configuration file.

Logging errors to a database using Serilog

Serilog is a third-party logging package for .NET applications. It focuses on fully structured events. It's known for simple APIs, easy setup, and lots of packages to log to various sources, such as files, databases, ElasticSearch, Raygun, and so on.

We will write log information to a database (an MS SQL Server database, that is) using `Serilog.Sinks.MSSqlServer`. We will add the following packages using the NuGet package manager:

```
Serilog: 2.5.1-dev-00873
Serilog.Sinks.MSSqlServerCore: 1.1.0
```

For database logging, we need a database server location, name, and table. Open `appsettings.json` to add these configuration settings:

```
"Serilog": {
  "ConnectionString":"Server=.\\sqlexpress;
  Database=MyWalletLogDB;trusted_connection=true",
  "TableName": "Logs"
}
```

Run the SQL script found at this URL on `MyWalletLogDB` to create a logs table. Refer to `https://github.com/serilog/serilog-sinks-mssqlserver` for more information.

In the `ConfigureServices` method of the `Startup` class, add Serilog to the DI to be used across the application:

```
services.AddSingleton<Serilog.ILogger>(x =>
{
  return new    LoggerConfiguration().WriteTo.MSSqlServer(Configuration[
  "Serilog:ConnectionString"],
  Configuration["Serilog:TableName"]).CreateLogger();
});
```

Open the `WalletController` web API to include the `Serilog.ILogger` to the DI and write the logs:

```
public WalletController(ExpenseContext context, Serilog.ILogger logger)
{
    _context = context;
    _logger = logger;
}
```

The source code attached contains the entire controller class. Now run the application and hit `WalletController` using Postman or Fiddler. Open the SQL Server to view the logs in a table. The result would look similar to this:

	Id	Message	Message Template	Level	Time Stamp	Exception	Properties	LogEvent
1	1	Daily Expense for 11 does not exists!!	Daily Expense for 11 does not exists!!	Information	2017-02-23 ...	NULL	<properties />	NULL
2	2	Erromeous input for Movie	Erromeous input for Movie	Error	2017-02-23 ...	NULL	<properties />	NULL

MyWallet logs in the SQL Server database

Exception management in a MyWallet project

Any web API project is not an application in itself. It is built so that popular frontends, either web or desktop, can consume it. It becomes essential for web APIs to handle any unexpected events (unhandled exceptions) or any business exception gracefully.

If unexpected events (unhandled or business-related) occur, then they should be logged and the appropriate response should be sent back so that clients can be made aware of it.

To achieve this, we require the following classes:

- `WebAPIError`: It acts as a response object to be used by clients.
- `WebAPIException`: It is a custom exception class for business or unhandled exceptions. It contains exception details, along with the status code.
- `WebAPIExceptionFilter`: It contains an exception attribute to be used as an attribute on the controller or actions.

Create a `ErrorHandlers` folder and create class files with the preceding names. Copy the following contents for each class:

- `WebAPIError`: It is used as a response object:

```
namespace MyWallet.ErrorHandlers
{
  public class WebAPIError
  {
     public string message { get; set; }
     public bool isError { get; set; }
     public string detail { get; set; }

     public WebAPIError(string message)
     {
        this.message = message;
        isError = true;
     }
  }
}
```

- `WebAPIException`: It is a custom exception class to carry exception details and status code:

```
using System;
using System.Net;

namespace MyWallet.ErrorHandlers
{
  public class WebApiException : Exception
  {
     public HttpStatusCode StatusCode { get; set; }

     public WebApiException(string message,
       HttpStatusCode statusCode =
         HttpStatusCode.InternalServerError) :
       base(message)
     {
       StatusCode = statusCode;
     }
     public WebApiException(Exception ex, HttpStatusCode statusCode
       = HttpStatusCode.InternalServerError) : base(ex.Message)
     {
        StatusCode = statusCode;
     }
  }
}
```

- WebAPIExceptionFilter: It is used as a filter to handle exceptions:

```
namespace MyWallet.ErrorHandlers
{
    public class WebApiExceptionFilter : ExceptionFilterAttribute
    {
        private ILogger<WebApiExceptionFilter> _Logger;

        public WebApiExceptionFilter(ILogger<WebApiExceptionFilter>
          logger)
        {
            _Logger = logger;
        }

        public override void OnException(ExceptionContext context)
        {
            WebAPIError apiError = null;
            if (context.Exception is WebApiException)
            {
                // Here we handle known MyWallet API errors
                var ex = context.Exception as WebApiException;
                context.Exception = null;
                apiError = new WebAPIError(ex.Message);

                context.HttpContext.Response.StatusCode =
                    (int)ex.StatusCode;
                _Logger.LogWarning($"MyWallet API thrown error:
                    {ex.Message}", ex);
            }
            else if (context.Exception is UnauthorizedAccessException)
            {
                apiError = new WebAPIError("Unauthorized Access");
                context.HttpContext.Response.StatusCode = 401;
            }
            else
            {
                // Unhandled errors
                #if !DEBUG
                    var msg = "An unhandled error occurred.";
                    string stack = null;
                #else
                    var msg = context.Exception.GetBaseException().Message;
                    string stack = context.Exception.StackTrace;
                #endif
                    apiError = new WebAPIError(msg);
                    apiError.detail = stack;

                context.HttpContext.Response.StatusCode =
```

```
                    (int)HttpStatusCode.InternalServerError;

                // handle logging here
                _Logger.LogError(new EventId(0), context.Exception, msg);
            }

            // always return a JSON result
            context.Result = new JsonResult(apiError);
            base.OnException(context);
        }
    }
}
```

You can break down the preceding code as follows:

- `ILogger` is taken in to write the logs.
- The `OnException` method checks whether this is a custom `WebApiException` type. If so, it prepares a `WebApiError` response with a status code. If it is an unauthorized access, it responds appropriately.
- With unhandled exceptions, it gets the stack trace details and responds with `WebApiError`, with full details of the release mode.
- The `ILogger` instance writes the log at the required place.

Our exception handling is ready in our `MyWallet` web API project. Let's incorporate the filter into our controller. You can either use an existing controller or create a new controller.

Firstly, decorate the controller with `WebApiExceptionFilter` that we created:

```
[ServiceFilter(typeof(WebApiExceptionFilter))]
[Route("api/[controller]")]
public class NewWalletController : Controller
{
    private readonly ExpenseContext _context;
    private readonly ILogger<WalletController> _logger;

    public NewWalletController(ExpenseContext context,
      ILogger<WalletController> logger)
    {
        _context = context;
        _logger = logger;
    }
    //Code removed for brevity
}
```

We are using `ServiceFilter` to use filter because we are using dependency injection to include `ILogger` in the filter so that it writes logs.

The `Get()` method can be written as follows to handle business logic failure, for example, if a requested record doesn't exist:

```
// GET api/values/5
[HttpGet("{id}")]
public IActionResult Get(int id)
{
  var spentItem = _context.DailyExpenses.Find(id);
  if (spentItem == null)
  {
    throw new WebApiException($"Daily Expense for {id}
      does not exists!!", HttpStatusCode.NotFound);
  }
  return Ok(spentItem);
}
```

Here is another example that illustrates that when the unhandled exceptions occur, the filter will handle them gracefully, and the error will be logged:

```
[Route("ThrowExceptionMethod")]
public IActionResult ThrowExceptionMethod()
{
  try
  {
    string emailId = null;
    if (emailId.Length > 0)
    {
        return Ok();
    }
    throw new WebApiException("Email is empty",
      HttpStatusCode.BadRequest);
  }
  catch (Exception ex)
  {
    throw ex;
  }
}
```

You can either log information to a file or a database. Once configured, run the application and use Postman or Fiddler to send a request and receive a response.

Here is a sample log written to a file using NLog, followed by a screenshot of Postman's response:

```
2017-02-13
17:13:59.9597|0|MyWallet.ErrorHandlers.WebApiExceptionFilter|WARN| MyWallet
API thrown error: Max movie expense limit is 300 and your amount is 2081
|url: http://localhost/api/newwallet|action: Post
```

Web API graceful exception

 Custom middleware can be written for gracefully handling the web API errors or exception.

Links to log management services

We can even move these logs to third-party log management services (trial and paid versions exist) to gather metrics about web API exceptions:

- **Seq**: Structured logging for .NET apps. It's an excellent tool for structured logs and log management services. Refer to `http://docs.getseq.net/docs/using-aspnet-core` to integrate it with the ASP.NET Core application.
- **Raygun**: One of the best tools for .NET apps for monitoring, reporting, and log analysis. Refer to `https://raygun.com/docs/languages/net/netcore` for integration.
- **Elmah**: Used for writing logs to their website, and for analyzing them later. To integrate, refer to `https://docs.elmah.io/logging-to-elmah-io-from-aspnet-core/`.

Summary

ASP.NET Core has greatly improved logging capabilities to any persistence source. The use of third-party tools for writing logs has been made simple. NLog or Serilog are the most widely used tools to manage writing logs.

We also learned how to gracefully handle web API errors, as well as how to log them to a log store in order to analyze them.

In the next chapter, we will learn about optimizing and improving ASP.NET Core performance using cache, asynchronous programming, and other methods.

11
Optimization and Performance

The real test of any web API begins when it's consumed by various clients (majority are frontend applications), increasing HTTP traffic with varying load. This is when we start to realize the web API performance has taken a hit, then the need for optimization and performance improvement comes into the picture.

The concerns for performance are mostly application-specific, but it's recommended to follow the best practices and techniques while building web API applications. Performance and optimization is a continuous process, and it needs regular monitoring to keep a check on bottlenecks.

As web APIs are exposed and consumed over HTTP, exploring various best practices to keep an application performing well, in case of light or heavy load, should be a top priority.

In this chapter, we will learn how to measure application performance, write controller action methods in an asynchronous way, compress HTTP response, and implement caching strategy for optimal usage of resources.

In this chapter, we will be looking at the following topics:

- Measuring application performance
- Asynchronous controller action methods
- HTTP compression
- Implementing in-memory caching
- Working with distributed caching
- Response caching

Measuring application performance

The web API application performance can be measured by using various techniques. One of the most important measuring parameters is running load test on Web API.

We will use **Apache HTTP Server Benchmarking Tool**, also known as **ab.exe.** It's a tool for sending hundreds of concurrent requests on endpoints.

The end point we will be targeting is /api/contacttype, the action methods are GetAllContactTypes and GetAllContactTypeAsync.

Both the action methods call stored procedures from the database using Dapper ORM using synchronous and asynchronous ways. In the next section, we will learn in more detail about asynchronous web API using the async await keywords.

Refer to the link, https://httpd.apache.org/docs/2.4/programs/ab.html, for usage of the ab.exe tool, and then run the application and perform the load test. Upon running the command, we should see similar test results (they differ based on system configuration):

```
Server Software:        Kestrel
Server Hostname:        localhost
Server Port:            61875

Document Path:          /api/contacttype/GetAllContactTypes
Document Length:        1007 bytes

Concurrency Level:      100
Time taken for tests:   104.133 seconds
Complete requests:      500
Failed requests:        0
Write errors:           0
Total transferred:      573000 bytes
HTML transferred:       503500 bytes
Requests per second:    4.80 [#/sec] (mean)
Time per request:       20826.557 [ms] (mean)
Time per request:       208.266 [ms] (mean, across all concurrent
Transfer rate:          5.37 [Kbytes/sec] received

Connection Times (ms)
              min  mean[+/-sd] median   max
Connect:        0    0   2.2      0      16
Processing:  1778 19553 7801.8  18951   40900
Waiting:     1420 17059 6988.9  17659   39134
Total:       1778 19553 7801.6  18951   40900
```

ab.exe for synchronous API endpoint

On examining the `Requests per second` parameter, we can see that `async` does show improved performance in load testing:

```
Server Software:        Kestrel
Server Hostname:        localhost
Server Port:            61875

Document Path:          /api/contacttype/GetAllContactTypeAsync
Document Length:        1007 bytes

Concurrency Level:      100
Time taken for tests:   98.114 seconds
Complete requests:      500
Failed requests:        0
Write errors:           0
Total transferred:      573000 bytes
HTML transferred:       503500 bytes
Requests per second:    5.10 [#/sec] (mean)
Time per request:       19622.705 [ms] (mean)
Time per request:       196.227 [ms] (mean, across all concurrent
Transfer rate:          5.70 [Kbytes/sec] received

Connection Times (ms)
              min  mean[+/-sd] median   max
Connect:        0     0   1.4      0      16
Processing:  3135 18962 4778.1  19089   31584
Waiting:     2839 15101 3969.6  14652   26176
Total:       3135 18962 4778.1  19089   31584
```

ab.exe for asynchronous API endpoint

Other ways of measuring applications:

- **Performance testing of REST Api using JMeter**:
  https://www.3pillarglobal.com/insights/performance-testing-of-a-restful-api-using-jmeter
- **Visual Studio 2015/17**:
  https://www.visualstudio.com/en-us/docs/test/performance-testing/getting-started/getting-started-with-performance-testing
- **Application Insights**: https://azure.microsoft.com/en-in/resources/videos/instrumenting-your-web-api-using-application-insights-with-victor-mushkatin/

Asynchronous controller action methods

ASP.NET supports asynchronous actions using **TAP (Task-based Asynchronous Pattern)**, this was first released in the .NET 4.0 framework and was greatly improved in .NET 4.5 and above using the `async` and `await` keywords.

In general, asynchronous programming in .NET helps to achieve a responsive application, improve scalability, and handles high number of requests in case of web applications.

.NET Core also supports asynchronous programming in the form of the `async` and `await` pattern. This pattern should be used when working with I/O or CPU bound or for database access.

As asynchronous means not occurring at the same time, any method called in an asynchronous way will return results later. To co-ordinate with a returned result, we use `Task` (no return value, that is, `Void`) or `Task<T>` (returns a value). The `await` keyword allows us to perform other useful work until `Task` returns results.

To understand more about the `async await` pattern, read through this link, `https://msdn.microsoft.com/en-us/magazine/jj991977.aspx`.

In ASP.NET Web API (Core or Web API 2), the `action` methods perform the asynchronous work, returning the result. The web API controller should not be assigned with an `async` keyword.

From the previous chapter's example of `MyWallet` web API demo application (*Chapter 10, Error Handling, Tracing, and Logging*), we will refactor the `WalletController` action methods to work asynchronously.

The `MyWallet` demo application was using EF Core In-Memory provider, we will extend it to work with Microsoft SQL Server database by following the *Integrating with EF Core* section of *Chapter 9, Integration with Database*.

Either create a new web API Controller or modify an existing one. The `WalletController` action methods are now refactored to work in an asynchronous way. Check the following controller code:

```
[Route("api/[controller]")]
public class WalletController : Controller
{
    private readonly WalletContext _context;
    private readonly ILogger<WalletController> _logger;
    public WalletController(WalletContext context,
        ILogger<WalletController> logger)
```

```csharp
{
    _context = context;
    _logger = logger;
}

// GET api/values/5
[HttpGet("{id}")]
public async Task<IActionResult> Get(int id)
{
    var spentItem = await _context.Wallet.FindAsync(id);
    if (spentItem == null)
    {
        _logger.LogInformation($"Daily Expense for {id}
          does not exists!!");
        return NotFound();
    }
    return Ok(spentItem);
}

// POST api/values
[HttpPost]
public async Task<IActionResult> Post([FromBody]DailyExpense value)
{
  if (value == null)
  {
      _logger.LogError("Request Object was NULL");
      return BadRequest();
  }
  CheckMovieBudget(value);
  if (!ModelState.IsValid)
  {
      return BadRequest(ModelState);
  }
  var newSpentItem = _context.Wallet.AddAsync(value);
  await SaveAsync();
  return Ok(newSpentItem.Result.Entity.Id);
}

//Complete code part of source code bundle
}
```

Now let us understand the code by breaking it down:

- All the action (GET, POST, PUT, DELETE) methods now have an `async` keyword indicating they are a part of the asynchronous call.
- All the `async` methods return `Task<IActionResult>` containing return values from method operations, typically values will be status code and response data.
- The `await` keyword is used for methods with the `async` implemented. We used EF Core as it provides almost all functions for asynchronous operations.

Best practice is to make methods asynchronous from top to bottom, that is, don't mix synchronous and asynchronous code.

Run the application and use Postman to test it. We won't feel the advantage of asynchronous methods for simple testing. It performs well when we have a good amount of load, but still writing the `async` methods will make the application load ready.

HTTP compression

Web API request and response are transmitted over the internet (HTTP-based data transfer). Network bandwidth is precious, it varies across regions. Web API responses are mostly in JSON form (a lightweight collection of strings). In these cases, even if we are sending a huge amount of data, it does matter a lot.

For quick transfer of response data over HTTP, it's good to compress the response before returning to clients. ASP.NET Core provides **Response Compression Middleware**, which compresses the response before sending it to clients.

Let's see it action, create `PersonController` with returns list of `Person` over the GET request (you can still continue using any Web API project from the book). I am using **GenFu**--the NuGet package to generate realistic prototype data, install this package or we can even connect to the database and return response of any table.

GenFu will give me a collection of the `Person` class, which I return when `PersonController` is called. Here is the code for `PersonController`:

```
using GenFu;
using Microsoft.AspNetCore.Mvc;
using System;
namespace compression_cache_demo.Controllers
{
```

```
[Route("api/[controller]")]
public class PersonController : Controller
{
    // GET: api/values
    [HttpGet]
    public IActionResult Get()
    {
        //Generate demo list using GenFu package
        //Returns 200 counts of Person object
        var personlist = A.ListOf<Person>(200);
        return Ok(personlist);
    }
}
public class Person
{
    public int Id { get; set; }
    public string FirstName { get; set; }
    public string LastName { get; set; }
    public int Age { get; set; }
    public DateTime DoB { get; set; }
}
}
```

Run the application, browse the `Person` controller in Google Chrome (preferred), and you will see the response size of 200 `Person` objects in JSON format over HTTP (size might differ on your machine).

Adding response compression middleware

ASP.NET Core provides a middleware to compress the response before sending it back. This middleware provider compresses different MIME types, for this example we are interested in JSON data.

This package `Microsoft.AspNetCore.ResponseCompression` is included as part of .NET SDK, interestingly we need not work at controller or action level, just include this middleware in HTTP pipeline processing.

Be default, a GZIP compression provider is used; we can use other compression providers or write our own.

Open the `Startup` class and make changes as follows in the `ConfigureServices` and `Configure` method:

```
public void ConfigureServices(IServiceCollection services)
{
    services.AddResponseCompression();
    services.AddMvc();
}
public void Configure(IApplicationBuilder app, IHostingEnvironment env,
    ILoggerFactory loggerFactory)
{
    app.UseResponseCompression(); //Before logging
    app.UseMvc(); //code removed for brevity
}
```

Run the application to view the size of response after compression. Refer to the following screenshot (it might vary on your system):

Response size before & after compression

Name	Status	Type	Initiat...	Size	T
☐ person	200	docu...	Other	17.5 KB	

Name	Status	Type	Initiat...	Size
☐ person	200	docu...	Other	5.2 KB

Response compression middleware in action

Implementing in-memory caching

Accessing resources is an expensive operation, it's even more expensive when the resource is requested frequently, and when it gets hardly updated. For a better performing Web API, it's essential to reduce the burden of accessing the least-updated resource by implementing a caching mechanism.

The caching concept helps in improving the performance and scalability of an app by reducing the work required to generate content.

ASP.NET Core provides a web server based memory caching technique called in-memory caching. The cache of content takes place on web server memory by using the IMemoryCache interface.

The in-memory caching is a good choice for limited use; applications that are not hosted on a web farm. It's fast, yet simple to use. Just dependency inject the IMemoryCache interface into the Controller/ class. The following code snippet illustrates this.

In this example, the Dapper (Micro ORM) is used to fetch the values from the database, and sends it as a response. To use Dapper in ASP.NET Core, refer to Chapter 9, *Integration with Database:*

```
[Route("api/[controller]")]
public class ContactTypeController : Controller
{
    private string connectionString;
    private readonly IMemoryCache _cache;

    public ContactTypeController(IMemoryCache memoryCache)
    {
        _cache = memoryCache;
        connectionString = "Data Source=..\\SQLEXPRESS;
        Initial Catalog=AdventureWorks2014;Integrated Security=True";
    }
    public IDbConnection Connection
    {
        get
        {
            return new SqlConnection(connectionString);
        }
    }

    // GET: api/values
    [HttpGet]
    public async Task<IActionResult> Get()
    {
        // Look for cache key.
        if (!_cache.TryGetValue("ContentTypeKey", out IList<ContactType>
          contentList))
        {
            // Setting the cache options
            var cacheEntryOptions = new MemoryCacheEntryOptions()
            // Keep in cache for this time, reset time if accessed.
            .SetSlidingExpiration(TimeSpan.FromSeconds(60));
```

```
            contentList = await GetAllContactTypesAsync();
            // Save data in cache.
            _cache.Set("ContentTypeKey", contentList, cacheEntryOptions);
        }
        return Ok(contentList);
    }
    //Complete code part of source code bundle
}
```

Now let's understand the entire code by breaking it down:

- Using DI, we are injecting `IMemoryCache` to working cache-related methods such as `TryGetValue` and `Set`.
- We are using the `Connection` property to connect to the database using Dapper ORM. We are using the AdventureWorks2014 database. You can use any example or real world databases too.
- In the `Get` method, first we are checking if a cache KEY entry exists, if so it returns the response from it.
- If the cache KEY does not exist, then we fetch the records using the `GetAllContactTypesAsync` method, and then add to memory cache using the `SET` method using `ContentTypeKey`.

Run the application. When `ContactTypeController` is accessed for the first time, data is fetched from the database and on any subsequent access, web API returns the data from the cache.

Working with distributed caching

Most real-world enterprise apps fetch data from various data sources such as third-party DB, web services, and most importantly the web APIs are deployed either on cloud or server farm environment.

In the preceding cases, in-memory won't serve the purpose of caching as it's web server memory-based. To provide a more robust cache strategy across a deployed environment, it's recommended to use a distributed cache.

The distributed cache stores the data on a persistent store instead of web server memory, in this way cache data is available across the deployed environment.

The actual data store gets fewer requests than in-memory, therefore distributed cache survives the web server restarts, deployments, or even failure.

Distributed cache can either be implemented with `Sql Server` or `Redis` using the `IDistributedCache` interface.

Using an SQL Server distributed cache

We will be using SQL Server for distributed cache; even Redis can also be used. To use SQL Server, use NuGet install the following packages:

> `Microsoft.Extensions.Caching.SqlServer: 2.0.0-preview2-final`

To use the sql-cache tool, add `SqlConfig.Tools` to the `<ItemGroup>` element of the `.csproj` file and run `dotnet restore` (optional):

```
<DotNetCliToolReference
Include="Microsoft.Extensions.Caching.SqlConfig.Tools"
    Version=" 2.0.0-preview2-final" />
```

Once this is done, verify that SQL tools for cache works fine by running the following command from the root folder of the project:

> `dotnet sql-cache create -help`

After that, run the following command to create a `Democache` table in the `PacktDistCache` database, this table stores all the cache entries.

Ensure that a `PacktDistCache` database is created before running the following command:

> `dotnet sql-cache create "Data Source=..\SQLEXPRESS;Initial`
> `Catalog=PacktDistCache;Integrated Security=True;" dbo DemoCache`

You can verify the table is created using SQL Server Management Studio.

Now that we are ready with Distributed Cache store in MS SQL Server, update the `Startup` class to inform it to use this location for distributed cache:

```
public void ConfigureServices(IServiceCollection services)
{
    services.AddDistributedSqlServerCache(options =>
    {
        options.ConnectionString = @"Data Source=..\SQLEXPRESS;
        Initial Catalog=PacktDistCache;Integrated Security=True;";
        options.SchemaName = "dbo";
        options.TableName = "DemoCache";
    });
```

```
         // Add framework services.
         services.AddMvc();
   }
```

We will create `CurrencyConverterController`, which fetches the daily currency exchange rates from public web API and stores it in the cache database. For any further access to `CurrencyConverterController`, the data is returned from the cache instead of a public web API. This reduces the burden on the server to fetch rates for every request:

```
namespace distributed_cache_demo.Controllers
{
  [Route("api/[controller]")]
  public class CurrencyConverterController : Controller
  {
    private readonly IDistributedCache _cache;
    public CurrencyConverterController(IDistributedCache cache)
    {
      _cache = cache;
    }
    // GET: api/values
    [HttpGet]
    public async Task<IActionResult> Get()
    {
      var rate = await GetExchangeRatesFromCache();
      if (rate != null)
      {
          return Ok(rate);
      }

      await SetExchangeRatesCache();
      return Ok(await GetExchangeRatesFromCache());
    }

    private async Task SetExchangeRatesCache()
    {
      var ratesObj = await DownloadCurrentRates();
      byte[] ratesObjval = Encoding.UTF8.GetBytes(ratesObj);

      await _cache.SetAsync("ExchangeRates", ratesObjval,
        new DistributedCacheEntryOptions()
        .SetSlidingExpiration(TimeSpan.FromMinutes(60))
        .SetAbsoluteExpiration(TimeSpan.FromMinutes(240))
      );
    }
    private async Task<RatesRoot> GetExchangeRatesFromCache()
    {
      var rate = await _cache.GetAsync("ExchangeRates");
      if (rate != null)
```

```
            {
                var ratestr = Encoding.UTF8.GetString(rate);
                var ratesobj =
    JsonConvert.DeserializeObject<RatesRoot>(ratestr);
                return ratesobj;
            }
            return null;
        }
    }
}
```

This is how the code works:

1. `IDistributedCache` is DI into web API controller class for `Set` and `Get` values.
2. The `SetExchangeRatesCache` method calls `DownloadCurrentRates()`, and then sets them to cache using the `ExchangeRates` key.
3. The `GetExchangeRatesFromCache` method reads the cache database to fetch the values from the `ExchangeRates` key.
4. The `Get()` method fetches the data and returns response if exists or else, it sets the data first and returns the cached value.

Running the application, accessing `CurrencyConverterController` will set values into cache database and any subsequent access will return the data from the database. The cache data is stored in the database as shown:

Id	Value	ExpiresAtTime	SlidingExpirationInSeconds	AbsoluteExpiration
1	ExchangeRates	0x7B2262617365223A22555344222C2264617465223A2232...	2017-03-27 19:56:57.3866186 +00:00	3600	2017-03-27 22:46:43.3394971 +00:00

Distributed Cache store

Response caching

In ASP.NET Core, response caching middleware allows response caching. It adds cache-related headers to responses. These headers specify how you want client, proxy, and middleware to cache responses.

To use this, we need to include its package using NuGet, as per .NET Core 2.0 latest version relevant packages are pre-installed:

```
"Microsoft.AspNetCore.ResponseCaching": "2.0.0-preview2-final "
```

After the package is installed, update the `Startup` class to add `ResponseCaching` to a services collection:

```
public void ConfigureServices(IServiceCollection services)
{
    //Response Caching Middleware
    // Code removed for brevity
    services.AddResponseCaching();
    services.AddMvc();
}
```

Also include the `ResponseCaching` middleware in HTTP pipeline processing:

```
public void Configure(IApplicationBuilder app, IHostingEnvironment env,
    ILoggerFactory loggerFactory)
{
    app.UseResponseCompression();
    app.UseResponseCaching();
    app.UseMvc();
}
```

Now the middleware, the `Startup` class is updated to use response caching, it's time to add them to the controller action method.

Response caching should be avoided for authenticated clients or data, due to this reason we are updating the controller action method with a `ResponseCache` attribute:

```
public class PersonController : Controller
{
    // GET: api/values
    [HttpGet]
    [ResponseCache(VaryByHeader = "User-Agent", Duration = 30)]
    public IActionResult Get()
    {
        //Generate demo list using GenFu package
        //Returns 200 counts of Person object
        var personlist = A.ListOf<Person>(200);
        return Ok(personlist);
    }
}
```

This attribute will set the cache-control header and set max-age to 30 seconds. Upon running the application, response header shows a cache-control header (either in Fiddler or Chrome tools).

Summary

In this chapter, we learned a great deal about how to write asynchronous Web API controllers, response compression, and improve response times by wiring caching mechanism.

We also learned about measuring the performance of web API application.

In the next chapter, we will look into different ways of publishing and deploying the application onto different environments and hosting providers.

12

Hosting and Deployment

We are nearing the end of this book. Over the course of this book, we have learned a lot of concepts about web APIs by creating ASP.NET Core Web API project, wrote controllers and actions, added routing, wrote custom middleware, unit tested the code, and handling exception, and performing some optimization. Now it's time for hosting and deploying the web API application.

With ASP.NET Core being cross-platform, hosting and deployment is not confined to the Windows environment (IIS and Azure) itself; environments such as AWS, Docker, Linux, and so on can be good alternatives.

In this chapter, we will focus on hosting and deploying a sample ASP.NET Core Web API project in a truly cross-platform way.

In this chapter, we will be looking at the following topics:

- Creating a demo ASP.NET Core Web API project
- Publishing a web API project
- Standalone web API
- Deployment strategy
- Deploying a web API to IIS
- Deploying a web API to Azure App Service
- Publishing a web API to a Windows virtual machine on Azure
- Publishing a web API to Docker
- Publishing a web API to EC2 on AWS
- Publishing a web API to Linux

Creating a demo ASP.NET Core Web API project

`PacktContacts` will be the demo project to be hosted and deployed on our various environments. This project is built using some of the features learned in this book, such as attribute routing, custom middleware, link generation, and route constraints.

Create an ASP.NET Core Web API project with the name `PacktContacts`, create a web API controller class `ContactsController` in the controller folder, and copy the following code:

```
namespace PacktContacts.Controllers
{
  [Route("api/[controller]")]
  public class ContactsController : Controller
  {
    static List<Contact> ContactList = new List<Contact>();

    // GET: api/Contacts
    [HttpGet]
    public IActionResult Get()
    {
      return Ok(ContactList);
    }

    // GET api/Contacts/5
    [HttpGet("{id:int}", Name = "GetContacts")]
    public IActionResult Get(int id)
    {
      var findContact = ContactList.Where(e => e.Id == id);
      if(findContact != null)
      {
        return Ok(findContact);
      }
      else
      {
        return NotFound();
      }
    }

    // POST api/Contacts
    [HttpPost]
    public IActionResult Post([FromBody]Contact contactsInfo)
    {
      if (contactsInfo == null)
```

```
        {
            return BadRequest();
        }
        ContactList.Add(contactsInfo);
        return CreatedAtRoute("GetContacts",
            new { Controller = "Contacts",
            id = contactsInfo.Id }, contactsInfo);
    }

    // Complete code part of source code bundle
    }
}
```

The complete source code is available in the code bundle.

Create a `Contact` class file in a `Model` folder and copy the following code. It acts as a complex object, but is used as model:

```
public class Contact
{
    public int Id { get; set; }
    public string FirstName { get; set; }
    public string LastName { get; set; }
    public string Email { get; set; }
}
```

You can break down the preceding code as follows:

- `ContactsController` is a web API controller performing CRUD operations on the `Contact` class.
- A static list property holds the records of `Contact`. In this example, it acts like a database.
- The `Get`, `Post`, and `Put` HTTP methods use `IActionResult` for returning a response. We can use HTTP code for various results.
- The `Post` method responds with `CreatedAtRoute`. This generates a link in the response header.
- The `Put` and `Delete` methods work only when contact exists; otherwise, they respond with the appropriate response.
- `Contact` is a POCO class that contains basic details.

`PacktHeaderValidator`--a custom middleware, mentioned in `Chapter` `6`, *Middleware and Filters*, can be used to check whether the request contains a custom header entry for the web API to respond to.

Publishing ASP.NET Core Web API project

We have created a demo web API project `PacktContacts`, tested it, and then run it in a local development environment. For production, the application should be published.

.NET Core or ASP.NET Core projects (either MVC or Web API) can be published using either CLI or Visual Studio tooling. We will learn both the ways to publish it.

Publishing by CLI

In `Chapter 3`, *Anatomy of ASP .NET Core Web API*, we learned various .NET Core commands. To publish an application, the .NET Core CLI provides us with the `dotnet` `publish` command. It generates the necessary artifacts for running the application.

Open the Command Prompt from the project folder and run the following command to publish:

```
dotnet publish --output "<output-path>" --configuration release
```

Breaking down the publish command:

- The `dotnet publish` command compiles the application by referring `*.csproj`. It collects all the dependencies and publishes them to a directory.
- The `-output` option specifies the directory path to publish the project.
- The `-configuration` option specifies which application should be published in the `RELEASE` mode. By default, it's always in the `DEBUG` mode.

Navigate to the output folder in File Explorer to view the published application containing the compiled DLL, `appsettings.json`, `web.config`, and other necessary libraries to run the application. The folder screenshot shows some of these files.

This `dotnet publish` command is sufficient for most cases, but .NET CLI provides many more options to use with the publish command.

Read through this excellent documentation on `dotnet publish`: https ://docs.microsoft.com/en-us/dotnet/articles/core/tools/dotnet-publish.

refs	31-07-2017 18:01	File folder	
runtimes	31-07-2017 18:01	File folder	
x64	31-07-2017 18:01	File folder	
x86	31-07-2017 18:01	File folder	
appsettings.Development.json	27-07-2017 14:41	JSON File	1 KB
appsettings.json	27-07-2017 16:15	JSON File	1 KB
Microsoft.AspNetCore.Mvc.Razor.ViewCompilation.dll	06-07-2017 17:16	Application extens...	55 KB
PacktContacts.deps.json	31-07-2017 18:01	JSON File	344 KB
PacktContacts.dll	31-07-2017 18:01	Application extens...	24 KB
PacktContacts.pdb	31-07-2017 18:01	Program Debug D...	5 KB
PacktContacts.runtimeconfig.json	31-07-2017 18:01	JSON File	1 KB
web.config	31-07-2017 18:01	XML Configuratio...	1 KB

dotnet-publish output folder

 The output folder containing the portable `PacktContacts` application can run on any OS with the .NET Core runtime already installed.

To run the published application, navigate to the output folder from the command line and run the following command, as shown in the following screenshot:

```
dotnet PacktContacts.dll
```

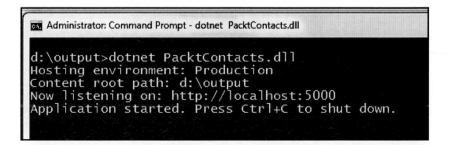

Running the published application

The `PacktsContacts` application runs the `http://localhost:5000`. This can be configured to any port. Use either the Fiddler or Postman tool to test the APIs.

Publishing by Visual Studio Tooling

Visual Studio IDE provides excellent tooling support for publishing applications. Just as older versions of ASP.NET perform the publishing step in Visual Studio, it's no different in ASP.NET Core.

Open the `PacktContacts` application in Visual Studio 2017, right-click on the project name, and click **Publish** to open the dialog window for publishing the project.

It provides us with three options to select the publishing target:

- **Microsoft Azure App Service**: Publish on Azure
- **Import**: Import an existing profile for publishing
- **Custom**: Publish either using web deploy, packages, FTP, or the filesystem

In this section, we will use the **Custom** option to publish the project to the filesystem, similar to the CLI approach. Click on **Custom** and give it the profile name `PacktPublish`.

Under **Connection**, select the **Publish** method as filesystem and select the **Target Location** as the filesystem, as shown here:

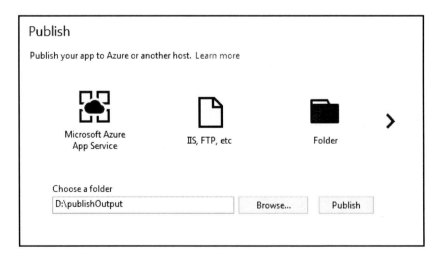

Select the Publish method and target location

Under **Settings**, select the **Configuration** option as **Release** and the **Target Framework** option as **.NETCoreApp**. The **Target Framework** field might show more options if different versions of .NET Core are installed.

We are not targeting any specific runtime here. In the next section, we will explore runtimes when we build standalone applications.

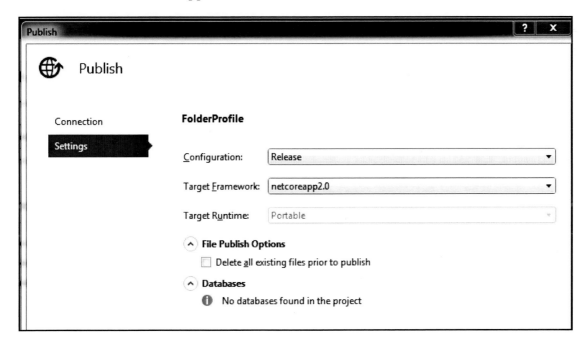

Setting the configuration and target framework

Click on the **Publish** button to start the publishing process. On completion, the target location provided will have all the files needed to run the application. A profile folder is created in the solution structure containing all the settings provided while using the publish wizard.

To run the application, just follow the commands as shown in the CLI section.

Standalone web API

In the preceding section, we published the ASP.NET Core application as a portable .NET Core application. On any OS (Windows, macOS, or Linux), the preceding portable application will run if the .NET Core runtime is installed.

The portable .NET Core apps run natively even if they are published on any OS. It's achieved by running **libuv** (a web server for ASP.NET Core apps) natively.

ASP.NET Core can be built as a standalone (self-hosted) application-that is, a published application with a runtime (.NET Core runtime) included with it. As .NET Core (ASP.NET Core) applications are inherently console apps, an executable file is generated when they are published as standalone, and running this file starts the application.

Let's publish `PacktContacts` as a standalone application and edit the `*.csproj` file to add `RuntimeIdentifiers` in the `PropertyGroup` section, as shown here:

```
<PropertyGroup>
  <TargetFramework>netcoreapp2.0</TargetFramework>
  <RuntimeIdentifiers>win7-x64</RuntimeIdentifiers>
</PropertyGroup>
```

Runtimes are also known as **RIDs,** that is, **.NET Core Runtime Identifier (RID)**. We need to mention the target OS against which the .NET Core application will be built as a standalone app.

I have used a Windows 7 x64 machine for building the ASP.NET Core Web API as a standalone app. Multiple RIDs can be targeted at once. The `dotnet restore` command should be run to restore all packages (you should explicitly call it if you are editing the `*.csproj` file in the editor).

 For a different OS runtime identifier, read through the documentation of the .NET Core runtime identifier at `https://docs.microsoft.com/en-us/dotnet/articles/core/rid-catalog`.

Run the following command from the `PacktContacts` folder to create a standalone application:

```
dotnet publish --output "<output-path>" --configuration release
```

Provide the appropriate output path to save the published application. On successful completion, you will notice that many files are copied, and that a `PacktContacts.exe` file is also created.

It contains the published web API, as well as the .NET Core runtime to run the application.

Now the `PacktContacts ASP.NET Core Web API` application can be run as an EXE, as shown here:

```
Administrator: Command Prompt - PacktContacts.exe

d:\packtContacts-standalone>PacktContacts.exe
Hosting environment: Production
Content root path: d:\packtContacts-standalone
Now listening on: http://localhost:5000
Application started. Press Ctrl+C to shut down.
```

Running as a standalone application

 It's recommended that you use the appropriate runtime identifier. As it's built for Windows 7 x64, it might work on a higher version of the Windows OS, but it won't work on Linux or macOS.

Deployment strategy

ASP.NET Core runs on a brand new web server called **Kestrel**, based on libuv.

 Microsoft recommends that Kestrel should be treated as an internal web server-excellent for development, it but shouldn't be exposed to the internet.

Then the obvious question would be how to host ASP.NET Core apps to expose them to the internet. The following diagram briefly illustrates the deployment strategy:

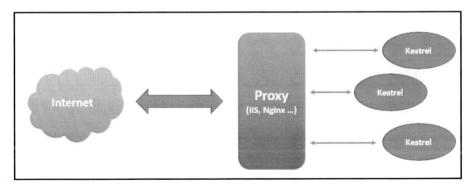

ASP.NET Core apps deployment strategy

The figure depicts the deployment strategy of having a proxy (aka a reverse proxy) in the form of IIS, Nginx, and so on.

These reverse proxies allow us to offload work by serving static content, caching requests, compressing requests, and SSL termination from the HTTP server.

Any requests coming from the internet will go through the reverse proxy (IIS or Nginx). The request is passed, and then the ASP.NET Core apps invoke the Kestrel server to take action on this.

In the next sections, we will deploy the `PacktContacts` web API using this strategy.

Deploying web API to IIS

Deploying an ASP.NET Core application to IIS is the preferred choice when hosting on different Windows OSes (machines or servers).

It's important to understand how IIS will work with ASP.NET Core apps. In the preceding section, we published the application to the output folder containing all the artefacts for running it.

The famous web.config also exists in the published folder. Examine the content to understand how IIS and ASP.NET Core work together:

```xml
<?xml version="1.0" encoding="utf-8"?>
<configuration>
  <!-- Configure your application settings in appsettings.json.
  Learn more at http://go.microsoft.com/fwlink/?LinkId=786380 -->
  <system.webServer>
    <handlers>
      <add name="aspNetCore" path="*" verb="*"
      modules="AspNetCoreModule" resourceType="Unspecified" />
    </handlers>
    <aspNetCore processPath="dotnet" arguments=".\PacktContacts.dll"
      stdoutLogEnabled="false"
      stdoutLogFile=".\logs\stdout" forwardWindowsAuthToken="false" />
  </system.webServer>
</configuration>
<!--ProjectGuid: d8d6c16d-f42a-4d87-a244-6484d6bffb5e-->
```

Breaking down the `web.config` file:

- `AspNetCoreModule` needs to be installed to transfer the request to Kestrel.
- `aspNetCore` tells `processPath` as `dotnet`, `argument` to be `PacktContacts.dll`. Logging is disabled as of now. This is same as the `dotnet packtcontacts.dll` CLI command but via `web.config`.

The `web.config` file is included in ASP.NET Core so that IIS can invoke the application and let Kestrel process the request. Note that IIS acts as a reverse proxy.

To know more about ASP.NET Core module configuration, read `https://docs.microsoft.com/en-us/aspnet/core/hosting/aspnet-core-module`.

Configuring a website on IIS

Assuming that IIS is already enabled on your machine, open IIS Manager and perform the following steps:

1. Under **Application Pools**, add a new application pool exclusively for ASP.NET Core apps. We are setting the .NET Framework version as **No Managed Code**.
2. Under **Sites**, right-click **Add Web Site**, provide the appropriate **Site Name**, assign **Application pool** created previously, and assign **Physical path** of the published folder (refer to the output path while executing the `dotnet publish` step)

At the end of this chapter, we will look at how to test the `PacktContacts` app:

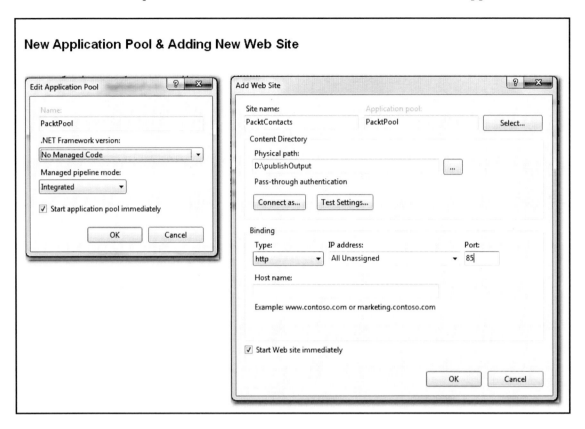

Creating a new application pool and adding a website

At the end of this chapter, we will look at how to test the `PacktContacts` web API.

Deploying a web API to Azure App Service

In this section, we will deploy the application using the Azure App Service. This example uses a free trial account. If you have access to any other subscription, you can use that here.

Follow these steps to deploy:

1. Right-click on the **project** in Solution Explorer and select **Publish**
2. In the **Publish** dialog, click **Microsoft Azure App Service**.

3. Click **New** to create a new resource group from Visual Studio. You could also use an existing one. In this example, an already existing Azure app under resource group is used.

4. Click **Ok** to web deploy the application to the Azure app.

5. Web Deploy will perform the operation of installing dotnet runtime, restoring packages, and copying the published web API application onto the Azure apps.

6. Once done, the browser automatically opens up with the link. You are ready to test it now:

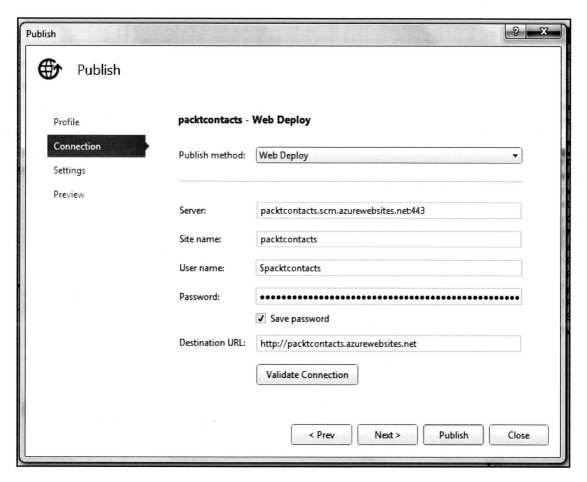

Web deploy to Azure App Service

Publishing a web API to Windows virtual machine on Azure

In this section, we will deploy the published `PacktContacts` web API to the virtual machine created on Windows Azure. We will be creating a Windows Server 2012 R2 Data Center as the virtual machine.

An Azure free trial account is sufficient. Go through the following steps to deploy the `PacktContacts` web API:

1. To create an Azure virtual machine, follow the steps mentioned at `https://docs.microsoft.com/en-us/azure/virtual-machines/virtual-machines-windows-hero-tutorial` to create a Windows Server 2012 R2 Datacenter.
2. After creating the VM, establish a remote desktop connection to deploy the application.
3. As it is a Windows server, we will be deploying the `PacktContacts` web API on IIS on this VM. Since it's a newly created machine, IIS won't be configured; to configure it, read through `https://docs.microsoft.com/en-us/azure/virtual-machines/virtual-machines-windows-hero-role?toc=%2fazure%2fvirtual-machines%2fwindows%2ftoc.json`.
4. After IIS is configured, install the `.NET Core Windows Server Hosting` (`https://aka.ms/dotnetcore_windowshosting_1_1_0`) bundle on the server. This will install the .NET Core runtime, the .NET Core library, and the ASP.NET Core module.
5. Copy the published web API project to the Windows VM either manually or through FTP and follow the steps described in the section *Configuring a website on IIS*.

Ensure that the deployed application on the VM is configured for access using a public IP address.

Publishing a web API to Docker

Docker is a tool used to create, deploy, and run applications by using containers. They work like VMs, but are more lightweight and use the host machine to provide better performance.

To understand more about Docker, read the article What is Docker? found at `https://www.docker.com/what-docker`. Docker can be installed on your machine by following the appropriate steps for your machine, found at `https://www.docker.com/products/docker`.
To use Docker, your machine should support hardware virtualization.

Once Docker is installed on the machine, go through the following steps to build a `PacktContactsAPI` Docker image and run it on a Docker container:

1. Right-click on the project name and go to **Add | Docker Support** to create the Docker file.
2. In the `PacktContacts` project, create `Dockerfile` and copy the following code:

```
FROM microsoft/aspnetcore: 2.0
ENTRYPOINT ["dotnet", "PacktContacts.dll"]
ARG source=.
WORKDIR /app
EXPOSE 80
COPY $source .
```

   It runs FROM the ASP.NET Core 2 with `ENTRYPOINT` of `PacktContacts.dll` (the same as if it were running under CLI) with no arguments. Copy the current directory content to the image.

3. Run the `dotnet publish` command once again; this will publish the folder with the Docker file that we created.
4. Now build the Docker image by running the following command from the Docker Terminal:

```
docker build D:\publishOutput -t packtcontantsAPI
```

   - The `D:\publishOutput` is the output directory referred to in the `dotnet publish` command:
   - `packtcontantsAPI` will be the Docker image name.

5. Run the following command to run the image on the Docker container:

```
docker run -it -d -p 85:80 packtcontantsAPI
```

Once everything is running properly, use the Docker machine default IP to access the `PacktContacts` web API.

Publishing a web API to EC2 on AWS

In the previous section, we build the Docker image `packtcontactsapi` for our ASP.NET Core Web API project. In this section, we will run this Docker image on the AWS EC2 container service.

Docker images are prebuilt with all required runtimes, which reduces the efforts of the published application to set up the environment.

Create an AWS account and move to the **EC2 Container Service** section. Follow the steps (they are quiet easy) and you will be presented with commands to push the Docker image to AWS EC2. The commands are shown in the following screenshot:

View Push Commands　　　　　　　　　　　　　　　　　　　　　　　　　　✕

Prerequisites: If you haven't installed the AWS CLI, please follow the instructions here to do so. If you haven't installed Docker, please follow the instructions here to do so.

1) Retrieve the `docker login` command that you can use to authenticate your Docker client to your registry:

```
aws ecr get-login --region us-west-2
```

2) Run the `docker login` command that was returned in the previous step.

3) Build your Docker image using the following command. For information on building a Docker file from scratch see the instructions here. You can skip this step if your image is already built:

```
docker build -t packtcontactsapi .
```

4) After the build completes, tag your image so you can push the image to this repository:

```
docker tag packtcontactsapi:latest 932462874879.dkr.ecr.us-
west-2.amazonaws.com/packtcontactsapi:latest
```

5) Run the following command to push this image to your newly created AWS repository:

```
docker push 932462874879.dkr.ecr.us-west-2.amazonaws.com/packtcontactsapi:latest
```

AWS push commands to Docker images

For more in-depth explanation of the steps involved in running Docker images on AWS EC2, refer to
`https://aws.amazon.com/getting-started/tutorials/deploy-docker-c`
`ontainers/.`

Create a Task Definition. Here, you will specify the Docker image to be used. The underlined text in the following screenshot indicates the push image that is used:

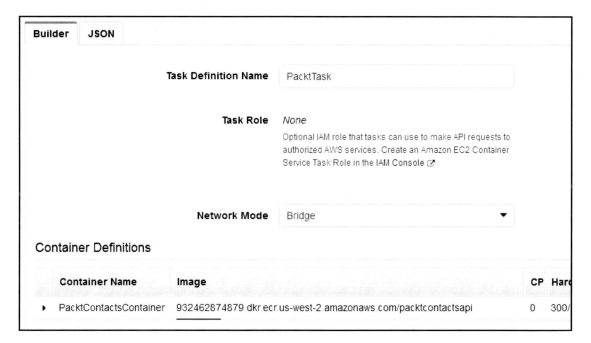

Creating the task definition in AWS

Configure a service to launch and maintain the task definition created previously:

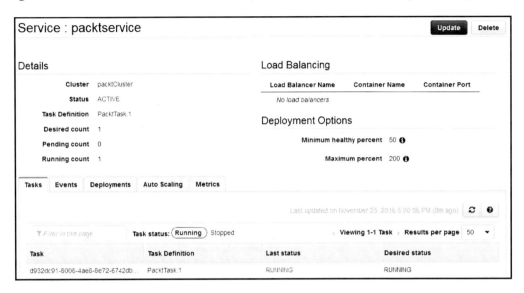

Configure the service to run the task

Configure the AWS EC2 cluster so that the services and tasks run on them. Clicking on the highlighted line shown in the figure will display the public DNS name needed to access the `PacktContacts` web API:

Configure and run the cluster on EC2

Publishing a web API to Linux

ASP.NET Core can be hosted on Linux OS. There are number of low-cost hosting providers using Linux OS. In this section, we will deploy the `PacktContacts` web API on a Linux machine run as a virtual machine.

We will be using Ubuntu Server 14.04 LTS Linux. There are numerous articles on how to run Ubuntu on a virtual box.

To install .NET Core for Linux, go to `https://www.microsoft.com/net/core#linuxubuntu`. Installing Visual Studio Code will help you to write your code, if needed.

There are two ways to deploy the demo web API project on this Linux machine: either transfer the published file or run the publish command from the source code.

I find that running publish from the source code is much easier. With the source code, you can work on the Linux machine as well. Push the source code onto the Git repository and clone the Linux (Git needs to be installed).

Once the source code is cloned, run the `dotnet publish` command, as shown at the beginning of the chapter. Run the application; it will start listening on port 5000.

Testing PacktContacts web API

ASP.NET Core applications can be hosted and deployed in numerous ways, with options such as Local IIS, Windows Azure, Docker, standalone, cheap Linux hosting providers, virtual machines, AWS, and many more.

Until now, we have only seen the hosting and deploying of a web API application, but we have never tested one. In this section, we will test all the CRUD scenario and custom middleware functionality. We will be using the Postman tool, however, Fiddler can also be used.

The following table shows the deployed location and the URL needed to access the application:

Deployed location	Access URL
Local IIS	`http://localhost:85`
Standalone	`http://localhost:5000`
Azure App Services	`http://packtcontacts.azurewebsites.net`

Docker	`http://192.168.99.100:85/`
EC2 on AWS	`http://ec2-35-164-207-251.us-west-2.compute.amazonaws.com`
Linux Host	`http://localhost:5000`

 These URLs will vary according to your setup.

Test case - Accessing a web API without the header

The custom middleware example from Chapter 6, *Middleware and Filters*, expects every request to have a custom header called `packt-book` with the value as `Mastering Web API`.

If there is no header, or the header is invalid, the web API responds with Bad Request error; otherwise, it responds accordingly:

Test web API without header

Test case - Accessing a web API with the header

In this case, we will be passing `packt-book` with the value as `Mastering Web API`. The web API responds with OK:

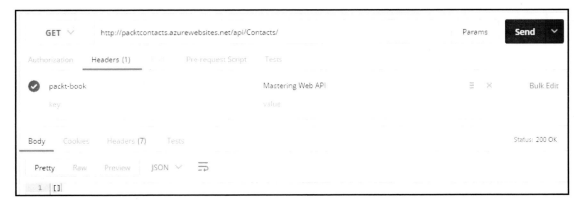

Web API responds with OK

Test case - Adding a contact to web API

In this case, we are passing the JSON request body to the `POST` method of `ContactsController`. It' must pass the custom header `packt-book`, as shown in the previous screenshot, to ensure that the `POST` request is processed. This example illustrates the middleware concept.

Here is the JSON request:

```
{
   "id": 20,
   "firstName": "Mithun",
   "lastName": "Pattankar",
   "email": "mithu@abc.com",
   "dateOfBirth": "1916-11-15"
}
```

Once the request is processed, the web API responds with a `201 Created` status in the response body. On observing the response headers, we can see the location header with the URL to access the created resource (contact, in our case).

The location header is an example of the link generation concept learned in `Chapter 5`, *Implementing Routing*.

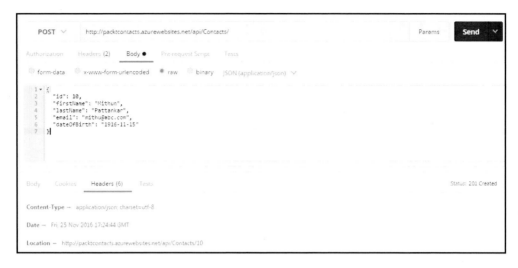

Post in action

Test case - Getting a contact from the web API

We will use the generated link to get the contact details:

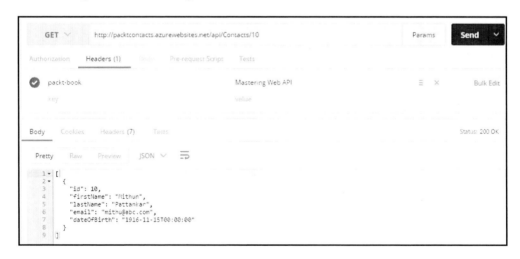

Get the contact details by passing the ID

Test case - Getting all contacts from the web API

This will get all the contacts that are present in the contact list, plus one more contact. The web API will return two contact details:

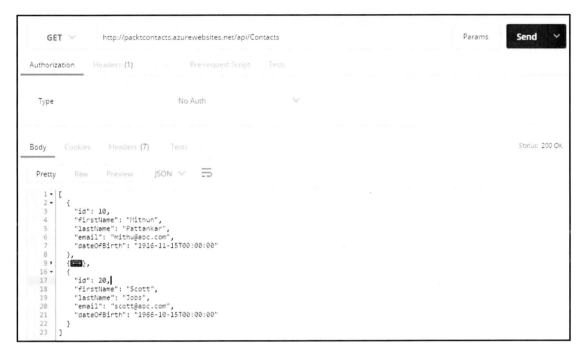

Get all contacts

Test case - Editing a contact to the web API

In this case, we are passing the JSON request body with the PUT method of ContactsController.

Here is the JSON request:

```
{
    "id": 30,
    "firstName": "Steve",
    "lastName": "Jobs",
    "email": "steve@abc.com",
    "dateOfBirth": "1966-10-15"
}
```

Test case - Deleting a contact from the web API

In this case, we will be deleting the contact by passing the ID with the DELETE method. Then we can call Get all Contacts to check that it's removed. If the ID doesn't exist then the Not Found response is returned:

Delete a contact

Summary

In this chapter, we learned the various hosting and deployment options for ASP.NET Core, right from the traditional approach to deploying published applications on IIS, to hosting them as standalone applications. The transition is really encouraging.

We learned that ASP.NET Core and Azure can be integrated so seamlessly by publishing using Azure App Services. There are plenty of low-cost Linux hosting options, and we explored those options as well. Truly, ASP.NET Core has emerged as a cross-platform technology from start to finish.

In the next chapter, we will consume these web APIs in modern frontends, such as JavaScript, JQuery, Angular, React, and Hybrid mobile apps.

13
Modern Web Frontends

We are in the last chapter of this book. We learned a lot of concepts in the previous chapters, such as how to create an ASP.NET Core Web API, write controllers and actions, adding routing, middleware, unit testing, and handling errors to optimization, and deploying and hosting on various environments.

The hosted web API was tested either using Postman or Fiddler tools, and it works fine. But the real use of ASP.NET Core Web API (and, in general, a web API built with any framework) lies in its ability to be consumed by front end applications such as web, mobile, or desktop apps.

Just as ASP.NET Core is cross platform, we have various web frontends that can be developed cross platform with open source technologies.

In this chapter, we will focus on building a web application with a modern web framework, such as Angular 4 (aka Angular), ReactJS, TypeScript (a superset of JavaScript), JQuery and JavaScript, Bootstrap, and Ionic 3 framework (a hybrid mobile apps framework). We will also look at how they consume the web API we developed in previous chapters.

In this chapter, we will be looking at the following topics:

- `PacktContacts` - Recap of the demo ASP.NET Core Web API
- Software prerequisites for web frameworks
- Consuming web APIs using Angular 4
- Consuming web APIs using Ionic 3
- Consuming web APIs using ReactJS
- Consuming web APIs using JavaScript
- Consuming web APIs using JQuery

PacktContacts - Recap of the demo web API project

In `Chapter 12`, *Hosting and Deployment*, we read about the demo ASP.NET Core Web API project known as `PacktContacts`, and hosted and deployed it on various environments.

The web API does a basic CRUD operation on the `Contact` model. We will be using this web API hosted on IIS as an end point for accessing it.

The `Contact` class file in the model folder acts as a complex object that is used as a model for data transfer over a network:

```
namespace PacktContacts.Model
{
  public class Contact
  {
    public int Id { get; set; }
    public string FirstName { get; set; }
    public string LastName { get; set; }
    public string Email { get; set; }
  }
}
```

Dealing with a cross-origin issue

When we tested the `PacktContacts` web API, either using Postman or Fiddler, they responded by calling with the appropriate response. When they hosted the endpoint URL of the web API that is used in modern web frameworks, it failed to work, resulting in a cross-origin issue.

Any web framework that uses AJAX requests to call the web API is prevented from making a call to another domain by the browser's security. It's popularly known as the same-origin policy in the web application world.

To elaborate in simpler terms, web API applications are hosted on the web server with an access URL of `http://www.abcd.com/api/packtcontacts`, and web applications are hosted on a separate domain (`http://www.xyz.com`). For example, a weather API exposes URLs and we consume those URLs in our application, yet it's obvious that they are hosted on different domains.

When we try to access the web API URL, a cross-origin error occurs. To avoid this, we need to enable the CORS feature in the `PacktContacts` project.

The CORS middleware comes into action here. It should be added to the `Configure` and `ConfigureServices` methods of the `Startup` class:

```
public void ConfigureServices(IServiceCollection services)
{
    // Add framework services.
    services.AddMvc();

    // Add service and create Policy with options
    services.AddCors(options =>
    {
        options.AddPolicy("CorsPolicy",
        builder => builder.AllowAnyOrigin()
        .AllowAnyMethod()
        .AllowAnyHeader()
        .AllowCredentials());
    });
}
public void Configure(IApplicationBuilder app, IHostingEnvironment env,
    ILoggerFactory loggerFactory)
{
    app.UseCors("CorsPolicy");
    app.UseMvc();
}
```

Now let's go through the code to understand it in a better way:

- In the `ConfigureServices` method, we are adding CORS to the web API using `AddCors`.
- We are creating `CorsPolicy`, which allows any origin call, any method, and any header to access the web API.
- The preceding policy is quite liberal for this demo project, but in a real-world example we can have a more strict policy. It acts at a global level.
- In the `Configure` method, we are using CORS middleware and passing in `CorsPolicy` that we created.

The rest of the code is the same as in the previous chapter (Chapter 12, *Hosting and Deployment*), as are the steps for testing the web API.

 `PacktHeaderValidator` - a custom middleware, mentioned in Chapter 6, *Middleware and Filters*, can be used to check that the request contains the custom header entry for the web API to respond to.

Software pre-requisites for web frameworks

We have been working on open source technologies right from the beginning, so we will end with building modern web frontends using open source technologies.

The following software needs to be installed as per the OS used- that is, according to Windows, Linux or macOS:

- **Visual Studio Code**: This is a lightweight cross-platform code editor. You might have already installed it if you're building an ASP.NET Core Web API on a non-Windows machine. If you haven't, then you can install it from `https://code.visualstudio.com/`.
- **NodeJS**: This is a package ecosystem for using open source libraries. We are using it to install packages. Install it from `https://nodejs.org/en/`.

You're free to work with the code editor of your choice, such as Sublime, Atom, or even Visual Studio IDE. We will be using **Visual Studio Code** (**VS Code**) as the code editor in this chapter.

Consuming web APIs using Angular 4

Angular (aka Angular 4) is an open source web framework built by Google to develop high performance single page applications (SPA). Google officially announced the latest Angular version, known as Angular 4, in 2016. It's completely rewritten, and doesn't resemble its previous version.

The Angular 4 documentation is extensive and in depth; you can read through it at `https://angular.io/docs/ts/latest/`.

The Angular 4 framework is written with TypeScript, its recommended language for writing web components for Angular. So what is TypeScript, then?

TypeScript is strongly typed, object-oriented script that generates JavaScript. TypeScript is designed to write enterprise-level web apps that use JavaScript. It's just like any other programming language, such as C#, or Java.

Some of the benefits of the TypeScript language are:

- Compilation to JavaScript
- Strong or static typing-you will see red underlines in the code editor if it's loosely typed code

- Popular JavaScript libraries are part of the type definitions that provide code completion
- Encapsulation

TypeScript alone can be used to develop web applications, as, in the case of JavaScript, it can be installed either using npm (node package manager) or the MSI installer. It can be used with any code editor or IDE, such as VS Code, Sublime, Atom, or Visual Studio IDE. To learn more about the language, refer to `www.typescriptlang.org`.

It's recommended that you learn the basics of Angular 4 and TypeScript before moving ahead in this chapter.

Angular CLI

The Angular CLI is a **command-line interface** (**CLI**) tool for creating Angular 4 applications, right from creating apps to creating services, components, routes, targeting builds, and running unit tests.

There are two different ways to create Angular 4 applications: through starter packs on GitHub or running the app from CDN. Frankly, the Angular CLI is the best tool available for creating Angular 4 apps, and I recommend that you use it in this chapter.

Install the latest NodeJS and npm to work with the Angular CLI. Install the CLI tool from NPM, and open Command Prompt to run following:

```
npm install -g angular-cli
```

After installing it, run the following command to create an Angular app with the name `ngPacktContacts` for creating a web frontend for our `PacktContacts` API:

```
ng new ngPacktContacts
```

This command creates an end-to-end Angular 4 application. There are numerous options to scaffold different application components. Use the information found at `https://github.com/angular/angular-cli` to generate these options appropriately.

When building an Angular 4 application, we need the following elements for working with the `PacktContacts` web API:

- An Angular service provider for calling the web API using HTTP verbs
- An Angular component for calling the preceding service provider and interacting with HTML
- An Angular component template for displaying the UI, such as HTML

We are dealing with a `Contacts` data model in our ASP.NET Core project. It would be great to have a similar data model in our Angular 4 application. Because we are using TypeScript, we can create a class called `contacts.class.ts` using CLI scaffolding options and copying the following code:

```
export class Contacts {
  id:number;
  firstName:string;
  lastName:string;
  email:string;
}
```

Note that TypeScript allows you to define the class and types to its properties, just like an object-oriented language.

PacktServices - Angular Service Provider

Let's create an Angular service provider by scaffolding the service from the CLI tool, and running the following command from the project folder:

```
ng generate service packt
```

This will create a service class with the name `PacktServices` in the `app` folder. Copy the following code to call the web API using different HTTP verbs:

```
import { Contacts } from './contacts.class';
import { Http, Response, Headers, HttpModule } from '@angular/http';
import 'rxjs/add/operator/map'
import { Observable } from 'rxjs/Observable';
import { Injectable } from '@angular/core';

@Injectable()
export class PacktServices {
  private actionUrl: string;
```

```
constructor(private _http:Http) {
    this.actionUrl = 'http://domain-name/api/contacts/';
}

public GetAll = (): Observable<any> => {
    let headers = new Headers({'Content-Type': 'application/json',
        'packt-book' : 'Mastering Web API',
        'Authorization': 'Bearer ' + this.token});
    let options = new RequestOptions({ headers: headers });
    return this._http.get(this.actionUrl, options)
    .map((response: Response) => <any>response.json());
}

public addContacts(ContactsObj: Contacts){
    let headers = new Headers({'Content-Type': 'application/json',
        'packt-book' : 'Mastering Web API',
        'Authorization': 'Bearer ' + this.token});

    let options = new RequestOptions({ headers: headers });
    return this._http.post(this.actionUrl, JSON.stringify(ContactsObj),
        options).map((response: Response) => <any>response.json());
}
//Complete code part of source code bundle
}
```

Now let's understand the code that we just developed:

- Import the Contacts class model that we created and the Angular HTTP module to call the REST-based API (web API in our scenario).
- The actionUrl parameter points to the ASP.NET Core Web API endpoint. This will be a hosted URL either from IIS, Azure App Services, AWS, or Docker, or even an application running on localhost .
- The headers object is created to set the content as JSON, and the custom header packt-book is created to work with the custom middleware created. The authorization header is also added to pass the JWT token.
- The GetAll method calls the web API using the HTTP GET verb to fetch all the records. We pass the headers object or else we get Bad Request as the response.
- The addContacts method receives the Contacts object from the UI to pass to the web API using the HTTP POST method.
- The updateContacts method receives the Contacts object and ContactsId from the UI to pass to the web API using the HTTP PUT method.
- The deleteContacts method receives the ContactsId object from the UI to pass to the web API using the HTTP DELETE method.

AppComponent - Angular Component

Components are the main way to build and specify elements and logic on the page. They create custom HTML elements (tags) to be used in the HTML page and start using the Angular features in them.

From the Angular-CLI-generated application, open the index.html page to see the `<app-root>Loading...</app-root>` HTML element. This isn't a regular HTML element-it's an Angular component with the selector name of `app-root`.

On examining the `app.component.ts` file, we would see the component declaration mentioning the selector name, template file (HTML file), and style sheet file path too:

```
@Component({
  selector: 'app-root',
  templateUrl: './app.component.html',
  styleUrls: ['./app.component.css']
})
```

The Angular docs will explain the `Components` concept in depth; read through these to understand more at `https://angular.io/docs/ts/latest/api/core/index/Component-decorator.html`.

We will be using this file instead of creating new components, to keep it simple. Copy the following code in `app.component.ts`:

```
import { Contacts } from './contacts.class';
import { PacktServices} from './packt-services.service';
import { Component, OnInit } from '@angular/core';
import {  FormGroup,  FormBuilder,  Validators} from '@angular/forms';

@Component({
  selector: 'app-root',
  templateUrl: './app.component.html',
  styleUrls: ['./app.component.css']
})
export class AppComponent implements OnInit {
  title = 'Angular 2 with ASP.NET Core Web API';
  recordsExists: boolean = false;
  formAddEdit:boolean = false;
  contactModel:Contacts;
  contactForm: FormGroup;

  public values: any[];
  constructor(private _dataService: PacktServices,
    private fb: FormBuilder) {}
```

```
ngOnInit() {
  this.LoadAllContacts();
}

LoadAllContacts(){
  this._dataService
  .GetAll()
  .subscribe(data => {
    if (data.length > 0) {
      this.values = data;
      this.recordsExists = true;
      //console.log(data);
    }
  },
  error => {
    console.log(error.status);
  },
  () => console.log('complete'));
}

onSubmit({ value, valid }: { value: any, valid: boolean }) {
  console.log(value, valid);
  let values = value as Contacts;

  if(this.contactModel.id === 0){
  //Insert
  values.id =  Math.floor((Math.random() * 100) + 1);
  this.AddContacts(values);
  }
  else{
    values.id = this.contactModel.id;
    this.UpdateContacts(values);
  }
  //Complete code part of source code bundle
}
```

You can break down the preceding code as follows:

- The `Contacts` class and `PacktServices` are imported.
- `AppComponent` is declared for `selector`, `templateUrl`, and `styleUrls`. There are a bunch of other options as well.
- The `AppComponent` class is defined, which inherits from the `OnInit` page cycle event. Other new properties are also declared.
- The `AppComponent` constructor takes in `PacktServices` and `FormBuilder` via dependency injection.

- The `ngOnInit` method gets called on the component initialization and calls the `LoadAllContacts` method.
- The `LoadAllContacts` method calls the `PacktServices` which in turn calls the web API and loads all contacts on the UI. The contact list is displayed only if the records exist.
- The `createContact` method sets up the contact form on the UI using the reactive forms technique in Angular 2.
- The `OnSubmit` method saves the contact details entered on the UI by calling `PacktServices` for both `POST` (add) and `PUT` (update).

The AppComponent template - HTML for Angular component

Every Angular component accompanies the UI template with its selector. In our example, the `aap.component.html` file is the template for displaying the UI.

To open the `app.component.html` file, copy the following code:

```html
<nav class="navbar navbar-default">
  <div class="container-fluid">
    <div class="navbar-header">
      <a class="navbar-brand" href="#">ngPacktContacts - {{title}}</a>
    </div>
  </div>
</nav>
<div class="container">
  <div>
    <button type="button" class="btn btn-primary"
      (click)="createContact()">Create Contact</button>
  </div>
  <br>
  <div id="contactlist" *ngIf="recordsExists">
  <br>
  <table class="table table-hover">
    <thead>
      <tr>
        <th>First Name</th>
        <th>Last Name</th>
        <th>Actions</th>
      </tr>
    </thead>
    <tbody>
      <tr *ngFor="let item of values">
```

```html
        <td>{{item.firstName}}</td>
        <td>{{item.lastName}}</td>
        <td><button type="button" (click)="editContact(item)"
           class="btn btn-primary btn-sm">Edit</button>
          <button type="button" (click)="deleteContact(item)"
            class="btn btn-danger btn-sm">Delete</button>
        </td>
      </tr>
    </tbody>
  </table>
</div>
<div id="contactlistform" *ngIf="formAddEdit">
  <form novalidate (ngSubmit)="onSubmit(contactForm)"
    [formGroup]="contactForm">
    <div class="form-group">
      <label>First Name</label>
      <input type="text" class="form-control"
        formControlName="firstname">
    </div>
    <div class="form-group">
      <label>Last Name</label>
      <input type="text" class="form-control"
        formControlName="lastname">
    </div>
    <div class="form-group">
      <label>Email Address</label>
      <input type="email" class="form-control"
        formControlName="email">
    </div>
    <div class="form-group">
      <label>Date Of Birth</label>
      <ng2-datepicker formControlName="date"></ng2-datepicker>
    </div>
    <button class="btn btn-success" type="submit"
      [disabled]="contactForm.invalid">Save</button>
    <button class="btn btn-danger" type="button"
      (click)="cancelForm()">Cancel</button>
  </form>
</div>
</div>
```

Let's dive deep into our code to get a better understanding:

- The `Create` button shows the form for entering the `Packt` contacts.
- The table showing the list of contacts is saved with the Angular For statement (`*ngFor`).
- Each record has an `Edit` and `Delete` button for its respective operation.
- There is a form to enter/update records for the `Packt` contacts. This form falls under the category of **Angular Reactive Forms.**

Now run the application using the command line `ng serve` and open the browser to view the application in action.

The demo project implements JWT-based authentication, leading us to include the login screen to perform authentication. When the login credentials are successfully validated, a JSON web token is generated. This token is saved in local storage to be passed along with subsequent HTTP calls as the `Authorization` header:

Login form in Angular 4

 Note that Angular CLI runs the application on `localhost:4200` port. This can also be changed.

The `Contact` form helps to enter the contact details and save them, as shown here:

Contact form in Angular 4

The **Save** button is enabled when all valid entries are filled in on the form, thus enabling you to save the valid data to the web API.

Once a contact is added, we can see the list on the UI with its action for the **Edit** and **Delete** button for each row.

Building hybrid mobile apps using Ionic 3

Ionic 3 is an open source framework for building hybrid mobile applications that can be built into mobile apps for Android, iOS, and Windows phones.

Ionic 3 is built on top of Angular and Apache Cordova with HTML5, CSS, and SASS. In this section, we will build a hybrid native app that consumes our `PacktContacts` web API.

Follow the steps found at `https://ionicframework.com/docs/v2/setup/installation/` to install Ionic 3. Be sure that the latest versions of NodeJS and NPM are installed.

Create a blank app for Ionic 3 with TypeScript by running the following command:

```
ionic start packtcontactapp blank
```

This creates an Ionic 3 project built on top of an Angular framework, so we can leverage the code that we wrote in the previous section.

`PacktService` is a service provider that talks to the web API using HTTP, and can be created by running the Ionic CLI command shown here:

```
ionic g provider PacktService
```

The Ionic CLI command can be found at `https://ionicframework.com/docs/v2/cli/`.

Since the provider is the same as the Angular 4 service provider, we can reuse the same `PacktService` web API we created in the previous section.

Home page - Ionic 3 page

Ionic 3 works by creating pages similar to Angular components and the template URL concept, but, in this case, they are navigated by the **Push and Pop** concept.

We can reuse most of the `app.component.ts` code from the previous section; copy the following code in `home.ts`:

```
import { PacktService } from './../../providers/packt-service';
import { Contacts } from './../../providers/contacts.class';
import { Component } from '@angular/core';
import { FormGroup, FormBuilder, Validators} from '@angular/forms';
import { NavController } from 'ionic-angular';

@Component({
  selector: 'page-home',
  templateUrl: 'home.html'
})
export class HomePage {
  title = 'Ionic 2 with ASP.NET Core Web API';
  recordsExists: boolean = false;
  formAddEdit:boolean = false;
  contactModel:Contacts;
  contactForm: FormGroup;
  public values: any[];
```

```
constructor(public navCtrl: NavController,
  private _dataService: PacktService,
  private fb: FormBuilder) {
}
ionViewDidLoad() {
  this.LoadAllContacts();
}
LoadAllContacts(){
  this._dataService
  .GetAll()
  .subscribe(data => {
    if (data.length > 0) {
      this.values = data;
      this.recordsExists = true;
      console.log(data);
    }
  },
  error => {
    console.log(error.status);
  },
  () => console.log('complete'));
}

// Code removed for brevity
// Similar to App.component.ts
}
```

This is how our code will function:

- It will import the `PacktService` provider and the Contacts class
- `ionViewDidLoad` is similar to `ngOnInit`, and this we will call the `LoadAllContacts` method
- The rest of the code is similar to `app.component.ts`

Home page - Ionic 3 HTML page

The Ionic 3 pages have a component and HTML to complete the page. We created the component for the home page; now let's make changes to the `home.html` file.

Open `home.html` and copy the following code from it:

```
<ion-content padding>
  <div *ngIf="formAddEdit">
    <form novalidate (ngSubmit)="onSubmit(contactForm)"
      [formGroup]="contactForm">
```

```
            <ion-list noline>
              <ion-item>
                <ion-label floating danger>First Name</ion-label>
                <ion-input formControlName="firstname" type="text"></ion-
input>
              </ion-item>
              <ion-item>
                <ion-label floating danger>Last Name</ion-label>
                <ion-input formControlName="lastname" type="text"></ion-
input>
              </ion-item>
              <ion-item>
                <ion-label floating danger>Email</ion-label>
                <ion-input formControlName="email" type="text"></ion-input>
              </ion-item>
            </ion-list>
            <button ion-button color="secondary" type="submit"
              [disabled]="contactForm.invalid">Save</button>
            <button ion-button color="danger" type="button"
              (click)="cancelForm()">Cancel</button>
          </form>
        </div>
        <ion-list *ngIf="recordsExists">
          <ion-item-sliding *ngFor="let item of values">
            <button ion-item (click)="editContact(item)">
              <h2>{{item.firstName}} {{item.lastName}}</h2>
            </button>
            <ion-item-options>
              <button ion-button color="danger"
                (click)="deleteContact(item)">Delete</button>
            </ion-item-options>
          </ion-item-sliding>
        </ion-list>
        <ion-fab right bottom>
          <button ion-fab color="secondary" (click)="createContact()">
            <ion-icon name="add"></ion-icon>
          </button>
        </ion-fab>
      </ion-content>
```

 The complete source code is available in the code bundle.

Now, let's understand how exactly this code will work:

- The `ion-header` tag displays the header information as either static or dynamic
- The contact form section will be displayed only on adding or editing using `*ngIf`
- The `ion-list` tag displays the saved contacts that are fetched from the web API
- The `ion-list` tag can perform the edit and delete contact tasks
- The `Create` button is displayed in the bottom for creating a new contact

From the command line, run the `ionic serve` command to see the application in action. It can be further built to create a native app for Android or iOS as well, by following the steps found at `https://ionicframework.com/docs/cli/`.

 Just as with Angular apps, don't forget to include `PacktServices` as Providers in the `app.module.ts` file of the Ionic app.

Ionic 3 app shows Packt contacts

Building web apps using ReactJS

ReactJs, or React, is a JavaScript library for building **user interfaces** (**UIs**). It was built by Facebook and later released as an open source library.

Its focus is more on a declarative, component-based way of UI development. It's equally as popular as the Angular framework for building modern web frontends.

A great starting place for learning about React is to go through the documentation, tutorials, and blogs at `https://facebook.github.io/react/`.

ReactJS in ASP.NET web application

You can find a number of ways for getting started or creating a basic application flow that uses React on the internet, and choosing one is quite difficult. In the previous sections, we created web apps using non-ASP.NET technologies; however, we will use an ASP.NET web application with React in this section to build a modern web frontend.

Using Visual Studio IDE, create either an ASP.NET empty website or an MVC 5 web application, and in that, install the ReactJS NuGet package. It creates a `React` folder in the `Scripts` folder section.

In the `Scripts` folder, go to **Add** | **New File** | `JSX file`.

Open `PacktContacts.jsx` and copy the following code:

```
var ContactsRow = React.createClass({
  render: function () {
    return (
      <tr>
        <td>{this.props.item.firstName}</td>
        <td>{this.props.item.lastName}</td>
        <td>{this.props.item.email}</td>
        <td><button class='btn btn-primary'>Edit</button> 
          <button class='btn btn-danger'>Delete</button></td>
      </tr>
    );
  }
});

var ContactsTable = React.createClass({
  getInitialState: function () {
    return {
      result: []
```

```
    }
  },
  componentWillMount: function () {
    var xhr = new XMLHttpRequest();
    xhr.open('get', this.props.url, true);
    xhr.onload = function () {
      var response = JSON.parse(xhr.responseText);
      this.setState({ result: response });
    }.bind(this);
    xhr.send();
  },
  render: function () {
    var rows = [];
    this.state.result.forEach(function (item) {
      rows.push(<ContactsRow key={item.Id} item={item} />);
    });
    return (<table className="table table-hover">
      <thead>
        <tr>
          <th>FirstName</th>
          <th>LastName</th>
          <th>Email</th>
          <td></td>
        </tr>
      </thead>

      <tbody>
        {rows}
      </tbody>
    </table>);
  }
});

ReactDOM.render(<ContactsTable
  url="http://localhost:50461/api/contacts" />,
  document.getElementById('grid')) }
```

Create the HTML file to be used with ReactJS to render the Contacts grid, namel
yReactUI.html:

```
<!DOCTYPE html>
  <html>
    <head>
      <meta charset="utf-8" />
        <title>Consuming Web API using ReactJS</title>
          <!--CSS-->
          <link href="Content/bootstrap.min.css" rel="stylesheet" />
          <!-- JS -->
```

```
            <script src="Scripts/jquery-3.1.1.min.js"></script>
            <script src="Scripts/bootstrap.min.js"></script>
            <script src="Scripts/react/react.js"></script>
            <script src="Scripts/react/react-dom.js"></script>
      </head>
      <body class="container">
        <div>
          <h1>Consuming ASP.NET Core Web API using ReactJS</h1>
        </div>
        <div id="grid" class="container">
        </div>
      </body>
  </html>
  <script src="Scripts/PacktContacts.jsx"></script>
```

Now, let us dive deep into the functioning of the preceding code:

- React's `CreateClass` renders a dynamic table
- `componentWillMount` calls the web API using an `XMLHttpRequest`
- The `PacktContacts` web API is called using fetch by passing the custom header required to return the proper response
- The contacts list is rendered on the UI on the grid `div` tag

Start the application by pressing *F5*; you will see the `Contacts` list:

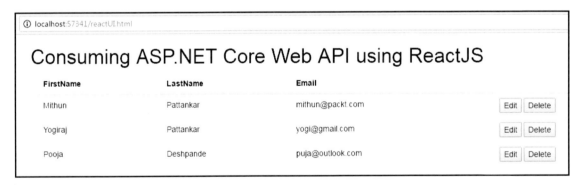

ReactJs fetching the PacktContact web API

Consuming web APIs using JavaScript

JavaScript is the programming language of HTML and the web. Every UI framework works with JavaScript. We won't be focusing on learning JavaScript, but if you're new to this, then I recommend learning it from the W3Schools website at `https://www.w3schools.com/js/`.

In this section, we will consume (call) the `PacktContacts` (ASP.NET Core Web API) using JavaScript and perform authentication and CRUD operations.

Create any web application (ASP.NET, MVC5, or any non-.NET web applications); the code bundle will use an ASP.NET empty application.

Create an HTML file to copy the following code to display the contact list, and add the contacts:

```
<body class="container">
  <div >
    <h1>Consuming ASP.NET Core Web API using JavaScript</h1>
  </div>
  <div class="container" id="divlogin" style="display:block;">
    <label><b>Username</b></label>
    <input type="text" placeholder="Enter Username"
      id="uname" required>
    <label><b>Password</b></label>
    <input type="password" placeholder="Enter Password"
      id="psw" required>
    <button onclick="doLogin()" class="btn btn-primary">Login</button>
  </div>
  <div id="contactsgrid" style="display:none;">
    <button onclick="AddContacts()"
      class="btn btn-success">Add</button>
    <div id="gridContent">
    </div>
  </div>
  <div id="contactform" style="display:none;">
    <div>
      <div class="form-group">
        <label for="usr">First Name:</label>
        <input type="text" class="form-control" id="firstName">
      </div>
      <div class="form-group">
        <label for="usr">Last Name:</label>
        <input type="text" class="form-control" id="lastName">
      </div>
      <div class="form-group">
        <label for="usr">Email:</label>
        <input type="email" class="form-control" id="emailid">
```

```
        </div>
        <button onclick="saveContact()"
          class="btn btn-primary">Save</button>
        <button onclick="doCancel()"
          class="btn btn-primary">Cancel</button>
      </div>
    </div>
  </body>
</html>
```

On running the application, we will see UI with the login page as shown here:

Login UI using JavaScript

Enter your credentials (username, `mithunvp` and password, `abcd123` as per the code bundle; you can change them too).

Using `XMLHttpRequest`, we will call the web API methods to perform login and CRUD operations on the `Contact` model. The JavaScript code looks like the following:

```
function doLogin() {
  var contactform = document.getElementById('contactform');
  var divlogin = document.getElementById('divlogin');
  var contactsgrid = document.getElementById('contactsgrid');

  var loginUrl = endpoint + "/api/auth/token";
  var xhr = new XMLHttpRequest();
  var userElement = document.getElementById('uname');
  var passwordElement = document.getElementById('psw');
  var username = userElement.value;
  var password = passwordElement.value;

  xhr.open('POST', loginUrl, true);
  xhr.setRequestHeader('Content-Type',
      'application/json; charset=UTF-8');
  xhr.addEventListener('load', function () {
    if (this.status == 200) {
      var responseObject = JSON.parse(this.response);
```

```
      if (responseObject.token) {
        //console.log(responseObject.token);
        localStorage.setItem("AuthToken", responseObject.token);
        getContacts();
        divlogin.style.display = 'none';
      }
    }
    else {
      bootbox.alert("Authentication Failed", function () {
      });
    }
  });

  var sendObject = JSON.stringify({ username: username,
    password: password });
  xhr.send(sendObject);
}

function getContacts() {
  var contactform = document.getElementById('contactform');
  var divlogin = document.getElementById('divlogin');
  var contactsgrid = document.getElementById('contactsgrid');
  var Url = endpoint + "/api/contacts";
  var xhr = new XMLHttpRequest();
  var authtoken = localStorage.getItem("AuthToken");
  xhr.open('GET', Url, true);
  xhr.setRequestHeader("Authorization", "Bearer " + authtoken);
  xhr.addEventListener('load', function () {
    var responseObject = JSON.parse(this.response);
    if (this.status == 200) {
      var responseObject = JSON.parse(this.response);
      console.log(responseObject + ' ' + responseObject.length);
      if (responseObject.length > 0) {
        contactsgrid.style.display = 'block';
        DisplayContactsGrid(responseObject);
      } else {
        bootbox.confirm("No Contacts exists, Click OK to create",
          function (result) {
          if (result) {
            contactform.style.display = 'block';
            contactsgrid.style.display = 'none';
            clearFormValues();
          }
          else {
            contactform.style.display = 'none';
            contactsgrid.style.display = 'block';
          }
        });
```

```
        }
      }
      else {
        bootbox.alert("Operation Failed", function () {
        });
      }
    });
    xhr.send(null);
  }
```

You can break down the preceding code as follows:

- The `doLogin` function uses `XMLHttpRequest` to call the web API using `loginUrl`. On successfully authentication, we save the `auth` token in local storage to be used with the authorization header.
- The `XMLHttpRequest POST` method takes the username and password. It then passes it on to the web API.
- The `getContacts()` function gets all the contacts from the web API, and uses the `auth` token to pass it so that the web API authenticates it as a proper request.

Run the application, log in, and add the contacts to view the list:

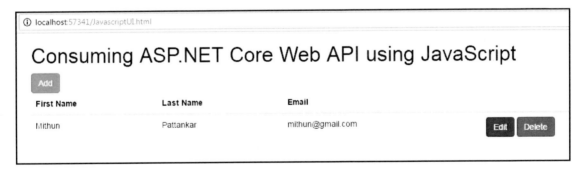

Contacts list using JavaScript

Consuming web APIs using JQuery

JQuery is a JavaScript library that greatly simplifies JavaScript programming.

To learn JQuery, read through the documentation at `https://www.w3schools.com/jquery/`.

We will be using the same project that we were working on in the previous section. Add HTML and JavaScript file to it.

The JavaScript file that JQuery uses to consume the web API looks as follows:

```
function doLogin() {
  var loginUrl = endpoint + "/api/auth/token";
  var sendObject = JSON.stringify({ username: $("#uname").val(),
    password: $("#psw").val() });
  $.ajax({
    url: loginUrl,
    contentType: 'application/json; charset=UTF-8',
    data: sendObject,
    method: "POST"
  }).done(function (data, status) {
    if (status == "success") {
      if (data.token) {
        localStorage.setItem("AuthToken", data.token);
        getContacts();
        $('#divlogin').hide();
      }
    }
    else {
      bootbox.alert("Authentication Failed", function () {
      });
    }
  }).fail(function () {
    bootbox.alert("Authentication Error", function () {
    });
  });
}
function getContacts() {
  var getUrl = endpoint + "/api/contacts";
  var authtoken = localStorage.getItem("AuthToken");
  $.ajax({
    url: getUrl,
    contentType: 'application/json; charset=UTF-8',
    beforeSend: function (xhr) {
      xhr.setRequestHeader('Authorization', 'BEARER ' + authtoken);
    },
    method: "GET"
  }).done(function (data, status) {
    if (status == "success") {
      if (data.length > 0) {
        $("#contactsgrid").show();
        DisplayContactsGrid(data);
      }
      else {
```

```
bootbox.confirm("No Contacts exists, Click OK to create",
    function (result) {
    if (result) {
        $("#contactsgrid").hide();
        $("#contactform").show();
        clearFormValues();
    }
    else {
        $("#contactsgrid").show();
        $("#gridContent").html("");
        $("#contactform").hide();
    }
    })
}}
}).fail(function () {
    bootbox.alert("Authentication Error", function () {
    });
});
}
```

You can break down the preceding code as follows:

- The `doLogin()` function uses the JQuery `Ajax GET` method to call the web API by passing the username and password, and saving the JWT token in local storage
- The `getLogin()` function uses the same JQuery `Ajax POST` method to get a list of contacts

After running the application and adding the contacts, we will see a similar UI, but built with JQuery:

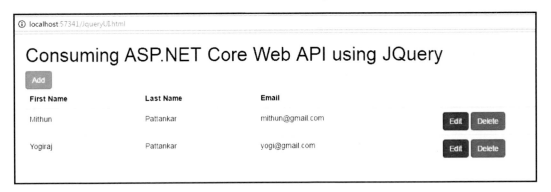

Contacts list consumed with JQuery

Summary

In this chapter, we focused on building modern web frontends in the form of Angular 4, Ionic 3, ReactJS, JavaScript, and Jquery consuming the web API built during the previous chapters. An in-depth explanation of each of the web frontend frameworks is a book itself. We have focused more on consuming the web API; however, the source code will help you understand all the concepts better.

It's been a wonderful journey, from understanding the concepts of HTTP and REST, to getting started with the ASP.NET Core Web API and its anatomy, and learning in detail about controllers and actions, unit testing web API applications, building routes, and middleware.

We learned how ASP.NET Core integrates with the various databases using ORM, and then we performed optimization of our web API. We also looked at exception handling. We applied various security measures for our web API application in the form of JWT, identity, and cookie authentication.

With the ASP.NET Core cross-platform concept, we looked into deploying web APIs on various heterogeneous environments, such as IIS, Azure App Service, NGINX, Linux, and even standalone applications.

Finally, in this chapter, we consumed these web APIs in popular web frontends (UI frameworks). It's been an amazing journey, writing this book, and I hope everyone benefits from it.

Index

X

Y